PATRICIA CLANCY was for many
years a senior lecturer in the French
Department of the University of
Melbourne. She is a winner of the
Victorian Premier's Award
for Literary Translation.

JEANNE ALLEN taught French at
La Trobe and Melbourne universities
and has published on the French
in colonial Australia.

The
French Consul's
Wife

*Memoirs of Céleste de Chabrillan
in Gold-rush Australia*

The French Consul's Wife

Memoirs of Céleste de Chabrillan
in Gold-rush Australia

Translation, with introduction and notes,
by Patricia Clancy and Jeanne Allen,
of *Un Deuil au bout du monde* (1877)

MELBOURNE UNIVERSITY PRESS

Melbourne University Press
an imprint of Melbourne University Publishing (MUP Ltd)
PO Box 1167, Carlton, Victoria 3053, Australia
mup-info@unimelb.edu.au   www.mup.com.au

First published 1998
Paperback edition 2003

Designed by Sandra Nobes
Typeset in 12/14 Centaur
Printed in Australia by BPA Print Group

National Library of Australia Cataloguing-in-Publication entry

Chabrillan, Céleste Vénard de, comtesse, 1824–1909.
    [Deuil au bout du monde. English]
    The French consul's wife: memoirs of Céleste de
    Chabrillan in gold-rush Australia.
    Bibliography.
    Includes index.
    ISBN 0 522 85066 9 (pbk.).
    1. Chabrillan, Céleste Vénard de, comtesse, 1824–1909.
    2. Actors–France–Biography. Victoria—Social life and customs 1851–1891
    I. Clancy, Patricia A. II. Allen, Jeanne, 1957– . III. Title.
    3. Goldmines and mining–Australia–Victoria. 4.
792.028092

Contents

Illustrations

Acknowledgements

WE would firstly like to thank all those who encouraged us to undertake the translation of the Australian memoirs of Céleste de Chabrillan, an extraordinary woman whose frank account of her experiences of this country have long deserved publication in English. At the University of Melbourne, considerable support and encouragement have been given to this project by the Department of French, in particular by Dr Colin Thornton-Smith, who has very generously shared much relevant research material. The committee of the Institute for the Study of French–Australian Relations (ISFAR) in Melbourne has also been most supportive from the beginning. We gratefully acknowledge the unfailing support and patience Jack Clancy and Shane McLean showed us throughout.

Research for this translation was carried out principally in the Bibliothèque Nationale de Paris, the Mitchell Library, the La Trobe Library (State Library of Victoria), the Baillieu Library (University of Melbourne), and the Public Records Office. The staff of all these institutions gave us a great deal of help throughout the project. Special thanks go to Ms Dianne Reilly, the La Trobe Librarian, for her generosity—above all in obtaining illustrations and facilitating our French–Australian research in general. Marianne Spindler of the Bibliothèque Nationale kindly searched obscure French reference material; while Kay Rowan, Local History Librarian, the City of Port Phillip, and artist Mirka Mora provided much useful information about old St Kilda.

Permission to reproduce illustrations has been sought and kindly granted by publishers wherever traceable.

Finally, we would like to thank Arts Victoria for their grant in support of this translation.

Introduction

WHEN Céleste de Chabrillan set sail from England in 1854 to begin a new life in Australia, she thought her past would never be known in a country thousands of miles away at the other end of the world. Taking with her, among other things, an adopted daughter, a maid, two lap dogs and a budgerigar in a cage, she had left her native France, her family and friends to become the wife of Count Lionel de Chabrillan, who was to take up his posting as the first French consular agent in the colony of Victoria.

Lionel's aristocratic family hoped that obtaining the consul's post would separate him from Céleste, but they were disappointed. The couple went to London and married before setting sail on the *Croesus*. However, just before her marriage, Céleste had sent the manuscript of her highly scandalous memoirs to the publishers. Her life up to then had been quite extraordinary, and the memoirs told it all in detail. Firstly there was her upbringing as an illegitimate child in Paris and the miserable adolescence which drove her first to vagrancy then to prostitution. She described how she went on to become a polka dancer, then quite a celebrity as an actress, a bareback circus rider, and finally a well-known Parisian courtesan. In fact, there are aspects of her life that could almost have come from the novels *Scenes of Bohemian Life*, written by her friend Henri Murger, and *The Lady of the Camellias*, written by the son of another great friend, Alexandre Dumas, which were made into the famous operas *La Bohème* and *La Traviata* respectively. Céleste tried desperately to get her manuscript back, but all her efforts to stop publication were unsuccessful, as the publishers knew a potential best-seller when they saw one.

When Céleste embarked for Australia, she did so in the belief that her memoirs would never reach such a distant land and that Lionel himself would never hear of them. As it happened, not only was word of the memoirs to reach Melbourne, but also the memoirs themselves were to land on those foreign shores just before she did. So, far from making a new start in Victoria, she would find that all her time and all her experiences here would be influenced by the life she had lived in Paris—the life she wanted so desperately to leave behind.

Of greater interest to Australian readers is her second set of memoirs, translated here. Entitled *Death at the End of the World* (*Un Deuil au bout du monde*—literally 'a bereavement at the end of the world'),[1] it deals with the time Céleste de Chabrillan spent in Victoria. She arrived in Melbourne with Lionel at the height of the gold rush, and spent two and a half years in Australia, before returning to France to try once again to extricate Lionel from the financial ruin that a disastrous commercial venture had brought upon him. She was reluctant to leave her husband behind, but not Australia. In spite of the fateful autobiography, it was in Melbourne that her literary ambitions began and grew—as she wrote copious entries in her diary, commenting on the country, people, places, events and gossip that made up life in the colony, as well as expressing her own personal thoughts and feelings. The second memoirs seem to consist, for the most part, of Céleste's diary entries, written up and published some twenty years later.

In Australia, Céleste certainly had time to think, write and observe, as she was ostracized by most of Melbourne society, which was extremely strait-laced. As the French Consul's 'harlot spouse',[2] she also had to endure snubs, censure and sometimes ridicule, in spite of her work for charity. When invitations came for Lionel, she was often not included—even though, trying to earn her title of countess, she behaved in a way she thought befitted a respectable wife. Governor Hotham, for example, did not see fit to invite her to his ball. Hurt and angry, Céleste commented that the same attitude did not seem to apply to the ex-convicts and even escaped prisoners from the Sydney penal settlement, who attended in significant numbers. She found society, especially the women, hard and unforgiving, and was immensely grateful to those, like the Mayor (Mr Smith) and the Judge (Mr Justice Williams), who were kind enough to acknowledge her.

Often left at home, Céleste described how she tried to make up for her lack of formal education, and occupied herself, for much of the time, by writing. In the end, it was through this writing that she had her revenge on the people of Melbourne with the publication of the novel she wrote here, *The Gold Robbers* (*Les Voleurs d'or*),[3] which was turned into a successful play; and much later with this second volume of memoirs, *Death at the End of the World*. The feelings and frustrations of this mentally and physically active woman, who could find little outlet for her energies, have come through clearly in what she wrote. If not in real life, at least in print, she was able to get her own back on those who had looked down on her, like her compatriot Mistress [*sic*] Brook (Mrs Brackenbury)—according to Céleste, the daughter of a bachelor soldier.

Not surprisingly, Céleste paints an extremely negative picture of life in Victoria—so negative that Hubert de Castella would write his book on Australian squatters[4] partly to counteract the picture she gave of the colony in *The Gold Robbers*. As she says herself, she was a Parisian to her fingertips, and there can be no doubt that Melbourne in the 1850s was a far cry from the Paris that this vivacious woman of the world had left behind. The culture shock was immense and immediate: we see her walking ankle-deep in mud for two hours to reach the couple's first lodgings—two rooms in a wooden hut—and paying a fortune for a simple meal of ham and eggs on the way. But before accompanying her any further as she begins her new life in Melbourne, we should perhaps know a little more about the life she had left. After all, the lurid details were already common knowledge not only in Paris, but also in Melbourne.

Céleste de Chabrillan was an extraordinary woman whose life was one of remarkable self-recreation. She was born Elisabeth-Céleste Vénard (or Vernard) on 27 December 1824, at 7 Rue du Pont-aux-Choux in the very poor and insalubrious 3rd arrondissement of Paris. Her mother, Anne-Victoire Vénard, the daughter of a furniture dealer, had been forced from her father's home by a jealous stepmother, and was distraught to find herself pregnant to a man who had since gone off to join the army.[5] Rather than give birth to this unwanted child, she tried unsuccessfully to take her own life, an action to which Céleste would later attribute her own extreme sensitivity and obsession with suicide.

Nonetheless Céleste had a reasonably happy childhood and was indulged by her mother, who allowed the young Céleste to do exactly as she chose, disregarding any notion of formal education. This was not uncommon at the time. Anne-Victoire was employed locally as a milliner,[6] and Céleste, left alone for much of the time, spent her days wandering around the area in which she lived, being entertained by the many acrobats, jugglers, dancers and the like, who performed in the streets. She also went to see productions in the local theatres and, at a very early age, professed a great interest in life on the stage. There was a wealth of entertainment in the area, with six theatres operating in the nearby Boulevard du Temple alone.[7]

Céleste admitted to having been a very precocious, proud and stubborn child and quite a tomboy, preferring the rough and tumble of street games to the more sedate, traditional pastimes that other girls pursued. Quite conscious, however, of her physical beauty and appeal, she liked to show off a new dress or hairstyle, and had little hesitation in displaying all her feminine charm when the need arose.

As a young child, Céleste had a very good relationship with her mother, but as the years passed, this became increasingly compromised by Céleste's extreme jealousy and intolerance of her mother's many affairs of the heart. When Céleste was just eight years old, her mother's lover attacked the girl during one of his bouts of drunken rage, and this caused Céleste and her mother to flee to Lyons. They made some of the journey on foot, being forced to stop at every town hall to collect the travellers' allowance for the destitute, which was three shillings a league.

Upon their return to Paris, Anne-Victoire took up with another disreputable character, a sculptor by the name of Vincent. Céleste was placed in an apprenticeship as an embroideress; she was eleven years old at the time. For several years, home life was intolerable, with Vincent constantly making sexual overtures to Céleste, and Anne-Victoire refusing to listen to her daughter's pleas for help. Bereft of the love and tenderness that she craved, the young Céleste suffered extreme mood swings and violent fits of temper which she could not control. There was constant quarrelling, and finally the situation reached crisis point when Vincent attempted to rape Céleste. She escaped and wandered the streets until given shelter by a young prostitute, who broke the law and jeopardized her own employment by offering the homeless girl shelter in a house of ill-repute.

Not long after this, there was a police raid of the premises, which led to their arrest and incarceration. Céleste spent five weeks in the women's prison of Saint-Lazare as a girl in moral danger and in need of care and protection. However, there was as much moral danger within Saint-Lazare as without. She joined ranks with one Marie la Blonde and a girl called Denise, who was biding her time until her sixteenth birthday when she intended to register as a prostitute.

Back home, after her mother finally bailed her out, Céleste lived as before. It was decided that she should be married off to one of their own class, but Céleste had greater aspirations, and so left home in search of her friend Denise, whom she found luxuriously dressed and full of enthusiasm for her new life in one of Paris's most fashionable brothels. Desperate for independence and tempted by the thought of getting to know the world of the rich, Céleste began work almost immediately. She writes of this day in her memoirs:

> In the morning, I was pure; in the evening, I was destroyed. Many women have fallen into this same abyss. I am arrogant enough to believe that I understood the depth of this abyss more quickly and more profoundly than any other before me. On that day, I realised that my life was over and that there could be no return to the world which I had always known. I would have given half my life to redeem myself but sometimes there is no going back.[8]

Two days later, with her mother's reluctant consent, Céleste joined the register of prostitutes at the Prefecture of Police.

The brothel in which Céleste worked attracted quite an elite clientele, including the well-known poet Alfred de Musset, who, as Céleste tells it, was particularly attracted to her. After about six months, and suffering from a severe bout of smallpox, Céleste was set up in an apartment by a rich admirer, and from then on she was supported by a series of well-to-do lovers. She also managed to get work as a dancer at the Bal Mabille, a very popular outdoor dance hall. It was here that she befriended the much-celebrated courtesan and polka dancer, Lise Sergent, known as Queen Pomaré, who was later immortalized by Emile Zola in *Nana*. However, she was still on the register of brothel prostitutes, and although she eventually managed to get her name removed with the help of Emperor Napoléon III's playboy cousin Prince Napoléon, this was a stigma that haunted her for the rest of her life.

It was from this time on that Céleste came to be quite well-known in Paris, where she started to mix with the artistic set. A dancing partner at the Bal Mabille gave her the nickname of 'la Mogador', after the North African town that the French bombarded in 1844, claiming it would be easier to defend the town than defend Céleste from her many suitors. This became the name under which she worked. Next, Céleste was given a dancing role at the Beaumarchais Theatre, and after that she could be seen performing as a bareback horse rider and chariot driver at the Hippodrome, a type of outdoor circus.

By this stage, at not much more than twenty years old, she was one of the star performers of Paris, living all the while as a kept woman. She took up with a Dutch baron, and the prominent Italian Duke of Ossuna, liaisons that gave her access to the high society of Paris. Things were going well until her circus career suddenly came to an end when she broke a leg in a chariot race. She was now without work or income, and her morale plummeted. Her stage friend Pomaré died at this time; and, upon learning of the suicide of her companion from Saint-Lazare days, Marie la Blonde, Céleste too attempted to take her own life.

Then, as Céleste tells it in her memoirs, she was dining one evening at the Café des Anglais, a restaurant favoured by the dandies of the time and a regular haunt of the demi-monde, when she was rescued from the jibes of a young reveller by a handsome and distinguished gentleman by the name of 'Robert'. This is the pseudonym she used for Count Lionel de Chabrillan.

Lionel belonged to an aristocratic family, a House of the former Knights of Dauphiné and pretenders to the throne of Monaco. He had worked in the French Legation in Copenhagen in 1838, but he was a bon vivant and an inveterate gambler who, it seems, had already managed to squander most of his large inheritance before actually coming into it. He and Céleste did not see each other again for some time and she began an affair with a Russian prince, but this ended abruptly when Lionel returned. The two then began what was to be a very volatile relationship, with numerous break-ups and reconciliations.

Upon the death of his father, Lionel inherited the then-huge fortune of 100 000 francs, but this hardly covered his debts. He decided that his best alternative was to marry someone rich and of his own class; so he broke up with Céleste, who continued her life as a high-class courtesan. After six months' separation, Lionel returned to find Céleste depressed and very weak, having just recovered from an overdose of digitalis. He immediately took her to his property in the Berry region[9] near the town of Châteauroux,[10] where she was astounded by the enormous wealth invested in the castle, the luxuriously appointed rooms and the extensive gardens. The disparity between their lives was driven home to her as Lionel led her around the estate with its immense stables housing seventeen prize horses and six emblazoned Chabrillan carriages, packs of hounds, and dozens of staff who waited on their every need.

However, the attraction of such luxury and the quiet country life with Lionel soon wore off for Céleste. Besides being frowned upon by the head butler, she became more and more frustrated by her lover's volatile and intemperate nature, and by his expectation that she play the role of the perfect mistress. Further angered by Lionel's long absences as he continued his pursuit of a suitable marriage partner, Céleste returned to Paris, to her Russian prince and her habits of old. When she was re-united yet again with Lionel, the count arranged for Céleste to purchase a small property near his own, much to his family's great annoyance. He was by now heavily in debt again and had been forced to sell off the most valuable contents of the castle, but continued to shower his mistress with expensive gifts, usually jewellery bought on credit.

Having finally become totally destitute, Lionel, like many desperate young men from all parts of the world, decided to set sail for Australia to try his luck on the goldfields. This was in 1852. He proposed marriage to Céleste before his departure, but she refused him, saying:

> Your count's crown would be my crown of thorns. I could never again face those poor lost souls who were part of my life, and I'd never have the right to face a decent woman. [. . .] There are two paths, yours and mine. I shall remain Mogador and you Robert de ***.[11]

Once Lionel had left, Céleste had to deal with his many creditors who descended on her. She managed to ward them off, in many cases by selling her own possessions. This would not be the last time she was called upon to do so.

Lionel wrote long letters of love and reproach from on board ship and then from Australia. These letters, if we are to accept Céleste's words, are quoted in their entirety at the end of her first set of memoirs. Letters, in fact, form an integral part of both sets. Lionel, however, who was never very lucky, had an unhappy and unfruitful stay in Australia, return-ing to Paris in 1853. In the meantime, Céleste had embarked upon a stage career and enjoyed a period of some success at the Variety Theatre, where she performed with Adèle Page in a dance called '*Le Pas de l'impé-riale*'. The well-known painter and teacher of Manet, Thomas Couture, asked her to sit for him and also made a plaster cast of her hand. Her earnings, however, could not cover the many expenses accrued in the legal proceedings still being waged against Lionel and which Céleste continued to fight in his absence. So, facing severe financial difficulties and acting upon strong encouragement from her lawyer, she set about writing her memoirs.

After Lionel returned from Australia, he was much more committed to Céleste. Their time apart had, this time, confirmed his love for her—and to prove it, he proudly showed his mistress her name that he had had tattooed on his arm during the outward journey. It was at this stage that Lionel's family connections procured him a position as the first French consular agent in Melbourne. It would seem that, like many an aristocratic family, they wanted to distance their black sheep as much as possible from an unsuitable match. What is more, his dissolute lifestyle could hardly have been seen as befitting the family name. Nonetheless, Lionel again asked Céleste to marry him, and to accompany him to Australia. Although it meant leaving behind the theatre and the gaiety and luxury of her life in Paris, this time she accepted.

It is at this point that the first set of memoirs, *Adieux au monde* (*Farewell to the World*), ends.[12] In the final pages, Céleste confesses that she has not yet told Lionel about their imminent publication. She writes:

> . . . if my memoirs are published after my departure, Robert [i.e. Lionel] will know nothing about them because we will be four months at sea. And then, who will read them? A few friends . . .[13]

Death in a Distant Land takes up exactly where the first set of memoirs stopped. Céleste begins by saying that she made desperate attempts to stop the publication of *Adieux au monde*, but her publishers knew they had a potential best-seller. Indeed it *was* a best-seller, and in fact caused such a scandal that this first edition was seized by the police soon after publication. Had Céleste been successful in suppressing the book, her accounts of Australia in the pages that follow might well have been different.

The gold-rush colony gave Céleste plenty to think and write about: apart from her own problems, there were the living conditions at the consulate—a four-roomed house in St Kilda—the intolerable weather, the news of the day, social and commercial life, problems of the French in Melbourne, the diplomatic circle and Government House, plus various trips in the country and on the bay. It is very interesting and quite revealing to compare her account of events with reports in the newspapers. Céleste's, naturally, are rather more dramatic, critical or flattering, being seen from a very personal point of view. One of the incidents that stands out is a public hanging near the new gaol, which she claims to have witnessed at close quarters—close enough to describe the distorted features of the victim in detail. She points out the barbarity of this type of capital punishment, suggesting that it is a reflection of the people by whom she is surrounded in Melbourne. Her views are also made quite apparent in the amusing account of Governor Hotham's ball, where there was little more to eat than ham and nothing to drink but a barrel of colonial beer. This earned the governor endless barbs in the press, where the event was dubbed the 'Beer Ball'. By contrast, the ball for the victims of the Crimea, which Céleste organized, donating all the prizes for the novel tombola, was from all accounts—hers and the newspapers'—a great success.[14]

Céleste also tells of Lola Montez's time in Melbourne and gives a vivid description of her theatrical productions. One of them presented on stage a melodramatic potted version of Lola's life; another was the famous erotic spider dance featuring Lola's frenzied movements as she becomes aware of the spider strategically placed in her underwear. It is hard to know whether Céleste is being disingenuous when she says she does not know why the good ladies of Melbourne got up and walked out of the theatre. She also describes in detail a burlesque parody of the dance by an English actor who also ran the bar at interval. Unfortunately, according to Céleste her association with Lola provoked new comments in the press about her past.

The pointed social snubs directed at his wife must have made life difficult for the French Consul, who, by contrast, is portrayed as a popular figure in Melbourne society. He is described as handsome and charming, although Céleste gently points out certain elements in his character that were not always so easy to live with: his aristocratic tendency to challenge her critics to the field of honour, regardless of the consequences; his stubbornness; his rash business ventures and, by extension, his complete inability to manage money. Nonetheless, Céleste paints a loving portrait of her husband in *Death in a Distant Land*. Indeed, the love story woven through the memoirs is almost as interesting as the people, places and events she describes. This is one of the things that distinguishes the book from most other accounts of life in the colony. For his part, Lionel seems to have been genuinely fond of the woman for whom he gave up a great deal; and she, perhaps for a mixture of reasons—not all altruistic—was never to remarry after his death. Céleste is quite aware of the effect of a love story on her readers, and, although never sentimental, she is often theatrical. We see her kissing Lionel's hand or throwing herself at his feet when feelings of love or gratitude overwhelm her. This sometimes gives the narrative an almost Mills-and-Boon flavour that is not without charm.

At the same time, it must be admitted that Céleste somewhat embellished Lionel's image both as French Consul and as a citizen. She seems to have fabricated some events and omitted to mention others. For example, there is no trace in the papers or the Registry of Deaths of Pierre P***, a French sailor arrested for the murder of a policeman during the Eureka Stockade. Lionel advised Pierre to use the same knife with which he had committed the crime to take his own life, so that the consul would not have to suffer the shame of seeing a Frenchman hanged. According to Céleste, the prisoner was found dead in his cell the next day. By his side was a note thanking the consul for his advice to carry out such a worthy act of courage. On the other hand, Céleste does not mention Lionel's intervention in a duel. In March 1856 the papers describe how the police arrested one of the men, but the other was offered consular protection and could not be taken into custody.[15] Both the police and the court were incensed by Lionel's interference and the papers were scathing in their criticism of the consul. Further, the *Argus* used this occasion to relate several other cases of Lionel's poor conduct, including his refusal to attend a theatrical performance because he was not reserved a front-row seat, and his publicly expressed indignation when one of the local papers published an unflattering picture of him.[16] Céleste describes her husband as proud and patriotic, but to residents in the colony, these obviously did not always seem to be virtues.

Céleste implies that Lionel and the photographer Antoine Fauchery were constant companions, and that Fauchery was a frequent visitor to the Chabrillan household, yet dates of events in Fauchery's life in Melbourne are often inaccurate.[17] Fauchery was at Lionel's deathbed, and it was he who advised Céleste of her husband's death and burial in a letter quoted in *Death in a Distant Land*. The newspaper reports of Lionel's funeral included in this letter are very interesting. They give a highly exaggerated account of the splendour of the burial when compared with those that appeared in the *Argus* and the *Age*.[18]

At the consulate, while Lionel went about his duties, which were mainly repatriating penniless French gold-seekers and interviewing French nationals who had fallen foul of the law, Céleste organised the household, embroidered, tried to educate herself and learn English, and wrote. She was very conscious of her lack of education, which must have been evident, at least to a compatriot like her malicious travelling companion on board the *Croesus*, Mistress Brook. The study she found very difficult, which is hardly surprising, as her only formal education had been daily writing lessons in the Saint-Lazare prison. She tried to cram knowledge, mainly from a large history of France by Anquetil. The consul presented a copy of this work to the State Library in 1856— probably the one Céleste had pored over. Writing came much more easily, and what she wrote on Australia, both in her *Death in a Distant Land*, and as fiction and theatre, would later give her not only a certain reputation as an author but also an income. More of that later. For the moment, it remains to preface Céleste de Chabrillan's Australian memoirs with some objective observations.

Céleste's style is direct, with many short sentences joined with colons and semi-colons. One has the impression, if not of a diary, at least of memoirs based on diary entries. There is also a great deal of reported speech, which gives life to the narrative. It is not an elegant style, although there are parts that strive for a more literary effect, and others where feelings are expressed in melodramatic terms to heighten the effect. Françoise Moser is the only biographer who claims to have seen the diary, which has since remained untraceable.[19] She comments on the bad spelling, and Céleste herself never hid the fact that she had a great deal to learn. Some of her Parisian literary friends probably advised her. In particular, her long-time friend Alexandre Dumas, who used quite a stable of minor writers to do hack work for him, may well have given Céleste a little help.

As the memoirs were published some time after her return to France, it is not surprising that there are inconsistencies in Céleste's notation of dates. The original notation in her diary was probably erratic. Especially during 1854, she often dates an event three to four weeks before it actually took place.[20] According to the official archives of the time, there is no record of the hanging she so graphically describes on 23 August 1854. There was one a month later, on 22 September, so it is feasible that she saw it.[21] By contrast, she is often quite assiduous in her recording of dates and details: the many anecdotes she gives about the arrival of British and French ships in Port Phillip Bay, for example, are generally verifiable and exact.

A close study of *Death in a Distant Land* reveals that it contains a number of exaggerated details and descriptions. Céleste bemoans the extreme length of her outward voyage on board the *Croesus* and tells of the great anxiety that was felt in Melbourne for the ship's fate, with all the newspapers concluding that it had been lost at sea. Articles did appear in the daily press expressing concern for the long-awaited *Croesus*, but they expressed no fear of the ship's untimely demise.[22] From her very early arrival in Melbourne, Céleste refers to the attention paid to her in the press, with many newspaper articles giving details of her past and questioning Lionel's wisdom in his choice of a wife. No such reports are to be found in the major Melbourne papers; even the *Melbourne Punch*, notorious for its lampoonery, made no mention of her. Indeed, the lack of interest shown in her by the press is quite surprising. None of the papers, including the *Ballarat Times*, refers to the Chabrillans' visit to the Ballarat goldfields, where, according to Céleste, the miners gave them a grand welcome and the many spectators expressed their admiration when she descended into a mine. It was during this same period that the governor and his wife, Sir Charles and Lady Hotham, made an inspection of the Ballarat goldfields. A number of newspaper articles mention the great impression that Lady Hotham made upon the miners.[23] Did these reports perhaps influence Céleste when she described her own visit, or should we doubt that she made the trip at all? It was not uncommon for travellers and immigrants-turned-writers to stretch the truth occasionally and mix a little fiction with genuine experience. As Colin Thornton-Smith observes, 'One rarely finds first-hand accounts, in what may be called a pure form, as a record only of what the author actually saw or experienced. There is an inevitable overlap with secondary accounts on one side, and with invented material on the other.'[24]

These and other examples of exaggeration, fabrication and omission generally appear when Céleste is describing the role that she and Lionel played in certain events. There is a seemingly conscious effort on her part to attribute a greater importance to their public lives in Melbourne than was actually the case. Just as she did in her first set of memoirs, Céleste presents herself as an innocent victim who has the courage to fight back against a cruel society. We can conjecture that she probably overstates the hostility that she encountered in Melbourne in an attempt to impress upon the reader her strength of character in enduring such painful social ostracism. Against the backdrop of a dissolute society, Céleste projects herself and her husband as models of rectitude. With what we know of both Céleste's and Lionel's past, there is perhaps room for doubt.

However, when we examine *Death in a Distant Land* for what it offers us as an account of colonial Victoria, we discover that Céleste is, on the whole, accurate in her recording of events. Melbourne life is of great interest to her and she often describes theatrical productions and visiting celebrities. She also gives us a valuable record of day-to-day living, citing accurate examples of the cost of food and accommodation, and of Melbourne's weather. She provides an account of the Ballarat goldfields, and documents the Eureka Stockade. So while we cannot always accept these memoirs as a true account of the role that Céleste and Lionel de Chabrillan played in Melbourne's public life, the reader can be certain that they do present an accurate and sincere account of events in Victoria at the time. When relating the difficulties of living in the colony, and when describing its countryside and inhabitants, Céleste's observations, though pessimistic, are generally supported by those of a number of her contemporaries. Her works deserve to be accepted as important accounts of life in Victoria during the 1850s.

One of the unique qualities of *Death in a Distant Land* is that it presents life in colonial Victoria from the point of view of a French woman. Several English women of high social standing were residing in the colony at the time, as were a certain number of Europeans, but Céleste seems to be the first notable woman from the European continent to stay in Victoria and publish a book about her experiences.[25] Like most new arrivals, she brought with her the prejudices of her background —not only those commonly held about the Aborigines and the Chinese, but also a particular French attitude to the English colonisers. The feeling seems to have been largely mutual. There was no one more self-consciously French than Céleste; her foreignness may well have engendered feelings of hostility among her Melbourne peers, a sentiment no doubt fuelled by her dubious past. Céleste de Chabrillan's own life, the way she presents herself, and the interpretation she gives to the events she experienced are as interesting as the events themselves, perhaps more so. And there was more to come: Australia would be present in her life and work for many years after she left our shores.

Part One:

___

Marriage and the
Journey Out

CHAPTER I

From Courtesan to Countess

LIONEL (for Robert was not Mr de Chabrillan's real name), had gone to London alone to publish our marriage banns, while I made my last preparations for departure here and approached Messrs Jacottet and Bourdilliat once again to try and get them to return the manuscript of my *Memoirs* . . . and destroy it. One after the other, I saw all the people who had encouraged me to publish these wretched *Memoirs*. In light of the new circumstances that I was about to enter, they were all as sorry about this publication as I was, but their intervention after the fact was to no avail.

Acting in my interest, Mr Emile de Girardin[1] had been so kind as to write me out a copy of the contract that I had entered into with the owner of Librairie Nouvelle. The publication of these *Memoirs* was to be split two ways: that is, half of all the profits each, once all the printing costs were paid. It seems that these profits were likely to be very high, and I was left with no transactional or repurchase rights, even judicially. I went to see my dear good friend Alexandre Dumas to ask him for one last piece of advice.[2] He welcomed me with his usual kindness. He had known Lionel for a very long time and tried to think of some way which would get us out of our predicament.

—I can't think of anything at the moment, he said as he held out his hand to me, but as I approve of your idea, I shall see what I can find out, I shall make inquiries.

A servant came and announced, in a hushed voice, the name of a person who was waiting in the drawing room.

—Of course! Perhaps luck is with you just at the right time: the person here is His Highness Prince Napoléon.[3] Like myself, he knew your Lionel in Italy, and if he takes your side, I assure you that you will win the day yet.

And without waiting for my reply, he went into the other room to announce me.

—Come in, he said as he opened the door, His Highness knows the situation.

—Yes, said the Prince with a smile, but there is simply nothing I can do. It's a business matter and the publishers are within their rights.

—But Your Highness, I am going to be married.

—And that is another act of folly. I have said so to your Lionel whom I have seen several times since his return from Australia, but he will go on with it unless you are more sensible than he is.

The meeting was not turning at all to my advantage, and I looked at my poor dear friend Dumas with such dismay that, after giving me a small sign of encouragement, he said:

—Folly or not, they have known each other for years, and their love has withstood the test of time; that is a mutual guarantee for the future. Every person should have the right to be happy according to his own idea of happiness. Besides, I don't know of any woman in the world who would refuse to marry the man she loved. He is handsome, noble and brave; she is intelligent and courageous. I can guarantee that she will prove herself worthy of him, but those wretched *Memoirs* must be withdrawn,—everything depends on that.

—They are likely to create a scandal, then? the Prince asked, addressing his question to the master. Have you read them?

—Yes, in manuscript. They are a kind of confession in the style of Jean-Jacques Rousseau—quite captivating—and they can harm no one but herself.[4]

—Well then, replied the Prince as he turned towards me, let matters take their course, and we shall review the situation after your departure.

The master saw me to the door and said:

—Be strong! There is strength in numbers, and we are here. You have nothing more to fear.

I returned home to the Rue de Navarin, where the only furniture I had left was two chairs, a table and a single iron bed. Henri Murger had been waiting for me for a long time.[5]

—You wrote to me and told me to come at two o'clock. I arrived at three and now it's four, he said with a smile. We are both as unpunctual as each other! Having said that, how are you and when is the great departure for Cochin China?

—Tomorrow.

—I hope for both your sakes that tomorrow never comes. Dash it! People don't go as far away as that, especially to get married . . .

—I shall have no regrets if good friends like you promise to remember me and write to me from time to time.

—I promise I shall remember you but, as for writing, I should be very surprised myself if that ever happened. I find it easier to contemplate things than to actually do them: I am very lazy when it comes to action!

—I shall still have the lines you dedicated to me at Philoxène Boyer's.[6]

—I don't remember them.

—Are you disheartened?

—Yes, somewhat, and quite disheartening to others. I'm very sorry that I never took up tailoring.

—You ungrateful soul! You have had great success with *La Vie de Bohème*.

—Yes, great success but very little money. But I did not come here to talk about myself, my dear Céleste. Everything is settled then, you really intend to leave?

—Yes, everything is settled.

—Well, you are making a mistake as big as the dome of the Invalides.[7]

—Why?

—Because you will miss the artist's life, your freedom, your country. The society in which you will be forced to mix will never forget your stage name. The title of countess will only serve to make you enemies and to make men and—what is worse—women jealous of you. Oh! if you were called to live unnoticed in the shadows, they would perhaps forget you in time, but with your husband being named Consul of France in Melbourne, you will be obliged to attend functions that are as hard to endure as they are to avoid.

—I thought the same as you, my dear Henri, and I myself have made all your very sound observations to Lionel, but he told me: 'I only accepted the position of consular agent in Australia so that I could engage in speculation which would make a lot of money in a short time. Once I am over there, I shall probably send in my resignation but, in any case, don't worry about anything. Love me as I love you and when you are my wife, the future will be my responsibility.

—Ah! if you don't need to depend on anyone, then . . .

—I trust Lionel because, after surviving so many ordeals, I have found myself again. I know the influence I have on him, and I am sure I can make good use of it to encourage him and support him in his new, positive resolutions. He would not leave without me: he would forsake everything to be wherever I am.

—Well, the alarmists will be wrong then, if time proves you right. Let me embrace you, and may all the happiness I wish you be yours!

He left. I went to the window to watch him and, as he walked away, he blew me a kiss and then disappeared. I stood there for a few minutes lost in thought. I was thinking that, once I had made up my mind, I should not have seen anyone.

I leave Paris on 3 January 1854 in dreadful weather. I arrive in London after a bad crossing, which does not make me look forward to the voyage I am about to undertake.

Lionel comes to meet me. He is so rugged up in furs that I don't recognize him at first and mistake him for a bear. I am chilled to the bone, and he covers me up with his pelisse. I want to walk. Marie, my maid, holds the hand of my goddaughter, Solange. The wind pushes them along, spins them around, and they collapse in a heap on the snow, but they don't hurt themselves in the slightest. We are still laughing when we arrive at the hotel, where a supper and a good fire await us.

Marie, this poor girl from the Berry region, who had clung to me, as oysters attach themselves to a rock, had had such a violent bout of sea-sickness crossing the English Channel that, while plying her with cups of tea, I offered to send her back to France.

—Never, she said to me with an air of determination that brooked no argument. I love Madam, the count and Miss Solange. I would rather die in their service than go back home and live in good health in the Berry.

Is it devotion or fear of poverty that makes her say that? I don't know, but I don't have the heart to insist on her going back.

She goes to bed. I put her into her bed like a baby in its cradle, and I can see that I am going to become my maid's maid, which will only double my responsibilities and my problems. Solange and Marie fall into a peaceful, deep sleep. I move away quietly and go into the drawing room.

Lionel does not hear me come in. He is sitting by the fireplace, perfectly still, staring at the flames, but not really seeing them. What is he thinking of? Two tears fall from his eyes and roll down his cheeks like pearls and disappear into his dark moustache. He is crying! He is suffering and yet I am here, by his side. I hold my breath as a host of wild thoughts go through my mind. He must have fears or regrets. I want to try one last test to give him back his freedom to choose. His lips move and he softly says my name, as if he was calling me in a dream. I run up to him, go down on my knees and cover his hands with kisses and tears.

—Where have you been? he says as he draws me into his arms. I thought I was alone and forsaken again, as I was before in this very place, when I was leaving on my first voyage. What a sad thing it is, this melancholy that comes back to haunt your memory at the time of my most complete happiness. You shall be my wife, mine, really mine, and for always, won't you? Get your things ready tonight, because tomorrow we must be at the town hall at ten o'clock, at the church at eleven, and at the French consulate at midday, he added, as if talking to himself.

Unable to find a word in reply, I open my trunk. Everything inside is all jumbled up. This trunk is the one that we closed last. Marie stuffed it with all sorts of things: books, a small bronze bust of the Emperor, a stationery set.

Our good spirits have returned nonetheless. Lionel pushes my white hat back into shape while I smooth out the flounces of my dress and spread out my cashmere shawl on the back of a chair. Lionel lights a cigar and I smoke two or three cigarettes. We wait for daybreak with an impatience that nothing can allay.

Finally, it strikes ten o'clock. We have each dressed in our own room. Lionel comes in to collect me, in his black suit and white cravat. He looks superbly elegant and distinguished. He is rather pale, but his lips are red and his eyes are shining, and he seems to be very happy. I make him wait for a minute. He says I am lazy and scolds me, then he kisses me and we leave.

Our civil wedding went very well. I think the magistrate made a fine speech for my benefit, but I understood absolutely nothing, not knowing a single word of English. As we left the building, I felt very moved, but still reasonably in control of myself. Upon entering the church, however, I was overcome with a nervous trembling which made my arms and legs

shake and my teeth chatter. The idea of making confession distressed me
to the point that I lost both my nerve and my memory. I said to Lionel
as I took his arm:

—Please let's go. We are married enough as we are.

—I have given you forgiveness for all your sins, he said to me with
a smile. The holy man who represents God on Earth will not be less
indulgent than I am. Besides, I have already spoken to him. Come now,
Céleste, be brave; we have faith to support us and prayer to comfort us.

We had almost reached the confessional where the priest was
waiting for me . . . I went down on my knees, but it was impossible for
me to collect my thoughts, to find anything else to say to him but these
words: 'Father, I have sinned . . . Father I have sinned.' I repeated it so
many times that the worthy man took pity on me, prompting both
questions and answers.

—Come, my child, he said to me as he leant towards me, show
yourself equal to the duties that lie ahead. Only remember the past to
help you lead a better life in future. Trust in God's mercy, and He will
never abandon you.

I was overcome with emotion and I was crying without really
knowing why, but those tears were sweet. Lionel had knelt down, his face
hidden in his hands. He was praying for me, I am sure.

They came to tell him that everything was ready. We went ·to the
Saint-Paul Chapel, situated at the far end of the church. Our witnesses,
some French people Lionel had found in London and whom he hardly
knew, and I didn't know at all, followed us in silence. After the usual
formalities, Lionel slipped on to my finger the ring that was to link his
destiny to mine.

—Never take it off, he said as he pressed my hand in his. If one of
us passes on first, the one who survives will wear both of them.

A few people had gathered around us. I heard someone say to a
woman, who was undoubtedly an old maid:

—The husband's a lord. He has youth, good looks, money and
rank, and he's giving all that to a harlot.

—It's not a real marriage, replied another shrew. I've already seen
many of that kind that haven't lasted.

Lionel had heard nothing, and I thought to myself: When the priest
absolves you and promises you the forgiveness of God and man, he can't
answer for the indulgence of women. If the war begins here in the
church, where will it end? . . .

We climb into the carriage and go to the French consulate. There is a foot of snow in the streets, and it's falling so heavily you can't make out the houses. We are shown into a large room where there are eight or ten people gathered around the fire. Not one of them moves to offer us a seat. We wait for an hour without it even occurring to us to ask what we are waiting for. A man enters. He has some papers in his hand and a pair of gold-rimmed glasses on his nose. He looks at us over the afore-mentioned glasses, goes into his office and calls: 'Count Lionel de Moreton de Chabrillan.' Lionel stands up and says as he moves forward:

—I am the Count de Chabrillan, sir.

—You wish to register with the French consulate the marriage you have just entered into, witnessed by the English authorities, with this young lady, Céleste.

—Yes, sir.

—Think for a moment! Later, he added, lowering his voice, you will perhaps regret having carried out this second formality. Your family . . .

—I have neither father nor mother, Lionel replied sharply. I am thirty-two years old, and quite old enough to understand the importance of the agreements I enter into.[8]

The man looks disgruntled but he sits down, puts pen to paper and hands Lionel a document which he then gives to me, saying:

—Here you are. This way we are married twice. If I were to die, no one would be able to cause you trouble over the name I am giving you. Ah! nothing is more precarious than life! Men pass on but legal documents remain.

These few words make me think again about some serious things which I try in vain to chase from my mind. Oh! how easy it is to preach philosophy and resignation to others, but how difficult it is to put them into practice oneself! Any good fortune that comes my way seems quite incredible . . . Is it a dream, a fairy tale? I am really his wife! For the rest of my life I have a friend, a companion in my old age. He has sworn it and nothing can ever separate us again. I marvel less at being a countess than being a wife.

I have just changed my clothes. They are calling me for lunch. I drink little and eat nothing at all. My wretched temperament is taking over again: I feel dreadfully unhappy without knowing why. Lionel is cheerful. He is making big plans, but I listen to him without replying.

This is another fault of my type of personality: I either say too much or too little.

Lionel allowed me to bring my goddaughter, this poor child whose mother died at my place in 1849.[9] He is bouncing her on his knees and says to me as he gives her a kiss:

—As the world we are going to enter knows nothing of our past, we must tell them that Solange is our child. Here we are with the start of a family. If others come along, he added, hugging the little girl who had wrapped her arms around his neck, you will still be our darling girl. We shall leave tomorrow for Southampton and go and visit the *Croesus* on which our passage is booked.[10] It's a magnificent 2500-ton ship. You will not find it tedious on board because life is very gay on the open sea: people laugh and sing and even put on shows in English. With your intelligence, you will learn the language very quickly.

—I hope so, but I don't feel at all confident.

—For you, where there's a will, there's a way, Lionel says, casting me that deep meaningful look which constantly compels me to unveil my most inner thoughts.

—I am afraid, I told him with some embarrassment, that I may not be a good sailor in any sense of the word.

—Your courage will make up for everything and, besides, I am here!

I ring and ask them to bring my menagerie, made up of two small Havana dogs, the size of your fist, that the mother of my dear Adèle Page gave me the day before my departure from Paris, and a small green budgerigar which talks like a school master.[11] My three companions in exile get on well in the same basket. These trivial things amuse us greatly.

CHAPTER 2

On Board the Croesus— *People and Places*

WE LEAVE at six o'clock the next morning. We arrive in Southampton; the town is a dreadful sight. It's completely obscured by coal smoke and dust. The snow is stained with mud. There is a commotion which is like an infernal gallop. We go on board the *Croesus*. Lionel shows me our cabin, a real dog's kennel; Solange and Marie's a mouse trap. I ask Lionel how much time we must stay in here and he laughs as he replies:

—From three to five months.

—You had better be joking, or I am leaving.

—That time is past, my dear Céleste, and will never come again: I am your lord and master in the name of the law!

—But we shall be like cloistered prisoners!

—We can go for a breath of fresh air on deck, Lionel says as he lights a cigar.

—We will need to take a great stock of it for the night. So where am I going to put our things?

—In the drawers, under our beds and up there on those ledges above the ventilators,—my cigars and the powdered seltzer water will be dry there.

I was dismayed at the sight of what I had for space in which to cram my things but, as one can always find someone more unfortunate than oneself, I was consoled on seeing the holes that are called second-class cabins. There was even one gentleman who came up with the idea of putting his children to bed in the drawers and closing them again afterwards! We are placed in the middle of the lounge. Coming out from our cabin, on the right, is the crossbeam of the stern; under this crossbeam there is a sofa and, in front of this piece of furniture, an enormous hollow column in which the helix goes up and down. This drum is encircled by a divan. A thick chain holds back the piano, just as our street singers suspend barrel organs from their necks. Above each door, there is a small gilt-embossed ship. I don't know yet but I have the strong impression that after this voyage, I shall only like ships in paintings.

The second-class lounge is a little less elegant than ours, but very comfortable. There is also a piano; the English put them everywhere. They want to convince themselves that they are not unmusical.

The odour which emanates from the ship's hold and the prospect of spending at least three months in these old sailing tubs contribute to preparing you for seasickness. And I think many people have cabin sickness, which is no less unpleasant.

On board the *Croesus* one must take care of one's own luggage. This was not the least of our troubles for, although we made do with only the most essential things, we only had the pleasure of two drawers. When I say pleasure, it's a very bad joke: these drawers are made of oak and are very heavy. It's often impossible to open them, particularly when the ship is leaning and the lock is in the air. Even were you to have the strength of a horse, you would have to abandon any idea of taking out an essential item. When the ship is leaning on the side of the opening, this same drawer opens all by itself and hurls container and contents against your legs.

Imagine my disappointment, not being used to long journeys. I had brought along some books, albums and other works which I had to send down to the hold. This was my first disenchantment. Oh! my poor books, I said to myself, they are going to be so badly stored!

The ship's deck this morning resembled the square of a vegetable market. There was an indescribable commotion. Right at the stern, on the side where the rudder is, the carpenters were constructing a half-rotunda which was to be divided into three parts: the middle one for sheltering the helmsmen in bad weather, and on each side another section forming a lounge for smokers. Some people were carrying rigging, others bags and trunks. The travellers were settling in, the sailors were loading goods and provisions. From all sides, they were bringing barrels full of vegetables, cauliflowers, coal, and all of it in the driving rain. You could not make yourself heard; when speaking, you had to scream out.

The sky was grey; the sea was black. The passengers were wet and muddy, and the surface of the deck looked like a sewer. The sailors were almost all drunk and were performing feats of strength to speed up the work because, despite the apparent impossibility of it, it was agreed that we would leave the next day.

Some men from the police brought back on board sailors whom they had been ordered to round up in the taverns where they would most likely have forgotten the day and hour of departure. Not one seemed happy to return on board and some must even have put up strong resistance to this reinstatement, for they had blood on their faces and their clothes were torn. I took these people for dreadful bandits, and I was not entirely at ease thinking that I was going to expatriate myself with them, and that once between sky and sea, they would be absolute masters on this floating island which was going to carry us very far away.

Lionel guessed all my thoughts. I have said it before: I have never seen such a gaze as deep or as penetrating as his. Often he would ask me questions and give my answers for me, and I must admit he rarely made a mistake when calculating what was going on in my mind. He said to me with that sudden brusqueness which was fundamental to his character:

—You don't expect to see those poor devils do the manoeuvre in white gloves and patent leather boots, do you? They have so many miseries to endure during the voyage that they get drunk to forget those that they have already suffered and those yet to come. You will see how good they look in times of danger!

It seemed to me that we had no hope of leaving on the advertised sailing day. Punctuality is not a priority in English companies, and they try to find a thousand ways to delay the time of departure in order to have a few more passengers. The *Croesus* did not have a full complement. It could hold 1000 and there were barely 500 of us. Lionel was making these remarks out loud to me when a man near us replied in fairly good French:

—It's shameful for an administration to make passengers leave in such a sorry state, but we shall leave tomorrow, make no mistake about that, even if it means risking the greatest of dangers.

Lionel was not as sociable with men who wear suits as with those who wear work clothes, and therefore he looked at this person speaking to us for a few seconds before replying. He was a man of about fifty with greying hair and a respectable look about him. He continued:

—You must know me, sir, by name at least. My name is Bonard and I am of French origin.[1] My brother is a banker in London and he had been recommended to you during your last trip to England.

—Yes indeed, replied Lionel as he held out his hand to him. I had the pleasure of spending a few hours in his company.

You would not believe how pleasant the prospect of having a friend can be when you are about to set out on a long sea voyage. Mr Bonard, what is more, was distinguished and educated, and we liked him from the beginning.

—We shall leave, he told us, because the company has received 25 000 francs from the government, on condition that it goes as quickly as possible to Lisbon to pick up the dispatches from the last mail.[2] They were left there by the ship that preceded us, which lost its masts on the Portugal coast and arrived so badly damaged that it can't go to sea again for up to six months.

Mr Bonard was right. The sailors spent the night cleaning up a bit. It's not exactly clean, but it's less dirty. We have just left the quay to go into the open harbour to wait for the moment of our final departure.

At two o'clock, the cannon fired its farewell to the town, and the steamers which had accompanied us a few miles out to sea, receded into the distance as they rocked from side to side. Handkerchiefs were waved about. One passenger blew kisses to her mother, another cried as she saw her husband and child grow distant. The English express their joy or grief by shouting frenetic hurrahs. They make a row that would waken the dead. The wind howls and puts an end to this unbearable shouting.

The *Croesus* moves away with so much speed that the seagulls can no longer follow it. The coast disappears into the horizon. Grey shadows engulf us . . . there is nothing, not a thing can be seen . . . it's night, we are in the open sea and this huge ship is taking us away, perhaps forever, to an unknown world . . . I sit down on the deck. Lionel is going to put our cabin in some sort of order, for I know nothing about how they are fitted out and, besides, I am overcome by fatigue and emotion. I need to be alone, to think, so that I can work out in my mind what I must do to radically change my way of living. Will I succeed? . . . I have been so poorly brought up, so ill advised! I don't know whether it's my courage or my heart that is weakening at the moment, but I am afraid that both are deserting me at once.

The *Croesus* had slowed its course but it jolted and tossed about on the waves so much that passengers and objects all came tumbling down on top of each other. All the people walking on deck crashed into each other as they lurched from side to side. You would have thought they were trying to dance a fantastical quadrille. The famous line 'hare you sichowek [*sic*]' (are you seasick?) went from one passenger to the next, some escaping to their cabins, others leaning over the side. The only reply one hears is moaning, groaning and retching.

I stay seated, clinging on to my seat. I feel the first effects of this horrible sickness, but I am fighting against it. The moon has risen and its light is as bright as day. Lionel comes looking for me. He is deathly pale.

—Are you coming? he says to me. I feel terrible.

—If I went down into our cabin, I would feel just as bad. I prefer to stay in the fresh air.

—Cover yourself up well. I can hardly stand up and I am going to go to bed with my head between two pillows. I shall feel better tomorrow.

All the passengers have disappeared as if by magic. I am the only one on deck, along with the sailors who are obliged to keep working. The wind whistles and stings my face; it dishevels and unplaits my hair but I don't let go of the seat which is firmly secured to iron rings.

I really don't know how we have lived through three days and nights. The *Croesus* runs by both steam and sail. They have furled all the sails and we are running on steam. The propeller thumps noisily in the stern. The sea is a little calmer. I have come through it but I have no more strength in my arms and legs. Lionel, Solange and Marie look like three drowned bodies recovered from the bottom of the sea. Lionel gets up, however, and says with a smile:

—Poor Céleste! I am the one who should have been looking after you. If I had been sick like this during my first crossing, the devil take me if I would have made a second one![3] Anyway, I hope it's over. We are in the Bay of Biscay; another bad strait to get through, but after that . . .

He could not say anything more and his expression changed dramatically. He reeled like a drunkard, gestured to me not to follow him and went back to our cabin, leaning against the ship's walls. I was distressed to see him suffer so and I could do nothing to bring him relief. When I stayed with him, he did not even see me. Lying still was the only thing that calmed him a little.

Our cabin is dark. Huge foaming waves roar as they crash against the sides of the *Croesus*. The wind is getting even stronger and comes whistling through all the openings. The ship is brand new; the planks, doors and masts crack as if thousands of woodcutters are cleaving them with axes. I can't bear to stay down below. I imagine the danger is worse than it is; I prefer to face the enemy and I go back up on deck.

The waves swell up before us to phenomenal heights. The *Croesus* wants to make headway nonetheless, and it's running at full steam. This constant fighting against the raging elements seems insane to us but the company has received £1000 to go and pick up the dispatches in Lisbon and we must arrive on the appointed day even if it means risking the loss of all hands. The captain's honour is at stake, and he risks his life which he doesn't seem to care about any more than ours. Driven on further in this way, in spite of all obstacles, the poor *Croesus* looks like a stubborn horse. It rears up at every assault from the sea that it takes on the bow and then it plunges from right to left. Some sailors laugh, others are afraid.

Moans from the passengers are increasing from all quarters. They are no longer conscious of anything. This morning, one of the people in a neighbouring cabin, a young man very much in love with his wife, refused to stretch out his arm to pass her a glass of water. The body suffers so much that the soul becomes insensitive to everything and everyone. Some long for land, others just want to die. It's a distressing sight.

I think that if it were possible to disembark whenever you wanted, few people affected with seasickness would complete a long ocean voyage. It has been a dreadfully bad night. I have not even been to bed, as I prefer fatigue to the suffering I see endured around me.

Marie and Solange are unrecognizable. I reproach myself for having brought them. The appearance of their room is indescribable. Solange is stretched out in the drawer which serves as her bed, with her head and arms hanging limply over the side. Marie is above, almost in the same position. They don't want to take anything and can't keep anything down.

The budgerigar is in a corner; it alone seems to recognize me and says in a doleful, nasal voice when it sees me half-open the door: 'Pretty sweetie! Have you had lunch yet, sweetie?' As for my friend Adèle Page's two small dogs, I don't know if they are still alive. They are curled up in a ball in the bottom of a wicker basket where they are playing dead, sleeping like logs.

When I have had plenty of fresh air above deck and when I feel I can safely go below, I go from one cabin to the other to see my poor patients. The rain is coming down in torrents and the wind is dying down. Lionel seems to be a little better but he is in such a state of exhaustion that he could be told: 'The sea has dried up, the sun has fallen into the water, the moon is asking for you, the *Croesus* is sinking . . .', and he would not say a word, would not move a muscle.

No living creature on board has escaped the storm. Cattle, a cow, the pigs, sheep, hens and ducks make pitiful noises day and night. I feel the strength of my resistance will not last much longer: I am at the end of my tether.

Thank God! the weather has just changed. Not a breath of wind any more but a fog which prevents you from making out surrounding objects five paces in front of you. This semi-darkness is as frightening as the storm.

People are talking, shouting, walking, running around me. Almost everyone has come up on deck. Whistles are being blown from stem to stern and the officers are using megaphones. They suddenly change the manoeuvre. Something extraordinary must be happening on board.

I look for Lionel and find him as he is trying to light a cigar so that he can feel himself again. He laughs as he tells me he is feeling better but he sits down on a bench, finding it impossible to proceed any further. I go and get Solange and carry her to him; they have not seen each other since we left.

—Have you have been sick, Daddy? she says as she hugs him. I don't want to leave you any more because I am afraid with Marie.

The fog begins to lift. Lionel puts the child on my knee and goes to make inquiries in English from an officer on board about what has just happened. After a few minutes, he comes back to me. He seems worried, preoccupied; they must have told him something unpleasant that he does not want to tell me.

The fog clears completely. There are a lot of passengers on deck. They have paid absolutely no attention to dress; it's like the walkway in an infirmary.

At five o'clock, the bell rings to announce dinner but the wind has risen and the *Croesus* is bobbing up and down ... nearly everyone has gone back to bed. Lionel takes the precaution of doing likewise. I go with Solange into the big lounge which serves as a dining room. There are a few people at the table but they look like death. I would like to have a little broth and I am forced to use sign language to a waiter who can't understand a word I say.

The captain, whom I had not recognized, tells me in French that he is entirely at my disposal and that it would give him great pleasure if I would ask him personally for anything I might need. For a start, I need to talk: four days of imposed silence for a woman, that is a real punishment, even when faced with danger.

The captain is not young. He is ugly, he has thinning hair, his teeth are black and his complexion is gingerbread yellow, but he speaks French! I find him charming, and ply him with never-ending questions. He is a well-educated, courteous man who has been sailing for forty years and yet he has rarely made a voyage without being sick for at least two or three days. When leaving port, he passes on his orders to the first mate, or issues them from his cabin.

Solange had fallen asleep on my knee and just as I was about to stand up to carry her down to bed, a wave hit the back of the ship with such force it shattered all the windows, which made an explosion similar to that of a violent clap of thunder.

Foaming water gushes in through the openings and the lounge is flooded. The captain jumps over the table; the passengers climb onto the seats and call for help. Everyone panics.

I go into our cabin. Lionel does not want to get up. He replies that it's nothing, that we shall certainly see worse than this. I can hear hammering, banging. I open the door to look: they have blocked the openings with mattresses. The carpenters are making wooden window frames. I am surprised to see how quickly they deal with accidents that occur at sea. Once again, I got off with a fright and soaking wet feet.

Solange has gone to sleep in my arms, her head leaning against my shoulder. I put her on my bed and go to see my maid. My budgerigar says good evening to me, my dogs growl, Marie is snoring. I feel tired out, worn out, exhausted. I return to my cabin and, for the first time, I lie down fully dressed on my bed, next to Solange. Tiredness overtakes me. I go to sleep, but I dream of the shipwreck of the *Medusa*[4] and I hear strange noises . . . a large hammer is striking without respite at the ship's stern. The doors open and close by themselves, the wood cracks, all our sails are in tatters and they whistle as they lash the air. I have had a nightmare, a temperature, and I wake up at daybreak, furious at having gone to sleep. I rub my eyes, I look around me and I am seized by a nervous laughter that wakes up both Lionel and Solange.

Everything that we had hung up in bags or put on the narrow-ledged shelves that go round the top of our cabin has fallen on top of us, between us, or on the floor between our beds, which stand opposite each other. A heavy pump for making seltzer water, a hundred packets of powder, two tins of cigars, combs, brushes, shoes, face powder, some eau de Cologne, astringent lotion: they have all been broken or mixed up as they came crashing down on top of each other. Poor Lionel sits down on our bed, spreads out his arms, and gives a real cry of despair upon seeing his cigars coated in powder like gudgeons rolled in flour. He leans forward and tries to save a few of them from the wreck.

I laugh more loudly, which makes him angry. He takes a washbowl, some water, washes his cigars, wipes them with a corner of his sheet, spreads them out carefully on his bed, looks at them tenderly and then, in turn, bursts out laughing, as he says to me: 'What does it matter! It's not important. I feel better . . . it's really not important.'

Someone knocks at our door; it's Marie who has come to get Solange. The weather is superb and the ship is not rolling any more. The poor girl is not yet steady on her legs, and she staggers a little as she walks, but she walks, and seems very happy with her lot.

There is one good thing about seasickness: an hour of calm makes you completely forget it. Everyone has been able to freshen up a little, and they are all out and about. People meet as they come out of their cabins; they greet each other and look at one another without being frightened by each other's pitiful appearance. The deck is covered with people. The 500 passengers are there, without counting the crew. They breathe in the air, opening their mouths like carp breaking the surface of the water. They warm up in the sun like sleeping lizards, for the mass of people is so dense that you can't move one step forward.

At daybreak, we leave the Bay of Biscay. If ever I think of it again, I am sure I shall not miss it. Until now, I have not had many observations to make about the people around me. They are starting to come to life, to talk a lot, but I don't understand them. Lionel is the centre of attraction. He has rediscovered his cheerfulness, his verve, and he answers all the people at the same time. Now and again, he blows kisses from a distance to Solange and me but he does not pay us much attention.

The bell rings to announce lunch. I am seated between the captain and my husband, my back turned towards the door of our cabin. There is a copious amount to eat and drink. The passengers don't eat, they devour. They drink everyone's health. The children and domestic staff are served after us. I am dazed by the noise that is being made around me. Leaving the table, there are a lot of drunken people.

The captain offers me his arm and invites Lionel to come and smoke a cigar in his cabin on deck. Everyone steps aside to let us pass. A few ladies look at me askance, with a rather starchy expression, which does not augur well for my future relations on board. I shall be on my guard.

The captain's cabin stands in the middle of the deck, at the foot of the mainmast. It has windows all the way round. Without leaving the cabin, one can see everything that is happening outside: passengers going for a stroll, sailors doing their work, the sides of the ship, the sea, the vastness.

The captain offers me his Voltaire chair,[5] and Lionel stretches out on a divan. There is a full range of astronomical instruments in here. As I am looking at them intently, the captain very kindly explains to me what they are used for. He studies the latitude, the longitude, marks a bearing on a map spread out on the table, points out to me all the preceding bearings and the one he has just added, and I can picture very easily the route that we have followed since the departure of the *Croesus*.

I am amazed and would love to have a geographic map and plot my position as well every day. The captain promises me that he will make a copy of his own and that we will record together.

—If you give in to her every whim in this way, says Lionel, laughing, I am warning you that you will have your work cut out. She will soon want to know as much about it as you do.

—I have done extensive studies and much research; approaching the coast, I have found airstreams favourable to navigation which have been named after me—the Hall winds are very well-known by our sailors. If you allow it, sir, I shall have great pleasure in being the countess's tutor. Ladies don't usually have much of a liking for this sort of study, yet it's a most captivating pastime and sometimes very useful.

Without waiting for our reply, he reaches out, opens a cupboard, takes out a bottle of sherry and three glasses, fills them and gives us one each, which we take together.

—To our speedy voyage! he says, saluting us.

—To our good health, says Lionel, returning his salute.

—To my future studies, I add, bowing in turn.

We talk about one thing and another. The captain congratulates me on the vigorous way I withstood the first ordeals of the voyage. Lionel replies that willpower is nothing and that the good management of a situation is everything. I claim the opposite while admitting some exceptions. He persists. The captain sides with me, and the discussion is about to become heated.

Lionel always has the same failing: he gets carried away by his ideas, becomes worked up and loses his temper to the point that he oversteps the mark, which often forces him to return to his starting point, defeated and embarrassed. Besides, I am determined never to give in whenever I am sure that I am right. That would give him too great an authority over my mind and my person. He would exploit it to the point of dominating me completely.

I stand up to free our captain who must need to return to the tasks of his occupation. He holds out his hands to us, saying:

—Treat this place as your own. Come and see me often. You shall not be disturbed, as I don't entertain anyone.

We went out, delighted to have made each other's acquaintance, but Lionel was rapidly inhaling upon his cigar which, to me, was an indication of some slight unexpressed annoyance. I let him be for some time without talking to him, and then I said, laughing:

—Be careful! you will burn your moustache.

—Céleste, my dear, I don't want to start off by making unpleasant comments, but you have an unyielding, uncompromising character, which is not becoming to a woman when her husband is with her.

—Must she bow to his better judgement, keep quiet or say amen to every remark, like an idiot or a little schoolgirl? You can really be unfair in a way that is quite peculiar to you; just pointing out that you are wrong is enough to annoy you.

—This is not just about being or not being seasick. You show surprise and astonishment at everything, which makes you seem ignorant.

—When one wants to learn, one must admit to knowing nothing.

Mr Bonard fortunately came up to us, and put an end to our not entirely affectionate exchange of views. He has been very sick and the hair on his wig is like a bundle of flax. I sit down on a seat so that I can see Solange who is dancing in a circle with a group of children. She does not understand them but all they are doing is jumping up and down and they get on very well.

There is a stir on deck. People are talking, pointing out something on the horizon, running to the bow. The captain appears with a telescope in his hand. People surround him and question him. I do the same.

—It's a dismasted boat, he tells me, but they are not sending me any signals . . . it must be abandoned.

Theories begin to fly. Everyone gives their opinion. Fifty lorgnettes and telescopes are trained on the same position, and nobody perceives the objects in the same way. The ship is still quite a distance away, but imagination takes over from reality; some say they see no one on deck, others are certain they can make out men.

—A few poor souls hit by the hurricane of these last few days, says Mr Bonard as he gives me his telescope. They must have been swept a long way from the coast, for they would not have ventured into the open sea with such a light skiff.

The weather is fine but there is a rising breeze and the boat's rocking motion keeps moving my lorgnette from the position on which I would like to fix it. At times, I see a dark silhouette between the sky and the water, but I can't make out anything that has a human shape. Mr Bonard claims he has just seen something white being waved in the air. Several people confirm what he says. They are very distressed and ask the captain what he is going to do to help these poor souls.

—Nothing, he replies, it's impossible for me to alter my ship's course to go to that boat and, besides, I haven't seen anything.

Everyone cries out at once in indignation. A moment later, the captain gives in to this strong moral pressure; he gives the order and we turn on our right and go full steam ahead to reach the boat.

—Ten years ago, Mr Bonard tells us, one of my friends was shipwrecked and lost part of his fortune for going, as we are doing now, to the rescue of a boat he thought was in distress.

—We will be luckier than your friend, says Lionel. Look . . . Look! we are getting closer but I can't see anything moving at all any more.

From this moment, the crowd becomes silent. Everyone cranes forward, looks intently, hardly daring to breathe.

—Perhaps they are all dead! I thought. We are going to see something awful.

I was waiting with great impatience, my heart heavy with anxiety. Suddenly, the captain began to swear, the sailors to laugh. A true comic revolution had taken place on board: we had just wasted our time and effort going to a wreck, a hull abandoned long ago no doubt, for there was moss on the deck. A little white poop deck catching the sunlight must have produced the mirage effects which Lionel and so many others had taken for signals.

The influence of the heart is so strong that it hates to waste any of its emotions. Like the others, I was sorry we did not have the opportunity to save a few poor souls dying of hunger and cold. The ship however must have been a scene of great desolation. On the deck, you could see men's clothes, tools and thick chains covered with rust. Water was pouring through all the cracks like tears.

We had drawn so close to this poor boat that, as we passed by, we dragged it along in our ship's wake. It followed us for a long time like those beggars who go running after carriages on the highway. The *Croesus* pulled away and picked up speed. It was as if it reproached that poor abandoned boat for the time it had just lost in going to its aid. It rocked as if to salute the giant that passed by, soon to disappear into the horizon over which the descending nightfall was already casting its shadow.

The night went well. Lionel can't keep still; he is very busy with Solange. Whenever we have a slight falling out, it's his way of getting back into my good books without talking to me. I go up to them, I kiss them and, with no further ado, we have made up. I take his arm, the little one gives me her hand, we hug each other and we are very cheerful, so happy that I would like always to stay at sea in the midst of these people I don't understand and who don't know me.

The captain keeps his word; he has given me a map that he has traced by hand. He is an extraordinary man and a true scholar: he speaks four languages, plays several musical instruments and draws wonderfully. He has some charming turns of phrase; his expression is sincere and his voice pleasant when he speaks to you privately. He makes you completely forget that he has a face ugly enough to frighten little children.

But when it's a question of his command, his whole being is immediately transformed: his hackles rise with rage, he shouts, swears, and threatens his men. His manner is abrupt, his eyes fiery and mistrustful, his voice strident. The sailors make way as he goes past and the children run away, calling him Mr Bogeyman. I understand the extent of his responsibility, but as I am just a little afraid of him myself when I see him in his explosive state, as he puts it, I wait until he comes to me, never going up to him. I think he is grateful to me for being reserved, for all his moments of leisure are devoted to me. Every evening, as we go for a stroll, he teaches me to read the stars. I already know the name of all the stars of our continent. Nature is such a wonderful book; it stays open and visible for all, but very few people try to decipher these beautiful pages traced by the Creator's hand.

Until now, I have paid such little attention to my fellow travellers that every time I see people coming towards me I take them for newcomers. There is a small colony of French people on board, or French-speaking people, of whose presence I was completely unaware. Mistress [*sic*] Mary Brook is one of them.[6] This morning, the captain came up to me on deck and said:

—May I introduce Mistress [*sic*] Mary Brook who is extremely eager to meet you?

—I am of French origin, this lady said, holding out her hand to me in the English tradition. My husband, Mr Brook, is a field officer in the service of Her Majesty the Queen of England. We lived in India for eight years. As the climate made me very ill, I had to make a trip to Europe and I have just spent two years there with my family. My husband has just been sent to the province of Victoria and I am going to meet him there. We shall be travelling together and if I can be of any help to you, I am at your disposal.

I thank her rather coolly: my position forces me to be very reserved. But this lady seems to me to have a lot of self-confidence or poise. She places her arm under mine and says: 'We shall go for a stroll together, shall we?' The 'shall we' is superfluous as she does not leave me time to say no. She talks to me about everything and everyone at once . . .

She looks about twenty-five to thirty years old. Her big round eyes are jet-black, her features fine, her teeth white and her lips thin and pale. Despite her voluminous dress, she looks almost transparently thin. She walks, skipping along on tip-toe, and this annoys me so I take my arm away from hers. There is something about this self-satisfied little creature which does not predispose me in her favour.

There is not a breath of wind and we are at a standstill. The captain is in an intolerable mood.

I would like to teach Solange the ABC but nothing seems to penetrate that skull of hers. Lionel reads to me out loud but he stops at the end of every line to make me admire the style of his favourite authors. I find that they make excessively long digressions, that they are deadly dull with their insistence on judging everything from their own point of view, and that by trying to prove so many things to me at once, they tire and bore me, without proving anything at all.

He is quite indignant; he closes his book and calls me Vandal between clenched teeth, but an hour later he bears me no ill will. He takes up his reading where he left off and, whether I like it or not, I have to swallow chunks of philanthropic, democratic and social prose which put me to sleep. I would rather study astronomy than human folly: judging it in action is quite enough. There are times when the days are so long on board that you need a few differences of opinion to help pass the time.

Mistress Brook, who often joins us, always agrees with him. He finds her very well-educated, a bit slight of figure, but refined nonetheless. He is delighted that she wants to look after me. It will leave him more spare time to play his interminable games of chess.

We have a group of strolling musicians: six strapping American lads who are going to try their fortune in Australia. They took jobs on board as domestics so as not to have to pay their passage. It's a service that leaves a lot to be desired, but there is one compensation: of an evening, they organize theatre-concerts. They smear their faces with black greasepaint, they make up costumes à la Robert Macaire;[7] some blow their instruments fit to burst them, others scrape their violins, gesticulating like epileptics; they sing negro songs, dance, punch and kick each other. Mistress Brook tells me that their repertoire is a bit risqué, but people laugh, and she more so than the others. She watches, listens and speaks all at the same time. She is very flirtatious and constantly preoccupied with the effect she is making or is about to make.

The young women avoid her. The men seek her out: they all seem to be playing up to her. Her seat was at the end of the dining-room table but, upon her request, a man gave her his seat opposite us. She insists on offering me her services. I can't say a word to my husband without her joining in our conversation. He loves to speak English and, most of the time, I don't know what they are saying. This irritates me and I have moments of bad temper that I can't conceal. Lionel makes fun of me, which does not help to calm me in the slightest. He ends up by asking me if I am foolish enough to be jealous of this plain, thin little person who chatters away like our budgerigar without knowing what she is saying. I don't say anything; I sulk.

—You know I adore you and you are the only person I love in the whole world, he adds as he kisses me; but we must humour her.

—Why?

—She is curious, indiscreet, untruthful. One day, she says she was educated at the Sacred Heart, another day, at the Convent of the Birds. She claims to be the legitimate daughter of a general who died a bachelor! Still, as it's impossible for us to avoid her completely, resign yourself to being pleasant to her.

—Yes, I shall try, but spare her your kindness and compliments.

—I am making fun of her.

—She doesn't think so, and the others will end up by believing that you are playing up to her.

—I ask her questions which, one day, will perhaps turn to your advantage. One never knows what might happen.

Obviously, he has changed his mind about Mistress Brook; he knows she is a scandalmonger and he fears her because of me. Since I can't distance myself from her, I am going to put someone between us— a woman she has told me she detests so much that she can't bear the sight of her. She is an elderly lady who occupies a cabin near mine. They call her Lady Gamby.[8] She must have been very beautiful, but unfortunately she has not known how to grow old gracefully. She has hung onto the clothes, the habits, the tastes and all the childlike airs of youth. She makes herself up heavily with mascara and uneven blotches of powder and rouge; her grey hair shows here and there under tufts of blonde curls; her neck and wrists are encircled with wide bands of black velvet, and she always wears gloves. She does not talk to anyone, and always walks alone, preferring to seek out places where there are the fewest people. She is, despite this, extremely gracious. She has an easy manner and a neat waist-line. They say she is a nice person; in a word, she must have great qualities because Mistress Brook hates her.

Lady Gamby knows how to play chess and gives Lionel tactical hints. She said to him:

—I am very sorry to have forgotten my French. I would have been flattered to talk occasionally with you and with Madam.

—Nothing is more simple, replied Lionel; you can exchange lessons, and in very little time, you will understand each other perfectly.

I had put off the introduction by replying to my husband: 'Later, we shall see.' I have changed my mind, and have just told him that I want to be introduced to Lady Gamby. Lionel offered her his arm and they have been walking on deck for an hour at least. Mistress Brook pulls a face which makes her look very ugly. Lionel and Lady Gamby come up to us, and Mistress Brook gets up and leaves. Lady Gamby takes her place next to me and says:

—I had a French governess, and if you would care to help me a little, it will come back to me very quickly.

I promised her to do my best. I asked my husband why I felt immediately at ease with this lady whilst I still could not get used to the ways of Mistress Brook.

—Because Lady Gamby is a real lady. In society, she would probably not have sought you out, but when you are seated next to her at the table, you will be spending a few hours together, and she will try and make things easy for you.

—Yes, but when she finds out who I am . . .

—She knows; I have just told her. I would never expose myself to a reproach by exposing you to an affront. For several days, Lady Gamby has been studying French in order to say the few words that she has just addressed to you.

I am perhaps a little too impressionable, but I am deeply touched and I feel that Lady Gamby is going to occupy an important place in my affections; and when I love, I love whole-heartedly.

—Well, Mistress Brook says to me in the evening as we are walking on deck, Lady Gamby has achieved her aim, and you will be a convenient friend.

—I don't understand you.

—Do you hope to understand her?

—Good-hearted people have a language which is easily understood.

—What a pity our young pianist is not as responsive to her as you are.

—Lady Gamby likes music.

—Is it the music . . . or the musician?

—Oh! madam!

—Haven't you noticed?

—I take no interest in other people's business and least of all when it's a case of inventing improbable stories.

—You must nevertheless take some interest in what is taking place around you.

—It would perhaps be better to mind one's own business.

—That would be no fun, admit it!

—That depends on one's personal resources.

—I haven't much imagination, she says, with a rather forced laugh.

—You don't really believe that. One always has enough without borrowing other people's.

She seems annoyed, which is fine as long as she leaves me in peace.

Lady Gamby gives me English lessons. I work with an intensity that makes me forget about eating and sleeping, but time passes so quickly and I want to make the most of it.

—You are getting on remarkably well with your neighbour, Mistress Brook has just remarked with a laugh. We can hardly get a minute of your time these days.

—Are you talking about Lady Gamby?

—Lady ... Lady ... she is no more Lady than I am. Her first husband was a nobleman, but her second husband was a merchant. The title was buried with the first husband.

—Excuse me, miss, replies a blonde lady who is sitting near us on deck, but in England a noble woman can remarry and keep the name and title of her first husband.

The person who has just addressed us has blonde hair the colour of a sheaf of ripe wheat. She speaks French with such a strong Alsatian accent that it takes all my concentration to understand her. She looks thoroughly miserable. The dress she is wearing is worn and faded. Mistress Brook looks at her askance, gets up and leaves without answering her.

This lady realizes that she is the cause of Mistress Brook's sudden departure and she says to me:

—That was wrong of me. Here one must never speak to anyone without first having been introduced, all the more so since I have only been with you here in first class since this morning. I booked my passage in second class to go and join my husband in Melbourne. I have with me my servant and my two children, the younger one is only six months old. The weather has been so bad that I fell sick feeding him and we were possibly both going to die, but the captain is so good that he invited me to come up to first class during the daytime and to take my meals at your table, which is more comfortable than ours. I lived in France, and I have heard here on board that the count is going to occupy the Melbourne consulate. He could be of great service to me in finding my husband down there, for I don't know exactly where he will be on my arrival. This is why I took the liberty of speaking to you in order to ask for your assistance.

—Mine would be of no use to you, but I am certain my husband will be delighted to be of help to you.

A little girl, blonde like her and delicate as a flower, is brought to her. I pat her affectionately and she responds. Then I take her to Lionel and Solange who find her delightful. After that we carry her back to her mother who has stayed in the background.

Lionel really does have a heart of gold. He comforted and encouraged this poor woman and promised to take care of her as soon as we arrived. She thanked him with tears in her eyes. Her expression, which had been so lifeless and her complexion so pale a few minutes earlier, lit up with joy. She is about thirty years old; she is not pretty but she seems gentle and kind.

An instrumental concert has been organized for this evening. The lady from second class sits down at the piano: she has a remarkable talent. Then the captain accompanies her on the flute at first and then on the cello. I have rarely heard such delightful music. People crowd around, congratulate and thank Mrs Wèbe [*sic*], for that is the name of our new recruit. We make her play the same pieces six times over.

Upon repeated requests from the captain, my husband sits down at the piano and plays a few polkas of his own composition. It's a daring thing to do, to follow on after such a successful performance, but energy replaces charm, the pride of the composer replaces the performer's technique, and he comes out of it very well. The honours are shared.

CHAPTER 3

In Port at Lisbon and the Cape

AT SIX o'clock in the morning, we enter Lisbon harbour—finally![1] Yesterday it was Winter, today it's Spring. The sky is blue, the breeze gentle, and there is sunshine everywhere. The Tagus is covered with painted ships decked out with flags of every possible colour, and pretty boats cross it in all directions. It's a wonderful panorama, but I prefer the sight of the charming town on our right to this splendour on the water.

There is no doubt about it, I would give all the rivers of the universe for one little garden. Lisbon is built on ascending terraces, in such a way that you think you are seeing a huge fan of a thousand colours opened out in front of you. They paint their houses black, green, yellow, pink or blue; it depends on personal tastes and they are very varied. There are flowers at every doorway, and the fragrance of orange trees perfumes the air. I am really looking forward to going ashore, and I get dressed at daybreak.

I already have my foot on the ship's ladder when some people coming up to us in a small boat signal me to stop. The boats that were to carry us ashore move away from the ship's side with such speed that they knock into each other. The man who prevented me from getting off is dressed all in black. The six oarsmen who accompany him also have crepe bands around their hats. The yellow flag bearing the Portuguese arms is covered with a large black crepe.

—What is going on here? I ask Lionel. Those people look far from happy.

—I don't know, he says to me as he goes up to the captain.

The captain exchanges a few words with the newcomer, and then the character in black moves away as solemnly as he had arrived. They remove the chains from the ship's ladder, and we look at each other in dismay.

—We have just been given notice of quarantine, Lionel tells me, tugging so hard on his moustache that he extends it by a centimetre.

—What for? None of us is sick.

—We have had a death in third class. The inhabitants of Lisbon are afraid of everything and they take exaggerated precautions. As they saw us make our entrance into the Tagus with our flag at half-mast, as a sign of mourning, they believe we have the plague or cholera on board, and have just sent us officers from the Health Department. Besides, it's the custom after all.

Since the Health Department boat has left, there has been a great deal of commotion on board the *Croesus*. The passengers are furious and express their annoyance through curses and wild threats. During this time, the captain has reached the open sea, and leaves us in the harbour where we shall have to stay until further orders.

I must admit that the prospect of remaining prisoner for forty days on board the *Croesus* hardly seems very entertaining to me and besides, even though we are not sick, we begin to have our doubts and we spend our time glancing surreptitiously at one another. They blame an officer for not having thrown the dead man overboard. He replies that when you are near a town, you must keep the dead on board in order to take them ashore. We are truly suffering the tortures of Tantalus![2]

In the evening, the town lights up, and we hear songs and music. This plunges us into a profound melancholy, but then we realize that the best thing to do is to resign ourselves to it. We organize a party. All the masts are lit up as if by magic. We make music and dance so much that the *Croesus*'s deck creaks and groans. Rockets are fired. There is a supper which the women don't attend. Lots of men fall over and sleep under the tables or on seats.

Day breaks. On the Tagus, there are many boats moving about, which are decked out by small traders of all sorts, but no one comes to us to offer us fruit, oranges or flowers. Our confinement on board is official, and despite our distance from the port, we are kept under surveillance. The coming day seems to be taking an eternity to arrive.

Mistress Brook has lost nothing of her verve. She is everywhere at once. She comes up to me and says, with the air of a thief who demands your money or your life:

—You haven't seen Mrs Wèbe for the past two days, have you?

—No.

—Well, it's because of her that we are going to stay here indefinitely.

—Why?

—Her baby is dying! You would have to be mad to set sail with a six-month-old child! Another death and we shall definitely be taken for victims of the plague.

Without answering her, I go straight to second class and knock on Mrs Wèbe's door. I find her seated, her arms hanging limply by her sides, her expression vacant, her breathing hoarse. Her child is lying on her knees; he is so white, so delicate, he looks like a wax doll. He has stopped breathing . . . I think he is dead! She looks at me, guesses what I am thinking, and lifting the child, she presses her cheek against the poor child's lips that are almost cold.

—It's not all over, she says to me as she bursts into tears, but very nearly! Ah! my poor husband, who would have been so happy to have a son! He will learn of his birth and his death at the same time!

—Don't give up all hope! What did the ship's doctor tell you?

—That I would be the reason why the *Croesus* will be left in quarantine. Cilia, she began again, addressing a beautiful young girl who was standing still in a corner despite the repeated rebellious cries by Mrs Wèbe's little girl, if your hands are not as cold as mine, try to warm him a little.

Cilia kneels down near her mistress. You could not possibly see anything prettier and more graceful than this young girl. She is about eighteen. Her big black eyes are filled with tears that she tries in vain to hold back. Her hair net falls off and her hair comes undone and falls like a mantle about her shoulders.

The young child doubles up and then relaxes. I think it's all over . . .

—Would you take Zine? Mrs Wèbe says to me, gently pushing away the little girl who is absolutely determined to force her mother to pay attention to her.

She doesn't want to follow me, so I carry her away. Solange is delighted, and she says to Zine in a cruelly naive outburst of joy:

—I wish your brother would die every day because then you would stay with me.

An hour has hardly passed when Cilia comes to tell me:

—It's all over! Madam's nerves have just given way. Please bring her daughter to her!

Mrs Wèbe has come round. Without shedding a tear, she stares at the ship's doctor with wild, piercing eyes. He is a man barely thirty-two years old with light blond hair and quite good-looking, very much concerned with himself, very little with his patients. He eats like a horse, drinks to excess, loves sherry and brandy with a passion that he can't control. He drinks from six in the evening to two in the morning, and the rest of the time he sleeps. What a strange practice to tolerate such a state of affairs on board ships where doctors have such a large responsibility.

He certifies the child's death. Mrs Wèbe opens a box, takes out a small christening bonnet, puts it on her son with a white robe and a blue cloak, carries him in her arms, gazes at him and puts him down on the bed, crying out: 'No, no! he can't possibly be dead!' The sight of this scene affects me terribly. I choke and I cry too.

Lionel comes looking for me and scolds me gently; he says I must not take such an active part in the events that take place around us at sea, because I shall end up turning into a hypochondriac or falling ill. We must try to find consolation in each other.

—For the moment you can't do anything. What consolation can you give a woman who is burying her child? Let this first wave of grief pass and then we shall see. What is most upsetting for us at the moment is being in quarantine.

—What would happen if we set fire to the ship!

—They would let us burn with it. They are supposed to send us a deputation of doctors tomorrow. If, after inspection, they are convinced we are not rabid, they will perhaps allow us to go ashore. While we are waiting for them, I am going to play my game of chess in the lounge. Come with me.

—No, I need air.

—Don't go back to Mrs Wèbe's cabin.

—No.

This long day has just ended. All faces are heavy with sadness and spirits are very low. No one is talking; people seem to be avoiding each other, but don't know why.

After dinner, our cheerfulness returns somewhat. I go up on deck with Lady Gamby. The sky is filled with bright, shining stars. We are talking about Mrs Wèbe at the very moment we see her appear. She is pale, unsteady, and has a lot of difficulty holding herself up, leaning against Cilia's arm. In a spontaneous reaction, we go up to her and offer her a place between us. Mrs Wèbe lets herself fall onto the seat. She looks as if she has lost all interest in life. Cilia moves away discreetly, leans on the ship's rail and hides her face in her hands: she is crying.

—Poor girl! Mrs Wèbe says to us, she misses him as much as I do! She was like a mother to him while I was sick. His first and his last smiles were for her! She followed me through a sense of devotion, for I am too poor to pay her for her services and, really, is one ever rich enough to reward such a loving soul? What would I have become without her? Oh God! Dear God! she went on in desperation; what have I done to deserve so much heartbreak and hardship!

—You have suffered a great deal, have you?

—Yes, a great deal.

I realized this poor woman would find some relief in telling us of her troubles and I asked her, in order to take her mind off her grief, why her husband had left her and what could have induced her to set sail with such young children.

—I was so young when unhappiness became a part of my life that I can hardly remember the day it arrived. My father was rich, indeed very rich. He saw to it that I received a full education, but he was an absolute authoritarian. I no longer had a mother to defend me and I had to obey all his wishes. I loved a young man who had given me music lessons. Not only did my father dismiss him from our household, but he made sure that he was sent packing everywhere else too. I followed him to England where we were married. We lived on the income from our work, but it brought in so little that we sometimes went hungry.

—And your father?

—He lost or squandered his fortune, and died without ever wanting to hear of us again. Poverty and deprivation quickly wear down your physical and moral strength. I fell ill and had to give up my students: I was giving piano lessons. My husband could not stand it any longer. 'I'm a coward! he cried. 'This miserable existence is killing you. You see, I can't make a living out of anything here, but there's a country where they are finding a lot of gold, and I'm going there.' I tried in vain to make him give up this idea. He left for Australia, leaving us, my daughter and me, in the care of a neighbour, Cilia's aunt. A few months later, I gave birth to my son. I received a letter from my husband, in which he said to me: 'I am lost without you: you are my strength and my courage.' By dint of hard work, I had accumulated a little money. Cilia's aunt had just died and the poor girl found herself all alone in the world; she suggested that she come with me. She loved my children, and said to me: 'I shall really earn my keep. I ask nothing of you but a little affection!' We left, happy that each of us could rely on some help from the other in caring for the children. Now one of them will never need anything ever again, and I wish I were in his place!

—You still have Rosine, a little angel who will console you for the loss of your other child.

—Poor Rosine! I dare not look at her any more: I seem to see the shadow of death hovering over her pale face.

—You are going to see your husband again.

—Who knows? I wrote to him but did he receive my letter?

—We shall help you find him. Don't start worrying about the future when the present is painful enough for you to bear. Be strong!

It's late and I am going back to my dog box of a cabin. Let us hope tomorrow will not be so sad.

This morning, the health officers came from Lisbon to pay us a call. After they did an inspection they told the captain he could let us disembark. School children at the start of holidays were never so happy! People of all shapes and sizes, young and old, sailors and passengers, they are all running all over the place, jumping about, exchanging handshakes and kisses.

We leave the ship as if we are scared of seeing Lisbon move away or sink into the ground. The stairway is narrow, the doorways small, and people jostle each other. A passenger and his wife, who were squeezed out by the crowd, have just fallen into the sea. They have been fished out but, far from being disturbed by the catastrophe, people are doubled up with laughter.

Mistress Brook seems to want to attach herself to us. Lionel has her understand that once he has left the ship he wants to have nothing to do with the passengers. But ten minutes later she sees us go past and shoots us one of her nastiest looks.

We drop in to the Braganza Hotel: when I say drop in, it's just a figure of speech, because to get there we have just had to make a veritable ascent. In my opinion, you have one of the most beautiful views in the world from the terrace of this hotel. The Tagus stretches away as far as the eye can see, and there are many small boats, all decked with flags, gliding over the silvery water or rocking to and fro. The air is filled with fragrant perfume, and all the gardens, one above the other up the side of the hill, are planted with orange trees in bloom. The appearance of the town centre is not as magical by a long way. Not many people wear the Portuguese costume. A few mules still make their little gold bells tinkle as they skip along on the wretched cobbles. The buildings, the streets, the shops have a profoundly sad appearance. All the inhabitants are dressed in black, as the queen has died.[3] Everyone has gone into mourning and a lot of people are feigning tears.

I look at Lionel with such disillusionment that he takes hold of my arm and says:

—I agree;—the town looks like a cemetery on All Saints' Day. Let's go and visit the surrounding areas. They are lovely.

We climb into a carriage and here we are, taking off alone like a pair of sweethearts. At the outset, everything seems splendid, but then we look at each other and talk about our plans and hopes, building such beautiful castles in Spain that the villages and estates of Portugal pass by unnoticed. It's impossible to begin the excursion again, as we have to shut ourselves up once more for the evening on board the *Croesus*. Lionel buys me whole baskets full of fruit, flowers and oranges. Everyone arrives at the same time with bunches of flowers and provisions, and they are all happy. We sort our things out and get organized as best we can and then wait for the signal for departure. The captain gives it, but not one member of the ship's crew makes a move to obey his orders.

After an hour of explanations and very heated discussion, we are told that while we were on land, the crew rebelled. The men had a meeting, after which they informed the captain that there were not enough of them to manoeuvre the *Croesus*, that they had to take on fifteen more sailors at Lisbon, and that they were to undertake to give them fresh meat at least once a week.

The captain cried out in indignation: he had not received orders to act. It's extra expenditure for which he can't assume responsibility. The conditions of enlistment were decided upon and signed by the company. He will have his powers and his right respected by reason or by force. In response, the sailors come together in a tightly packed group and go on the defensive. They have arms. The officers move in around the captain. Women scream and children cry. Panic takes over. People are fleeing, jostling each other. Flowers, fruit and even children are rolling around on the deck and are trampled underfoot. Two or three hundred people try to go down to the lounge at the same time and they tumble down on top of each other.

This mutiny frightens me, but I am even more afraid of being suffocated while going down with the others. I stay on deck where there remain about 100 passengers who seem to be discussing the arguments for and against. Lionel is with them in the bow. I can't hear anything of what is said and would not understand anyway. I am worried to death. I climb up on a seat. Lionel sees me and comes over to offer to take me back to our cabin because, the way things are developing, it does not seem as if they will be worked out amicably.

—The sailors are right to refuse to continue a duty beyond their capabilities. Everyone's safety is at stake. The Company makes us pay dearly enough for our tickets: it should not make too much of a fuss. Basically, I think the captain agrees with the sailors.

—Why doesn't he give in?

—Because he wants it to be noted that they have used force against him.

—Are they going to fight then?

—No; the numbers are too unequal. It's impossible to send them to prison or to put them down in the hold. We would be left without a crew. Everything will work itself out. Go back.

—Come with me.

—No, I want to see.

—Well then, I'm staying too. The ship's barrier is far enough away from the bow for me to be quite safe.

After a very loud discussion which lasted two hours, Lionel comes back over to me. He is very pale and seems to be troubled by something. I ask him what has happened.

—Nothing of concern. If you want to go ashore again, we shall not be leaving before tomorrow.

—Are they going to take on more crew?

—Yes, fifteen.

—Where will they find them?

—In Lisbon. There is no shortage. The Portuguese were the world's first sailors.

—You are hiding something from me.

—Don't be silly. I shall go and get our bag and toiletries. We will leave Marie and Solange on board.

Whenever he does not want to answer me, he always has a ready excuse to leave me.

People are moving around again. In general, they seem to be delighted to return to land. The captain looks downcast. As for the sailors, they are beaming. People give them cigars and shake their hands. One of them who speaks French is talking close by with Mr Bonard. He says:

—I knew they would decide in our favour. The sails are not secure, the engine is too strong for the hull, and there will be draught and damage on the way. I've seen the hold myself and I know as much about it as the captain.

Lionel comes looking for me. We spend our evening at the hotel. It's impossible to go out to enjoy ourselves anywhere as all the public places are closed. At daybreak we return on board.

A few hours later, four Portuguese boats draw alongside the *Croesus*. Two bring us fifteen sailors enlisted in Lisbon while the two others carry livestock. All of it is loaded in a flash, and they get down to work to weigh anchor. Everyone is on deck. The weather is fine but the air is cold and this gives everyone a sullen appearance and makes them look sad and dispirited.

When the sailors have a difficult job to do, they all sing the same shanty so they can pull on the cables in unison. In this way, they focus all their effort and energy on the spars of the wheel which is used to raise the anchor. The work is hard and they need more than the shanty this time, so one of the leading seamen asks for a musician. A waiter arrives with his violin and marks the beat. The sailors work even harder. On the third turn, one of the spars snaps and strikes a young officer between the shoulders. He had joined the other sailors to help them as much as to urge them on. He lets out a scream, throws out his arms and falls under the feet of the men who are still turning the wheel and can't stop short.

When they lift the poor officer up again, he is already dead, blood streaming from his nose, mouth and ears. They ask for permission to bury him in Lisbon and permission is granted. Our departure is set back again by two days.

The next evening at eight o'clock, we watch the approach of a small boat whose pointed, intersecting sails resemble the wings of a bird. They lower the coffin into a dinghy which then glides away across the Tagus like an eerie shadow. The passengers are asked to make a contribution so that enough money can be left in Lisbon to erect a memorial to this unfortunate young man. Everyone gives readily.

Céleste Mogador in a male role (J. Richardson, The Courtesans*)*

Madame la Comtesse Lionel de Chabrillan. Céleste at the time of her marriage,
1854. (F. Moser, Vie et aventures de Céleste Mogador)

Céleste in retirement, 1896 (Moser)

The Count de Chabrillan's bookplate (Collection J. Thibault)

Céleste's visiting card, showing the Count de Chabrillan's coat of arms (Moser)

The next day they weigh anchor at dawn, but it's a dark, miserable day and the sailors' shanty is as miserable as the weather. We sail full steam ahead. The bobbing up and down begins anew and lots of passengers disappear again. I ask Lionel whether he shall cope better with our second ordeal. He assures me he will and stays close by me on deck. As for Solange, as soon as she felt the ship's first motion, she said to Marie:

—I feel sick in my tummy; let's go to bed. And Marie took the precaution of lying down too.

An Indian domestic comes over with a deck chair and puts it down beside us. He straps it to a bench, places some cushions on it and then stands and waits. A stooped old lady, leaning on the arm of a young man, walks nonchalantly across and sits down in the chair that has just been prepared.

—Who is that lady? I ask Lionel. I haven't seen her before.

—Mrs Liston. She came on board in Lisbon.

—Is that her son with her?

—Goodness, Céleste, imagine if she heard you! That is her husband!

—She looks thirty years older than he. It really makes you wonder. Heavens! what an ugly sight she is with her large eyes, sallow complexion and big teeth. Her sight must be very poor to peer at us like that with her monocle.

—Yes, I think she is short-sighted.

—I think she is impertinent.

—She wants to see whether she has reason to be jealous of you: she is a tigress!

—So you know her then?

—Yes and no. I told you that in Lisbon I met a friend of mine who is attached to the French Embassy there. He knows these newlyweds and, because he knew we were going to travel together, my friend told me about them. The man looks like an old woman and the woman like an old fairy. She acts so pretentiously . . . if only it were just an act! but it seems she thought she was the most beautiful woman in Lisbon. I have been told we would be most entertained by her. But you are staring at her!

—Well, she has done nothing but peer at me.

—Look away!

—I would rather leave.

—They are like us: they are going to Australia to hide their happiness. We shall meet up with them again.

Lady Gamby is as charming as ever towards me, but she is overly fond of music. She spends hours leaning on the piano, watching and listening to a young passenger who thumps away from morn till night and who sings either from his throat or through his nose. People make fun of her; she is becoming the laughing stock of the ship. I tried to broach the subject tactfully but she does not understand, or pretends not to understand,—which is worse.

Solange cut me on the hand while she was playing with my scissors and now I can't sew or write. I shall carry on with my diary later.

It's the eve of a big event: we are approaching the equator, and the question on everyone's lips is whether they will have the crossing the line ceremony or not. The captain was against the ceremony but the sailors and many of the passengers were in favour of it so he had to relent again. On this day, the captain and officers abdicate all power and Neptune is king of the ship. King Neptune is either a hideously got-up dummy or the oldest sailor.

There is some buying and selling takes place on board ships but the sale of wine and spirits beggars the imagination. Every passenger was therefore expected to give money to help cater for the ceremony because for English sailors, the more there is to drink, the better the occasion.

The captain looked on unhappily as his ship was turned upside down by all the preparations taking place. He knew from experience how these things turn out. They tied a huge tarred sail to the front of the *Croesus*, from starboard to port side, and then left the pumps on all night to fill it up like a huge bath. At daybreak, the ceremony began. There was a procession. All the crew were in fancy dress, that is, they had smeared their faces and bodies with every imaginable colour and had made themselves wigs using sheep skins. They were carrying pitchforks, shovels, sticks and wooden sabres. They walked in two rows with the novices—those about to be baptized—in the middle.

Then they made those poor souls sit down, blindfolded, on a plank across the middle of the improvised bath. They smeared their chins with tar and, while this was going on, the others talked to them and told them the silliest and sometimes the funniest things imaginable to try and get them to open their mouths so they could be forced to eat tobacco, soap, or even bits of candle. When one of them was caught out, they made him do a somersault. The men in the water (the Tritons) caught him and made him drink as much salt water as they could until he was almost drowned. Then they all embraced him. He was baptized.

Needless to say, all this involves a good deal of rough play which generally ends in serious quarrels. The passengers are not exempt from this so-called little ceremony, but they can buy their way out of it with a bottle of brandy.

One poor ship's boy was so afraid of the ceremony he had hidden down in a cabin. But they found him and dragged him out. He screamed and cried but it did him no good: those half-crazed men were merciless and baptized him even more roughly than the others. When they let go of him, the poor fellow looked like an imbecile: he was pale, his teeth were chattering, and his arms and legs were trembling uncontrollably. The more he seemed to suffer, the more the audience applauded. There is no doubt about it, these people have instincts of savage brutality.

Lionel asked the captain why he had not intervened in the face of such rough treatment which was bound to have unfortunate consequences.

—I can't do anything before sunset, he told us. If I got involved in what they call their games, they would be capable of making a fool of me as they did that poor wretch who made the mistake of trying to resist. You can take an interest in these people from a distance, he went on, nodding in the direction of the sailors who were dancing in a circle around a half-barrel of brandy, but see them at close quarters and while they are working, and they are wild beasts that can only be controlled by threats and blows.

The captain must have been exaggerating; he was probably remembering the violence he had suffered himself, but I must admit that, at the time, I rather agreed with him.

Solange derived no pleasure at all from the ceremony. A French sailor, the only one on board, and who had made himself a red, yellow and green-coloured mask, came over to carry her to the baptism. I think they were going to sprinkle a drop of salt water on her head but she was dreadfully frightened and let out the most piercing screams.

—But I'm Jacques, you know that, Jacques from Brittany, he said, trying in vain to console her. She hid her head in my skirt and we had to take her away.

During the night the ship's boy, who had been the hero of the ceremony, had a bout of fever. The sailor on watch grabbed hold of him just as he was about to throw himself overboard. He was just sixteen years old. His parents had made him enlist against his wishes, for he loathed both the sea and sailing.

—Well, what did you think of the English festivities? Mr Bonard asked us at lunch.

—I think it's a very poor reflection of the supposed progress of our civilization, but how can you hold it against those poor creatures? Lionel replied. If they had the slightest intelligence, they would not take on a trade as beasts of burden. They are badly housed, badly fed, badly treated and exposed to cold and danger. They get drunk so they can forget, and are more to be pitied than blamed.

—You are a philanthropist, sir.

—I feel strongly for all those who have heart and courage. When I see those poor people snatched from their sleep, being forced to climb in dark, stormy weather to the top of those tall masts where their lives hang by a thread, by a puff of wind, I am overcome with pity and admiration.

—I have only admiration for your soldiers, Mr Bonard replied kindly. Being a sailor is a profession.

—Profession, ambition, it's all the same. Whether you work for glory or to earn your keep, you are still working to satisfy one need or another. In wartime, our soldiers come into their own: they have an enemy to fight, whereas sailors battle the elements, the vast distances, the invisible, the unknown.

—We are going to have a theatrical performance, Mr Bonard told us confidentially. It's a surprise.

—It's not much of a surprise, laughed Lionel. Mistress Brook told me she is playing two roles in the same performance. The doctor is taking part, but how will he avoid getting drunk?

—He will get drunk.

—Well then, how will he be able to play his part?

—We shall find out the day after tomorrow, Mr Bonard replied. The performers are rehearsing with great enthusiasm.

Lionel interrupted, saying:

—Mistress Brook is going to great pains to teach the doctor how to make a declaration.

—Of war?

—Of love! She only wages war against women.

I pointed out to Lionel that, probably without realizing it, he was constantly attacking Mistress Brook, and that in the long run, all these remarks would be turned against me.

—Do you think I would be foolish enough to ever start a war of words, especially against a woman? She has done everything possible to turn people against you on board, and I have heard her telling some home truths about us.

—So?

—So! Some truths are sometimes better left unsaid, and I shall teach her that to her cost. She had better behave herself or I will show her no mercy. You must be beyond reproach yourself to judge the conduct of others!

I realized then that Mistress Brook was waging a fierce underhand little war against me. A few ladies who had been extremely friendly at first had later shunned me. As I had not sought them out, I had no regrets in watching them distance themselves from me.

The saloon was divided in two by a curtain. A stage had been improvised with scenery, a centre light and footlights. At seven p.m., the three knocks sounded and the performance began, to the great satisfaction of the crowd, for the second and third class passengers had been invited.

They began with an English play interspersed with songs. Mistress Brook had a pretty costume and a self-assurance which revealed the boldness of her character. The first piece was quite well acted, but the lover was tipsy in the second and completely drunk in the third.

Mistress Brook was so sure of her success that she accepted the many compliments paid to her from all sides with the greatest of ease.

A supper was put on for the actors. They never want to miss an occasion to eat and especially to drink. Lionel and I would have preferred not to go to the dinner but alas! we were bodily apprehended—and that is the right word for it—and forced to occupy seats of honour. I had the chief steward on my right and the captain on my left. My husband was seated between Mistress Brook and a lady who had played the role of a grandmother in a white muslin dress and blonde curly hair cut in a bob.

The supper consisted of baked potatoes and slices of toasted bread spread with butter so strong that the taste of it overpowered the red pepper sprinkled on top. But, as I have already said, as the whole business of eating was only an excuse to drink, they drank everyone's health with cheers loud enough to wake all the fish asleep at the bottom of the ocean.

I don't know whether Mistress Brook was trying to make the doctor jealous with her melting looks and moist eyes, but she was so charming towards my husband that it really set me thinking, especially as he seemed to be responding to her. I returned to my cabin with a rather heavy heart, but I did not say anything to Lionel for fear of annoying him.

The heat was oppressive and the *Croesus* had not made any headway for a week. Flying fish and porpoises leapt up around us. As there had been a strong breeze, the steam had been turned off in order to proceed by sail. However, the wind had since died down completely and the engine was not being stoked up so, after much idle talk amongst themselves, the passengers called a meeting to ask the captain for an explanation. He hummed and hawed and gave improbable excuses which did not convince anyone. They enjoined him to tell the truth. He asked for four delegates to whom he could give his reasons in private.

My husband, Mr Bonard and two other men went into the captain's cabin and stayed with him for more than two hours, which seemed a very long time to us. Our anxiety was at its height, yet we had only the merest inkling of the danger surrounding us on all sides. When Lionel came out of the captain's cabin, I ran up to him and bombarded him with questions. He was pale and I thought I saw tears in his eyes, but he made an effort to smile and said:

—We are condemned to intoxication,—there is no more drinking water.

—What do you mean?

A window had not been shut in time and a sea swell had dumped some waves into the tank. The supply of fresh water was totally ruined.

This was certainly not good news but I could not understand why Lionel was so affected by it to the point that his voice was trembling. After all, he had told me himself that, with the help of machines, they could condense steam and make a large supply of fresh water daily.

—The machines are broken, he said in a low voice, but you must not tell anyone.

—I think everyone suspects as much already since we are sitting here at the equator, dying of heat and impatience.

There was indeed a general feeling of great concern on board and the precautions taken by the captain had only disturbed the passengers even more. They were all making their own assumptions and conjectures, and would most probably have exaggerated the seriousness of the situation, if it could have been exaggerated. Anxiety, the heat and the lack of water were making almost all of us ill.

As soon as he had been told, Lionel bought me some bottles of soda water but this effervescent water can cause dysentery, an illness which in the tropics is so similar to cholera you can die from it in a few hours. On the third day, we had to drink beer and undiluted wine which burned our stomachs without quenching our thirst.

We were hoping for some rain but the sky was wonderfully clear and the sea was limpid and blue with not a breath of wind to ruffle its surface. In the position we were in, this calm was much more to be feared than the storm. The livestock were dying of thirst, the crew were suffering horribly, and I imagine we would have given all our food for one barrel of water. Engineers, carpenters and stokers worked down in the hold while the sailors and officers manned the pumps day and night.

On the fourth day, we were sitting on a bench against the captain's cabin which was situated on the deck. His window remained open and though the captain could not see us, we could hear everything that was said inside. His first mate came in and said:

—If God doesn't help us, the *Croesus* is finished.

—What about the repairs? the captain asked in a subdued voice.

—Hopeless! As soon as we seal up one leak, a larger one develops alongside. The hull was not strong enough to cope with the motion of the propeller, and all the planks at the stern are moving apart. It would take four hours, and more, at the pumps just to empty out the water we have taken on in one hour.

Lionel looked at me in dismay.

—You have known about this for a long time, I said, and I have suspected as much. He drew me into his arms and began to weep.

—Come now, don't cry; keep calm. You know very well I have never lacked courage in the face of danger. We have just heard them pronounce what amounts to our death sentence. We can't escape our destiny, you know that, so let God's will be done.

The captain said in French:

—We must try to reach the Cape of Good Hope. We are only three days away.

—We will never get there, the officer replied. Tell the men to get the lifeboats ready and order the second-class passengers to stay on deck tonight.

—That would alarm them too much.

—Better to alarm them than drown them! cried the officer angrily. I told you in Lisbon the ship was leaking. You wanted to economize the company's time and money and now here you are responsible for the lives of 700 passengers and sailors who are not going to be faced with death without calling you to account.

—Keep your voice down, replied the captain, becoming angry in his turn. You are forgetting that I am the one who gives the orders. I don't take them!

—That is where you are wrong, interrupted Lionel as he suddenly stood up and appeared outside the window. You have chosen a bad time for this outburst of pride! If you were incapable of avoiding this situation, then admit your incompetence!

—Sir, exclaimed the captain, turning pale, this is my domain.

—In the eyes of your crew perhaps, but to me you are like a bad coachman. You are going to tip us all over, and I am going to warn everyone!

Some people had gathered around us. Lionel was carried away in one of those fits of anger that he can't contain. He recounted what he had just heard so that everyone would be put on guard. There was widespread consternation.

—I knew it! said the sailor who had been talking with Mr Bonard in Lisbon. I was down there, I saw the hold!

We spent the night on deck. At daybreak, we saw them throw the cow overboard; she had died during the night. Two large sharks came to fight over her. The water was so clear we could see them following us for part of the day.

I shall not try to describe the terrible state of mind we were in. Lionel and all the other passengers set to work on the pumps, and what did I do? I set about crying! I shed all the tears I had been holding back for days. Not for myself, I was not afraid of dying, but watching our poor little girl as she ran about me, laughing and playing, I had a feeling of great despair. I blamed myself for having brought her and I was overcome by the thought that, even if I were to sacrifice my own life, I could not save hers.

A light nor-westerly breeze came up and we began to move slowly, but at least we were moving forwards, towards the Cape.

Once again we spent the whole night on deck. Solange fell asleep on my lap. Exhaustion, deprivation and fear had drained us so much that we were scarcely recognizable. Poor Lionel's cheeks and lips were pale but his eyes were red and his hands bloodied.

The *Croesus* was rolling from side to side but making no progress. It sat ten feet deeper in the water than when we set sail, yet they had dumped ballast, and our consumption of provisions had significantly reduced the ship's 400-ton load.

We noticed a ship on the horizon ... We were saved! Land was coming to us! but it disappeared without responding to our signals, and our disappointment now was much greater than our hopes had been. Unknown dangers are much more frightening than those one faces, and I believe that people who fear an earthquake or a flood are much more wretched than those who face a sword.

Every time the ship moved, we could not help shuddering with fear, as it seemed we could feel the *Croesus* sinking and dragging us with it into the abyss. We huddled against each other and tried to remember our prayers! But we did not all feel the same sense of resignation. I put on a very brave face so that Lionel would not despair. I could see that he was almost mad with grief and that, at times, he wanted to kill himself rather than see me suffer. Women cried and men quarrelled. They had all lost their heads.

The engine was repaired. They proposed to try and use steam to reach the Cape which was no more than a few leagues away but, with the movement of the propeller still separating the planks with each jolt, we were going to take on an even greater amount of water and increase the danger. But the desperate situation and intolerable anxiety into which we had been plunged made us stake our all, and most of us decided in favour of using steam. They stoked up the engines to bursting point.

The next day, at dawn, we entered the bay of the Cape of Good Hope. Not before time! The *Croesus* would not have lasted six more hours at sea!

—We were lucky to get out of that with our lives! said Lionel as we stepped ashore. Come along, we must go and give thanks to God!

And without giving me time to have the glass of water I needed so badly, he led me firmly into a little church and began praying with such fervour that I began to feel it too. We really did look as though we had been shipwrecked!

Our arrival at Cape Town caused a great sensation, and people came to visit us at the hotel, partly out of interest but mainly out of sheer curiosity.[4]

We had a bath, we went to see the running fountains and we drank water like fish. Then we started to think about where we would stay, as the repairs to be done to the *Croesus* would take a month at least. The passengers had all dispersed throughout the town. Upon my husband's invitation, Mrs Wèbe had come to stay in the same hotel as us, in a room adjoining our apartment.

From my room, I could see the gigantic Table Mountain whose peak is often so shrouded in clouds that you can't tell whether it's rising from the earth or descending from the sky. Climbing the mountain is perilous: parts of the rock sometimes give way as hands and feet try to get a hold on them. Still I wanted to climb it. From up there, I thought, I should be able to glimpse at least a shadow of the French coastline.

—I have absolutely no intention of courting danger, Lionel replied. We are going to take a coach and go and visit the town of Constance. That will be more enjoyable and not nearly so tiring.

We set out in a barouche drawn by four horses. We travelled through magnificent countryside and through Kaffir and Hottentot villages.[5] There was too much for me to take it all in. When I say villages, I am talking of flat open country that looks as though it has been ploughed up by gigantic moles. The Hottentot huts are mounds of dirt covered with straw. The Hottentots themselves are hideous. If it were not for the fact that the women wear skirts, it would be impossible to tell them from the men. They smoke enormous pipes, their hair is close-cropped, and they have thick lips, flat noses and ugly black skin.

The Malay women are tall and well built with sleek hair and fresh faces, and those who don't dress themselves up in our fashions are pretty. But most of them wear pink dresses and white bonnets so that they look like monkeys in women's clothes.

Constance has nothing unusual to offer: the town's only interesting building is a wine-maker's shop which has very nice cellars. The road is lined with private homes, surrounded by camellias, geraniums, cactus and aloes. This is the main reason people come to see Constance. The travellers all bought some of the famous Constance wine, which has the advantage of being processed in France, but here it has a smell of liquorice or molasses and makes your stomach turn.

The owner of the main establishment showed us round his garden, a very fine orchard with apples the size of melons and melons the size of pumpkins. He let us take with us all the flowers and fruit we wanted. Marie, my maid, wanted to take everything, but the funniest sight of all was Solange who was biting into a pear much bigger than her own head. She had to leave it behind in the end because she could not carry it any longer. We got back into the coach, laden with fruit and flowers, an invaluable treasure for people who have just spent two months at sea.

The Malays who were driving our coach, for there were always two of them, climbed back onto their seat and drove us to the place where Signolo's prison is. He is a Kaffir king who is one of the sights of the Cape.[6] They put him on show for the travellers in the same way you would display a tamed lion or a dog with two heads.

On the way, our Malayan drivers pointed out a snake about six foot long emerging from the ditch by the side of the road. It was starting to cross, slowly and majestically, when one of the Malays, as quick as a cat, jumped from his seat and killed the reptile with one crack of his whip handle. We drew to a stop and I bravely decided to go and look at the ugly creature, once they had assured me it was dead. The Malays put it in the trunk of the coach and took it with them, which caused me great concern for the rest of the journey.

When we arrived at King Signolo's residence, we asked whether we could still go in as it was almost six in the evening. The guard replied that it was up to him, so Lionel gave him a few shillings and he ran off to announce our visit to the prisoners, as the king had a queen.

We waited for the guard in a courtyard about twenty feet square. In one corner there was an old negress squatting on the ground, her elbows on her knees and her closed fists pressed into her hollow cheeks. She had frizzy, greying hair which escaped in great tufts from under a gaudy checked kerchief, and her clothes were in rags. There was something wild and distraught in her penetrating stare. She started to search about the ground where she was squatting and covered her bare feet with bits of her skirt, then hid her face in her lap. She was a madwoman, and we were as frightened by her as she was by us.

Four or five small doors opened onto the courtyard. We were shown to one in the middle from where we entered a room about ten feet square that was like a cold, damp, dark dungeon. The only light came in through two window panes above the door and the only piece of furniture was a wooden bench.

The prisoners were lying on the ground on a pile of rotting straw, both covered by the same blanket. Despite the tanned colour of their skin, it was easy to see how much they had suffered! My husband, who had seen them during his last voyage, said he could hardly recognize the woman. She stretched her bony hands towards us; her arms were like a skeleton's. Her big black eyes were filled with an expression of indescribable gentleness. The man seemed tall to me. There was still a look of pride in his eyes: he might only be a savage but they were afraid enough of him to hold him captive. He had a reputation for bravery that the English knew and feared. He fought like a lion, and therefore when he was caught they treated him like a wild animal.

The sight of these poor souls made my heart bleed. They live, they feel, they suffer as we do. God gave them the instinct of self-preservation, and when they are attacked in their homelands in the mountains and in the deserts they defend themselves. In all countries of the world, people make war, man is destroyed by man.

I imagine, in fact I am quite sure the government would not be at all interested in my thoughts on the matter and this encourages me to say exactly what I feel. Well, I think it's appalling to treat a defeated enemy, whoever he might be, in this manner. All these tribes who are constantly being hunted down and dispossessed will one day revolt. The Kaffirs have already begun, others will eventually follow, and there will be a war of extermination in which the fierceness of the savage will be justified by the cruelty of the civilized man. It's cruel leaving these poor creatures to live like this in their mire, to be abused with impunity. We were told that a drunken Englishman had hit them with his riding crop!

The Kaffir king looks intelligent. His big black eyes become as red as rubies when they insult him; his nostrils flare and his thick lips part, showing his fierce-looking teeth. But he knows he is powerless to do anything and his muscles go slack. The fanatics then spit in his face, beat him and jab him with their burning cigars, but he never moves.

They have given him a suit of livery. The Kaffir has taken off his pearls, plumes and all the gaudy royal rags of his tribe, and put on the braided suit that keeps out the cold.

I gave my flowers and fruit to the prisoners and left, seriously regretting having come.

—Well then, what did you think of them? Lionel asked me when we were back in the carriage.

—I thought their living conditions were awful.

—Do you expect them to be given a palace? Come now, those people are very dangerous! If only you knew how many English troops they have killed!

—Why do the English go after them?

—To increase their territory.

—What would you do if someone tried to take your house or garden away from you?

—I no longer have either, Lionel replied with a laugh. Listen, don't get angry; I agree with you! I think it's wrong that they are treated so harshly but, don't worry, they know how to retaliate, and it's always an eye for an eye.

The carriage stopped opposite our hotel and Mrs Wèbe came out to meet us with Cilia.

—I have been waiting anxiously for you to return! she said to me in a low voice. Misfortune has struck once again; it seems to be hounding me.

I looked at the little girl but she was happy, with bright eyes and rosy cheeks. Then I realized from the direction in which Mrs Wèbe was looking that it concerned Cilia. She was walking with her head down and a doleful look in her eye. A bitter smile hovered on her parted lips. She was holding back tears and choking on sobs that she could barely suppress.

—You can go for a walk with the child, Mrs Wèbe said twice before Cilia heard. I have to speak to the countess. I shall join you in a minute.

Cilia walked off without replying.

Mrs Wèbe went with me to my room, closed the door, then spoke to me with such distress in her voice that I became concerned.

—It will be the end of her, unless you can help me save her.

—The end of her! Who do you mean? I asked in great surprise.

—Cilia! she said as she walked over to the window. Here you are, come and look.

Poor Mrs Wèbe, she has gone mad, I thought without moving from where I stood.

—Do come and look, she said as she drew me towards the window. He is with her, he follows her like a shadow.

—Who are you talking about?

—Mr James, the young officer from the *Croesus*.

—That nice boy. I saw him several times during the crossing. Lionel says he is very well educated.

—He is a young man of means.

—Well, what of it?

—He is in love with Cilia.

—That doesn't surprise me. She is the loveliest girl.

—But he won't marry her; he is rich.

—Good! Then he shall have the pleasure of making his wife's fortune.

—You don't understand society. The aristocracy makes bargains with marriages.

—Personally, I have no real quarrel with that. But how did all this happen? For the past hour you have been talking in double Dutch! First of all, does she love him?

—Yes.

—You have told me she is a good honest girl, so her conscience will protect her.

—No, Cilia is a passionate soul with an impetuous nature. The first words of love spoken to her set her heart on fire and when she loves she spares nothing. It was affection that made her follow me, and it's love that will be the ruin of her.

—Have you spoken to her about him?

—Yes, and to everything I said she replied: 'I love him and I told him so on board the *Croesus* because I thought we were going to die together.'

—That is more serious and, as you can't refuse anything to a person under sentence of death, they perhaps exchanged some things that are difficult to take back.

—They pledged eternal love.

—They didn't commit themselves too far as they thought they were about to die.

—They didn't die and James promised everything except marriage.

—We must talk to him.

—I did this morning.

—What did he say?

—That he comes from a good English family and that he could not marry a servant.

—Did you tell Cilia this?

—She overheard us and I later found her lying face down on the floor in her room, unconscious.

—Then she can't be in love with him any more.

—You saw him by her side. He will tell her she was mistaken in what she heard.

—She won't believe him.

—She will believe him because she loves him, said Mrs Wèbe sadly.

—If her heart is her own worst enemy, you will find it difficult but you must do everything possible to save her from herself. Don't ever let her go out alone.

—I could do that here but on board intimacy is unavoidable.

—We are not ready to go back on board the *Croesus*. Between now and then you can try to work something out. You can tell the captain if need be.

—The captain would not know anything about matters of the heart, said Mrs Wèbe after a moment's hesitation. If you could talk to Cilia and ask the count to speak to James, perhaps by reasoning with them, we would achieve what the closest supervision never could.

The idea of setting myself up as a moralist or as a guardian of virtue seemed quite novel to me but, as I felt the experience would ultimately serve some purpose, I promised Mrs Wèbe I would talk to Cilia as soon as I found the right occasion, after having first consulted my husband, however, for I was always afraid of displeasing him, even while doing the right thing. And actually, the supervision of Cilia's behaviour which I had thought would be very easy was at present if not impossible, at least very difficult, because she did not eat with us as we took our very leisurely meals at the residents' table. She therefore had three hours a day of total freedom.

The hotel where we were staying had two main buildings, two exits. The first floor of the front building was for the masters, the second for the European servants, as all the Indian, Greek and Italian servants sleep on a mat across their master's doorway. Some claim it's out of devotion, others say it's for the sake of economy. In either case it makes it very difficult to return to one's room at the end of the passage. These servants have fine outfits, but they walk bare-foot and in general they are the epitome of grubbiness.

Mistress Brook is staying in a neighbouring hotel. When we come across each other, she crosses the street to avoid having to greet me. As for my husband, that is a different matter entirely: she introduces him to her friends at the Cape. And she has many of them, officers who had served with her husband in India. I don't know whether her dislike for me stems from her liking for my husband, but I am beginning to think so.

For the week that we have been at Cape Town we have not stopped. I don't like the towns because they are inhabited. It's the open country that I love. There, I can breathe freely. Animals are less to be feared than women: if you avoid them, they leave you in peace. What is more, these remote countries seem cursed; they are all afflicted with one or more blights. There is a red dust which strains the eyes terribly, a sun that devours plants and then the mosquitoes which do to the inhabitants what the sun does to the plants. These insects love European blood and they attack new arrivals with unbelievable fury. Nature has its wonders but also its monstrosities. We are kept awake during the night by gnats constantly flitting around us.

We walk about like the Wandering Jew,[7] but in no time we become blasé about these great mountains and faraway horizons and very quickly want to escape from them. The ship carrying you to your destination becomes your homeland; happy to leave it initially, you then begin to long for it. So every day our main concern is to find out whether they are making progress on repairs to the *Croesus*, and we go and see it, just as if we were paying a visit to an invalid.

On one of these daily walks we saw the flag at half-mast. The captain had said he was not well; we thought he had died. Fifteen of us set out in a dinghy to go on board the *Croesus*. Various stories, tales and versions circulated freely during the trip. A few passengers had known since the day before that the captain was dead but they had forgotten to tell us. Everyone spoke highly of the deceased. This man who, just yesterday, had been called a tyrant was now reputedly a saint. He was a great captain, a brave man, a hero and I don't know what else besides. Fortunately, we got off with nothing more serious than lamentations: the captain himself came to welcome us on board. We very nearly asked him why he was not dead, and we asked him why our mainmast was showing the sign of mourning.

—Because during repairs to a large ship that had arrived in the Bay, he told us, the engineer and an officer were killed as they were helping to put the propeller back into place. As we were leaving the harbour, all the ships followed the example set by ours: all their flags were set at half-mast as a sign of mourning.

It had suddenly become dark. Just as they were telling us that night brought forward the tide by several hours, a storm was brewing on all sides. The cannon boomed. It was like a battle at sea, and we reached our hotel only just in time. The noise of the explosions sounded twenty times over in the mountains: it felt as if the earth was shaking. The storm opened up the heavens and set the sky alight. The sea roared and thunder answered the cannon fire. It was like a declaration of war between man and God. From my window, I could see the Lion Mountains from one side and from the other the harbour, which presented a fearsome sight. Ships were being tossed by the waves to phenomenal heights where they crashed together and smashed. Water poured down the mountain side, forming a torrent at its foot.

All this disturbance did not stop them welcoming the arrival of the new fortress commander.

These things are all so very frightening and, if there were another way, I would choose to go by land. Lionel thinks the whole thing is marvellous.

—Aren't storms magnificent! he said, drumming on the window pane. Do come and look! What strength, what force it must take to set all those elements in motion.

—At the moment it's all dreadful as far as I am concerned. If this continues, the mountain will come crashing down and crush us underneath as it falls, or else the hotel will collapse under the force of the rain.

—The hotel, quite possibly, but I can vouch for the mountain. Whoever created it . . .

—Also created the trees, and there are some very big ones out there being splintered right now by the Creator's passionate caress. It will be a scene of disaster in the bay tomorrow. The fortress commander can be none too happy. It's an awful day to make his official entrance into the town.

—Yes, I hope the weather will be better for our departure.

It took only one night to repair all the damage. Steam rose from the earth as it dried in the scorching sunlight. The sea was a silvery calm, and if it were not for the wrecks washed up here and there along the shore, you would think it incapable of causing harm to even the smallest boat.

The commander is at the same hotel as us for the time being. He is a man of about fifty but he believes he is much younger and does his utmost to make sure others are of the same opinion.

In situations where one cannot get angry whatever happens, one has to laugh at everything. When I say everything, it's a manner of speaking as I can't help but become very annoyed about the washerwomen. They work hard, very hard in fact, but here is their system: they beat even the finest embroidered muslin on sandstone (that is what they use as a washboard here) and they bring everything back to you in tatters.

I had been told Cape Town was charming. The town looks like a box of children's toys put down higgledy-piggledy at the foot of the Obelisk.[8] Even when there is not a breath of wind you are blinded constantly by a fine, impalpable dust: it's like powdered brick. We have looked like Red Indians since our arrival here. We have to change our clothes up to three times a day. Oh! my beloved France! I don't think there is anything on earth that could make me forget you.

Lionel has paid some official visits and he has received invitations to a number of balls, receptions and dinners. As life is lived mostly indoors at Cape Town, they entertain a great deal. Lionel declines all invitations because of me.

The damage to the *Croesus* has finally been repaired. We have been told of our imminent departure, and we are going back on board tomorrow. God knows how time has dragged for me here. The passengers don't seem too pleased to be going back to sea for they are worried about the soundness of the ship.

The captain has had a notice attached to the mainmast: he says he values his life as much as we do, and that if repairs had not been carried out as they should have been, he would not have fixed our departure for the next day. In general, it takes very little to alarm a ship's floating population and even less to reassure it. This proclamation worked wonders, and they all seemed to believe they would be perfectly safe. I don't know why, but in all manner of things I am incapable of overcoming a feeling of mistrust and the captain's protestations did not convince me at all. I kept my thoughts to myself, though, as they could do nothing to change our situation.

CHAPTER 4

The Last Leg of the Journey

THE SAILORS were furious as they were forced to weigh anchor on a Friday! But there had already been so much time lost. We were carrying dispatches and besides, everyone was anxious to reach their destination. On 10 March they fired the cannon, and we set off at full steam. The *Croesus* made a superb exit, but it cost us dearly a few days later. We had what the sailors call a squall. You had better make out your will if you have hopes of surviving one.

The waves, illuminated by lightning, rose up in a hellish dance around us to the sound of the thunder. Every wave felt like a block of stone being hurled at the wretched ship's sides. The propeller broke again and there was a headwind, so our hopes of using sail were in vain. Three sails were torn apart as if they had been made of paper. The shreds of cloth beat against the masts with frightening force. It was as if the wind was imitating the cock's cry and the snake's hiss in turn. Those hours are indescribable: we lived a hundred years in one night.

The manoeuvring of the ship was terribly difficult. We feared for our lives and for those poor souls perched on top of the yards swinging violently in the air above the depths. A moment's dizziness, a foot that slips, a rope that snaps and that is the end of everything, their lives are over.

We felt we were in such great danger that we spent all night on deck. I saw Cilia in the darkness: she was as still as a statue, her eyes staring, her breath coming in gasps, her arms and legs trembling. When I followed the direction in which she was looking, I saw James receiving orders from his officers and passing them on to the sailors while he himself was taking an active and dangerous part in the procedure. For sailors, a storm is a day of combat with all its dangers and glories. Poor Cilia's heart was also suspended up there in the yards. I had not spoken to her at Cape Town as Lionel had asked me not to get involved in anyone else's business.

The girl was unrecognizable. She had hollow cheeks and bluish circles under her eyes, her shoulders were hunched forward. A heavy swell suddenly keeled the *Croesus* over to port. Cilia gave a heart-rending scream. A wave had just engulfed James and his companions. They were submerged for barely a second, which seemed like a century to us. When they reappeared, Cilia was unconscious. Mrs Wèbe was by her side and was trying in vain to bring her round. They carried her to her cabin.[1]

Nobody paid any attention to this small incident, as they were concerned only with themselves.

—Well, what do you think of the courage of these good sailors? Lionel asked me. Listen how they sing as they reef their sails.

—To me they look as though they are defying death.

—Death does not come before its appointed time, my dear Céleste. Since we set sail it's come close many times without touching us. You must be fatalistic at sea because then you have the courage to have absolute confidence in what must be, and what can't be avoided.

The squall has passed and now there is a biting cold. We don't walk on the deck any more: we run to warm ourselves up.

The English drink to excess. If you put a light near their mouths, I am sure they would catch fire. We are surrounded by some really strange types but when I try to draw a portrait of one, I feel just like an employee in the passport office must feel: they all look the same.

Mr Bouchon, the chief steward, is a fat, portly little man in serious danger of killing himself through his excessive personal hygiene. He is always clean-shaven, his hair dressed with pomade, and I think he wears a corset. He has the mannerisms and all the refinement of an old woman. He is very kind and helpful, but only to those he likes.

The chief steward is an important person on board, so it's good to get on well with him. He is responsible for maintaining orderliness and good relations between the servants, and that is not an easy task. It's probably why they chose a steward built like Hercules. He is also responsible for the food supplies, a job which to be well done requires him to be on constant lookout. You have no idea of the stealth with which boys, lower class passengers and sometimes sailors steal a ham, onions, apples, etc. The steward does his round every evening, a lantern in his hand and a bunch of keys by his side. The supply rooms are above our saloon and the air is filled with the very unpleasant smell of colonial produce.

So, the chief steward is the enemy of the thieves and prowlers. They detest him heartily and are always dreaming up ways of playing dirty tricks on him. At about nine o'clock we heard a scream, a dull thud, then silence. We all looked at each other with concern.

—What is it? I asked Lionel.

—Mr Bouchon has just played Bertram's scene in *Robert the Devil*; he has fallen through the trap door.[2]

—But how can you laugh? He could have killed himself!

—He won't have hurt himself. He's fat and well-padded.

—What if he were to hear you?

—God forbid! He would put me on dry bread and his bad, second-quality beer.

—Here he is. Try to look very concerned when you ask him how he is.

But that was easier said than done.

—That was a fine thing to do! laughed Lionel. How can you have lost your balance after such a fine dinner? You were looking pretty sprightly to me!

This simple joke threw us into disgrace, and Mr Bouchon refused to have anything more to do with us. I did not exactly lose my appetite or any sleep over this, but I worry though about how tactless Lionel can be: I think he would risk his life to make a clever remark.

Sea voyages, it seems, bring out the loving feelings in women on board. Some of them are totally smitten, either with other passengers or with officers. There are love nests in every nook and cranny. The husbands go for walks, smoke, and play along with the loving couples. Yesterday a man at our table, mistaking my foot for that of his sweetheart, kicked me twice so hard that I could hardly keep it to myself.

Cilia is sick and no longer leaves her cabin. Mrs Wèbe does not come to play the piano any more. I am working so relentlessly at learning English that I don't concern myself at all with other people. The only reason the bad weather frightens me now is that it stops me from working. At the moment it's dreadful and our nights are awful. The dancing of the ship has started again and it's more frenzied than ever. It's becoming unbearable; our joints feel dislocated.

We have been accompanied for several days now by black and white birds which look like swallows. They call them sailors' souls. The sight of them always has a profound effect on the crew. When one of these birds flies over the deck or swoops down on the ship, they say it's a soul coming to call another one. Some of the men laugh about it, others tell what they claim to be true stories.

At six o'clock this morning, one of these birds flew over the deck and, with the tip of its wing, almost touched the head of an officer, the same officer we had heard talking in French to the captain, not long before we were run aground at the Cape. He came down and told us we would lose a crew member before very long. As no one seemed to believe his prediction, he sat down next to us and said:

—I have travelled the seas for thirty-five years, and it would take me six months to tell you about all the accidents I have seen. Here is the first one:

I was a novice on board a whaling boat. I had a friend from the same home town with me whom I loved like a brother. We were playing quoits on deck. Despite the noise we were making, one of these birds came and circled above us. After our game, my friend went to lie down in a boat attached to the side of the ship. Not seeing him at dinner-time, I looked everywhere for him. I went to look in the dinghy where he had gone to lie down: it had capsized! The poor boy had fallen into the sea! The helmsmen hadn't seen or heard a thing.

Two years later, the crew were being given their ration of grog on the deck when the soul flew between them. No one dared take a drink. Then a novice raised his glass and said: 'Who cares! It's the smell of the grog that's attracting them. Your good health, little bird!' That evening the wind changed. It was as black as pitch and we had to reef the sails. I had climbed up in the yards when I heard a long moan that was lost in the wind. A man had just fallen overboard and there was no way we could save him. We had to reassemble to find out who the victim was: poor Roger Bontemps didn't answer to his name. He had drunk his last drink to the health of the very one that had come to take him.

Lionel smiled as he inhaled on his cigar but I listened with great interest because I am superstitious. I believe in all premonitions, and my own are not often wrong! He continued:

—A few years later, I was on a merchant ship trading in India. One morning, ten or so men were pulling on a cable and singing in time when the soul flew between them. When they had finished, one of my cabin-mates said to me: 'It's me it came looking for. If something happens to me, I want you to take care of my watch and all my things. My mother is so poor!' We all made him drink to take his mind off it. He drank and then, feeling the need to go to the bow, he was holding on to the rope when he lost his balance, fell overboard, and we lost him too!

I was on a voyage to Bombay. I was an officer at that stage and I had a sailor on board who sang well, and who sang from morn till night. One day the soul flew over his hands. A cabin boy who was busy pulling up buckets of water on a rope lost his balance and slipped and was dragged overboard by the weight of his bucket. The singer—that's what we called him—swam like a fish. He threw himself into the sea to rescue the boy. It was a calm day and his friends called out to him, laughing: 'You'll catch a cold! There'll be no singing from you tonight!' He kept on searching as he moved further away from the ship. The boy reappeared at the ship's side, grabbed one of the ropes they had thrown to him and was heaved back up on deck. As for the singer, whether he ran out of strength or a shark got hold of his legs, he went under and didn't come to the surface again.

I went over to Lionel. He squeezed my hand as if to say: Don't interrupt him; he enjoys talking. I remained silent, and our storyteller continued:

—A few years ago, I was captain of a ship and when we were at the equator my passengers asked me to lend them a dinghy so they could go swimming. Just as they were moving away from the ship, the soul flew several times over the dinghy. Two of the crew wanted to come back on board but the others teased them, and they set off. One of the bathers, who had swum away from the dinghy, disappeared suddenly. One of my men rushed to help him, but the poor devil had already lost his head and pulled the man who was trying to save him down with him.

The officer had hardly spoken these words when a jolt like that of an earthquake shook the *Croesus*, and we had to hold on to each other to stop ourselves from falling. Then we heard the grating of the pulleys: the *Croesus* was doing twelve knots an hour and they were trying to slow it down.

No one knew how, but one of the Portuguese sailors who had been taken on in Lisbon had fallen overboard. We only saw him being dragged along by a rope that he had grabbed. But he could not hold on for very long, as the *Croesus* was going too fast. They threw him seats and chicken cages but he could not catch hold of anything.

For a long time after, we could see the lifebelts that they had thrown the unfortunate young man floating on the surface of the water.

He was only twenty-two. It's a dreadful thing to lose a man at sea, and, improbable as the story of the bird heralding a death had seemed to us, for a very long time we were frightened of seeing others appear.

Every evening, Lionel goes and smokes his cigar in the ship's bow. He speaks perfect Spanish and the poor Portuguese sailors are grateful to him because he tries to console them a little for the loss of their friend.

James was quite seriously hurt as he was checking one of the pieces of the steam engine. A stopper hit him right in the chest and almost smashed his ribs. He is vomiting blood and they say he will not survive. Cilia is beside herself with worry. In spite of appearances, everyone is now convinced she never gave in to him. She said to the captain, in our presence: 'An honest girl might die for love, but she guards her honour so that she will never be despised by the man she loves.' They granted her permission to look after James.

—I shall save him, she said to Mrs Wèbe, or I shall kill myself if he dies!

Everyone is concerned with James's state of health. He is a young man just twenty-five years old, very good-looking and recklessly brave but an unfortunate youngest child born too late, depriving him of his father's title and fortune. He set sail at fifteen and he has never seen his homeland since. The tenderness and care Cilia lavishes on him seem to comfort him in his final hours. This morning we had given up hope but this evening there is some improvement.

The passengers have a new subject of concern: the *Croesus* has sustained more damage. As it's dead calm, they are working day and night on the repairs. Perhaps we shall arrive at our destination but it will not have been without all manner of suffering! There must be cases of madness on board; poor Lady Gamby has most surely lost her head. She has become quite assiduous in her attentions to the pianist, and she writes him notes folded into paper hats. The doctor found one of these notes and it's now in the hands of Mistress Brook who has it read aloud to everyone. Lionel does not want to hear another word spoken of the poor woman. He says of all the outlandish things he has seen, he has never come across anything so ludicrous.

They have just had a meeting to vindicate a man who stole ten shillings gambling—as if such people can be vindicated. He is a very rich man and he spends enormous amounts of money on extra wine. The speech makers (and there were quite a few of them) defended him, pleading monomania and temporary insanity. The extenuating circumstances were accepted and the verdict of not guilty was pronounced unanimously minus one voice—that of Lionel, who no longer speaks to him and who leaves the gaming table when he comes and sits down at it.

Last night a passenger who was feeling unwell left his cabin to go and find the doctor, but he was not in his room. Having heard voices, he listened, watched and supposedly saw the doctor, without a light, coming out of the cabin of one of his lady patients. The passenger was probably tipsy or half-asleep and so thought he saw what he actually dreamt. This joke has become the main topic of conversation. The heroine has not been named but, as Mistress Brook believes they think it's her, she is creating the devil of a rumpus to prove the contrary, which only serves to give absolute confirmation to the rumours.

Lionel had the unfortunate idea of jokingly congratulating the lucky doctor, and Mistress Brook who, until then, had accused her detractors collectively, now loosed her fury on us. She went to complain to the captain. He replied that she was not careful enough of her behaviour for a married woman and that he had no power to stop gossip on board, but that if he did, he would have already stopped her from speaking ill of everybody.

This threw her into such a state that she is now in danger of becoming jaundiced. But she obstinately refuses the doctor's care, and the awful man, who was not at all concerned at having what was considered to be such good fortune, makes constant fun of her as he continues with his excessive drinking.

I really don't know how people can concern themselves with running each other down when there are so many dangers threatening us at every moment. The wind has risen and is soon blowing fiercely. Everything has been overturned and broken. One of the cannons has come loose, as well as a cupboard and meat safe on deck. They are all sent crashing into each other and it's some time before the crew is able to grab hold of them and attach them again. The men have lost control of the helm. One poor sailor has just had his leg broken and he is crying out pitifully from the pain.

Added to this commotion is another noise no less frightening. The second class passengers are almost all drunk. They spend most nights drinking, swearing and fighting each other. Some have been put in irons in the hold, but this has had no impact upon the others. What a strange world! My courage fails at the thought of having to live in a country whose population is entirely made up of such people.

The captain has just put up the notice: 'Anyone disturbing the peace will be put in the hold.' They pay no attention to the warning for there are large numbers of them and they know it's impossible to put a hundred men in irons. The captain refuses them the right to buy grog; they are on the point of strangling the chief steward, so he has to give in and their drinking gets worse.

With my overly vivid imagination, I shall go out of my mind if I have to spend two more months here. I feel the same way about things as I do about people: I either love them or I hate them. I curse the *Croesus* every minute of the day.

The captain has just given me a very beautiful watercolour that he did for me. It's a view of the Cape of Good Hope with the *Croesus* painted in the foreground. I would be only too pleased to forget the ship, but the drawing is lovely and I shall keep it always, in memory of our poor captain who is really to be pitied. It's the first time he has had a bad crossing, and he feels seriously dishonoured at having experienced so many delays beyond his control. It's mainly thanks to him, though, that I am starting to speak English and Solange no longer says one word of French.

Another dreadful night. They come one after another and never vary. We are exhausted and almost resigned to it all. There are times in life when one no longer has the strength to complain or the strength to hope.

James is not out of danger but he is a little better. He has just had them send for the captain. They talked for a long time and, as a result of this conversation, they are going to have what is called a marriage in extremis on board. Nothing could make the sick boy change his mind: he wants to marry Cilia. The captain has the right to conduct marriages on his ship. He seeks Lionel's advice, and I am the one who gives my opinion in favour of this union:—one can't refuse anything to a dying man.

They draw up the documents. Lionel and several others act as witnesses. In less than an hour it's all over and in proper form. Mrs Wèbe is weeping for joy. Cilia prays on bended knees and covers her husband's hands with kisses and tears. Everyone present feels moved. James smiles sadly and says in a very faint voice: 'I want her to have the right to wear mourning for me.' He closes his eyes; we rise in silence . . . but suddenly we hear wild cheering. Pretty little birds, lost at sea, have just landed on our rigging: we are close to land.

—We will enter Port Phillip tomorrow, the captain tells us, but I am very much afraid that my ship will never leave it again.

We don't go to bed at all that night. Day finally breaks, but it's heavy with fog and we can't see a thing. It starts to clear up a little, however: they signal and a pilot arrives and climbs on board. The captain hands over all his authority to him. He is now nothing but an ordinary passenger like us.

The entrance to Port Phillip Bay is very dangerous. There are reefs which only just break the surface of the water, and many ships have been wrecked on them because the captains had not asked for a pilot.

The joy of the other passengers makes me feel sad. I can't help myself—my eyes are filled with tears. Yet we are going to land.—Yes! the land of exile, for I am five thousand leagues from France—France that perhaps I shall never see again. But come now! The homeland can be anywhere, provided you are with those you love. Lionel is happy, and Solange and Marie are delighted. It will all be for the best, if we don't run aground in the port.

Part Two:

Life in Gold-rush Australia

CHAPTER 5

First Impressions and
Settling In

OUR disembarkation in Melbourne.[1]

When one arrives at one's destination after a long voyage, the activity on board is even more frenetic and more confused than when one came on board. People sort out their bags and clamour on all sides for their trunks. On deck, there are mountains of parcels. They roll all over your feet, catch your legs, tear your clothes. People argue and lose their tempers but, because there is no order on board, it doesn't get them anywhere.

—There's no point in hurrying so much, the captain says in a low voice; I don't dare start the engines, and we have a headwind so we won't be able to enter the harbour today.

The pilot does, in fact, change the manoeuvre and we end the day and spend the night turning round on ourselves without moving a mile forward. In the distance we can see the Mauvant [*sic*] lighthouse blinking on and off, and that is all we can see.

I would like to rest a little but I find it impossible. I have hardly closed my eyes when I start having terrible thoughts. I call out . . . I choke . . . I begin to cry . . . Lionel gets up and takes me in his arms.

—Come now, try to calm down a little. Dreams are often nothing more than the result of things that have worried us during the day. Cheer up! Don't give in to gloomy thoughts. Just tell yourself that, as long as I live, no serious harm can ever come to you.

—And if you were to die?

—I have no intention of doing that, he said with a smile. Just try to live each day without thinking of tomorrow, since tomorrow is beyond our control.

Promising to be calm costs me absolutely nothing and I promise him in good faith, but my wretched nature will not allow it. At the slightest mental strain, my nerves become irritated and I start to suffer. I feel gripped by an emotion that my willpower and determination can do nothing to overcome. The past, the present and the future all confront each other in my thoughts, in a wild rush of ideas and bad memories that distress me and make me want to hurt others in turn. Because of the inevitable changeability of my character, my confidence and cheerfulness do not come naturally: changes of mood always produce a feeling of deep melancholy within me. I believe I have too much strength and too great a need for physical activity to be happy seeing others act without taking any part in the action myself. When my body is forced to rest, my mind works in such a ferment that I fear I may be mad or going mad. I do everything within my power to rid myself of what Lionel calls my faults, but I fear they result from an hereditary illness, and that I shall carry them to my grave.

At daybreak we finally enter the harbour. A hundred boats and steamships surround the *Croesus*. Cigars and newspapers are handed around. Our ship had been declared lost with all hands. The best informed papers even gave details about our tragic end.[2] Believing us dead, there was no need to treat us with tact or consideration, and they gave us none. They wrote at length about the French Consul who had been foolish enough to marry his mistress and yet believe that society in the colony of Victoria would welcome the notorious Céleste Mogador,—who, what is more, had left behind her very strange *Memoirs*, of which the first two volumes have been published by Librairie Nouvelle in Paris, and which can be bought in Melbourne at M***.

As Lionel was skimming through these newspapers, in English fortunately for me, I could see his features tense up, his cheeks go pale, his hands tighten and screw up each page as if he wanted to reduce every one of them to dust.

Mistress Brook went back and forth in front of us with a look of triumph which at any other time would have caused me to ask questions, but I had just promised to be calm. My usual perceptiveness had been lulled and I suspected nothing. Ten ships which left Europe well after the *Croesus* had preceded it to Melbourne.

We enter Port Phillip Bay at midday. From a distance, the view is glorious: the coastline is fresh and green like new hope, the harbour like a forest of masts. There is a great stir aboard, but we are approaching the centre of the Bay and disillusion is quick to follow. Ah! what ugly, dirty ferry boats, and what men work on them! They wear big boots covered with mud: we are told that you can't take a step in town without getting your own in the same condition.

There are a few hackney carriages but the cab men charge 100 francs for one trip. It's impossible to go ashore together to go and find accommodation. Lionel goes alone. I stay on board with a heavy heart and my eyes full of tears.

Although I have felt no particular attachment for the passengers on the *Croesus*, I watch them leave with regret. A few still remain, however: Mrs Wèbe, James, whose health is improving every day, and that intriguing girl, Cilia. Then the guards arrive in great numbers. Sentries are placed everywhere. They are afraid of the frequent daily desertion of sailors arriving in Port Phillip Bay.[3] It seems they all try to escape to go to the gold mines. The *Croesus*'s deck looks like the inside of a barracks.

I go down to my cabin with Solange and my two little dogs who are not at all in good condition but who are very sweet. Lili, the female, had convulsions during the crossing and they tried to force me to throw her overboard. I did not want to, so I hid her by shutting her away in the cabin. As for Mr César, her brother, he is a real devil: he devours everything he can catch, even our hands.

We were playing together when Mrs Wèbe knocked on my door. She came in carrying some newspapers. She looked very unhappy as she showed them to me, saying:

—My poor countess! how you must have suffered when you read all these horrid articles.

With all the presence of mind of which I am capable when I am about to find out something distressing, I put on an expression as aggrieved as hers and said:

—I speak English very badly, but I can't read it at all. This morning my husband told me only what he wanted me to know, but I would like to know the whole truth. Would you please read me the articles that concern me?

She looks in Solange's direction. I understand, and send her to play with Marie.

Mrs Wèbe slowly translates for me the interminable screeds written by those gentlemen of the English press who must have copied them from our own. I can feel my poor face turning all the colours of the rainbow, one by one. My heart races, my throat goes dry; I find it impossible to cry . . .

I thank Mrs Wèbe and ask her to leave me alone. I want to write to Lionel, to kill myself. I start ten letters, then tear them up. He is not to blame for anything; he has suffered because of it without a complaint, without one word of reproach. I must follow his example of courage and live for him, in spite of everything.

I write to my mother, to Prince Napoléon, to Dumas, Murger, Adèle Page, Ernest Baroche.[4] I suddenly become feverish . . . I complain bitterly about the dreadful repercussions that the publication of these *Memoirs* will have for us. I tell them I want both the book and the publishers burned: anger gives me wild ideas.

Marie enters, as alarmed as if she was running from a fire. She is carrying Cocotte the budgerigar in his cage. The bird is screeching at the top of his voice. I ask what is the matter.

—Nothing, she replies in a trembling voice; the rope that was holding up the cage snapped. Cocotte had a fright.

—And you did too. You are terribly pale.

I hear a dull thud, confused shouts, the sound of people rushing about on deck. Marie implores me with a woeful look not to go up on deck because a fight is about to break out, and with guns. I think she must be out of her mind, and I go up.

Several shots whistle and go off together, but they are fired into the air to sound the alarm. Sailors, stokers and shipwrights are fighting man to man against the soldiers who are trying to tie them up; but their plan of escape has been discovered and they know they will be punished, so they are fighting like demons. As long as there are only punches being exchanged they don't use arms, but at the first sight of blood, it's a fight to the death.

Thank goodness! Reinforcements sent by the police arrive in time to quell the revolt. Nonetheless, there were injuries on both sides, and there are large bloodstains on the deck. Two thirds of the crew are in irons. In their fury, some say they are going to set fire to the *Croesus*, others that they are going to sink it. Lionel has not yet come back. I do hope he does not leave me too long in such dangerous company! They all look so very determined to do what they have said they will. At nightfall, large boats arrive to take them to the pontoons. I am very happy for them, for they will be better there than down in the hold, and I shall feel safer. I quickly lose sight of them. It's late and the night is dark.

Lionel will not be back this evening. The steamboats that service the harbour don't run after eight o'clock. Mrs Wèbe is very upset as she had hoped her husband would know of our arrival and that he would come and meet her on board. I urge her to draw on all her patience, but I have no reserves of my own. I walk back and forth along the deck and I walk alone: no one would be able to keep up with me.

Ten o'clock strikes and all the lights go out. I go back into my little hole which seems the size of a desert without Lionel. I go and get Solange, Marie, the budgerigar, the dogs. They are all asleep, but I take no notice; I carry those that don't want to come with me. I don't go to bed as I am too afraid of sleep. I talk all night before I am totally over-come with tiredness, but no one hears me. I make up my own questions and answers. My nerves are as taut as violin strings. My arms and legs feel as if they are about to break. At daybreak I begin to fall asleep.

They start banging and nailing down boards above my head. I go up on deck, furious: I would like to have an excuse to shout at someone, but I am confronted with a coffin that they are just finishing. I ask who has died and they point out a long shape lying on the ground, covered with an English flag. The thought comes to me that it might be Cilia's husband, but one of the men lifts up a corner of the flag and I recognize what looks like the sleeping face of the young novice they had treated so badly when we crossed the Equator.

—He received his baptism and Extreme Unction at the same time, said the man as he covered him over. What a fine job his father did! He forced him to leave. When the lad found himself on the open sea, he was the saddest sight I've ever seen. I'm sure he's glad to be finished with sailing. We're going to take him ashore, which means that he'll be pleased with us in the next world, and I'm pleased with him because he stopped me being nabbed with the others. All the same, the *Croesus* never brings good luck to anyone.

I move away sadly. Mrs Wèbe comes up to me but we don't exchange a word. We gaze into the distance towards the shore. We are waiting with the same impatience, she for her husband, I for mine. At last we see a small steamboat coming towards us, a real old tub. Mrs Wèbe lets out a great cry of joy and says:

—There he is, it's my husband!

They throw themselves into each other's arms, kiss, weep and talk all at once. Lionel is not there. Mrs Wèbe's joys and illusions come to an abrupt end. Her husband earns hardly enough to live on and she can't stay in Melbourne where it would be impossible for her to give lessons. She is going to continue her voyage on the same ship as far as Sydney. I do pity her!

Finally another boat arrives. I can see Lionel from far in the distance. He tries in vain to smile at me but there is sadness in his bright, intelligent eyes. He looks worn out, discouraged. He clasps my hand and says:

—My poor dear Céleste, what changes have taken place here in the year since I left Melbourne! The whole place has been turned upside down, and I can hardly find my way around. It's impossible to find accommodation; rents are exorbitant. I have found two small rooms though, but in a dreadful area. It will alarm you, because we have to go there on foot. The roads are impassable to carriages.

—Is that all?

—Yes.

—You have no other reason to be sad?

—The Duke d'Esclignac, our old friend from the Berry, has just died here in the most dire poverty, and the awful thing is that they threw him like a dog into some corner of the cemetery without even marking the place where he is buried, but I shall find it.[5]

They pile our luggage in with us on the very small steamboat that has just brought Lionel. Mrs Wèbe says farewell to us, and promises to write. Cilia is staying in Melbourne with her husband, and she will come and tell us how she is getting on.

One can't help but feel deeply apprehensive when one leaves a big ship to board a steamer that is not very solid, is very badly fitted out and is always overloaded with parcels and passengers. We huddle up against each other without saying a word. We leave the harbour to go onto the river. The Yarra-Yarra is narrow but deep, for it carries ships. There is traffic congestion and we nearly get crushed between two large boats which pass regardless.

The fields which line the river are uncultivated. We see scraggy, sickly livestock and dead animals abandoned on the ground. They are left to rot in the sun until rain and fine weather drive their carcasses back into the earth. The few trees we come across are misshapen; we see them here and there, lined up in battle formation like a regiment of hunchbacks.

Finally, after spending three hours on this awful skiff, we arrive at the Worf [*sic*] dock. They put us ashore in a great hurry so they can save time and we are all thrown out pell-mell—passengers, trunks and parcels—on to a type of quay made of loosely-packed sand. We are abandoned to the porters who demand whatever ransom they please from us. After a great number of inquiries, we find a handcart to carry our trunks. We follow behind, paddling through the mud like poodles. The roads are full of potholes; in the most difficult spots, Lionel helps push. We look like acrobats moving house on a rainy day.

The streets are strewn with old shoes, old clothes, pieces of broken crockery, tin hoops, in short, with everything that has been imported and unpacked, for this country produces absolutely nothing.

After walking for an hour and a half, we stop for lunch at an extremely unpleasant eating-house. They serve us stale bread, strong-smelling butter, suspect eggs, fermented sauerkraut, rancid ham, sour beer and coffee. Oh! what coffee! This nice little feast costs us sixty-eight shillings!

We set off again. I carry Solange who carries the budgerigar. Marie holds a dog under each arm. The poor girl's bewilderment is beyond description, and she pulls such a funny face that we laugh uncontrollably. She tells us that she had imagined arriving in a land where everyone was carried about on palanquins.

After having spent ninety-five days at sea, we have forgotten how to walk: we take one step forward and two steps back.

5 April 1854

We cross the main street of Melbourne: it looks just like a fairground except that the shopkeepers are not dealing in gingerbread but in gold. They are almost ape-men, these shopkeepers who stand beside their open-air shops, grimacing and contorting their bodies to attract the attention of successful miners and to buy their gold. There is movement everywhere, everyone yells; it's exactly like the Paris money market. There are a few brick houses surrounded by huts and tents.

As for the shops, when you need to enter one you must lift your dress with one hand and hold your nose with the other. Not that there is any need to be too hard to please: they sell everything. Dresses made from antique moire, York hams, ladies' hats, miners' boots, candles, perfumery, pickaxes and children's toys; they even trim beards. Attached to the doors there is a huge striped pole bearing the words written in large lettering: 'Men shaved here.'

Everyone runs, jostles and knocks into each other without even apologizing. 'Times [*sic*] is money', the English tell us, and they don't waste any, even to reply when we ask for directions. Since there are no signposts to distinguish the tracks that have been haphazardly cut through the woods, we lose our way. Our carter does not want to walk any further and, as he was paid in advance, we resort to the use of force and threat. After a quarrel which lasts an hour, Lionel pulls out his gun and threatens the carter with a bullet in the head. He reluctantly continues on but Marie and I have had such a fright that we can hardly walk. We must, however. We cross a small wood without meeting anyone. Night is approaching. Finally, we catch sight of some huts.

—There it is, Lionel tells us. Just a bit further!

We arrive at the door of a house made of very badly-joined wood—temporarily erected in a makeshift street in the middle of a forest. All the same, we are in high spirits as we settle in. We have the use of two rooms on the ground floor and one on the first. The kitchen is shared with the owner.

—They leased me the lot, laughed Lionel, for the modest sum of 1200 francs per month and that is nothing compared with other lodgings. They will provide meals when there is something to eat. I can't promise you that will happen every day, but we shall work something out.

—Where will Marie and Solange sleep?

—Above us.

—But that's the attic. You reach it by a ladder! Oh well, we shall have to take the rough with the smooth. The beds are terribly hard but what does that matter? If we are tired enough we shall sleep well anyway.

The next day we have a breakfast of bread, cheese and tea. Our very unpleasant landlord—he is horrible—comes to see us. He tells us that he was a master mariner, and that he married his wife for love because all she possessed were her two lovely eyes. With her, he had two charming daughters to whom he is going to introduce us.

The furnishings in our bedroom consist of an iron bed, two chairs, a wash-stand and our trunks. Nothing shuts, the doors are warped, the locks broken. The paper on the ceiling is covered with large yellow and dark stains. The sash windows are made of very small panes of multi-coloured glass. They have no metal catches so they need to be held open by hand or wedged up to allow a little air to flow inside.

We are surrounded by people who are probably very honest but who look like veritable bandits. All are armed. Is it to attack or defend? Time will tell. They have begun to macadamize the road in front of our house. This consists of throwing broken stone into the deepest ruts in the road. The men employed for this type of work wear a uniform of grey cloth with their number written across the chest. Those who guard them are armed with muskets. The men have chains on their feet and are shackled like horses in a field, none of which prevents them from appearing reasonably happy with their lot. These are the thieves and murderers who are put to work rather than being fed to do nothing but while away their time in prison. But I think to myself as I watch them from behind the curtains: 'Heavens! I only hope their chains are strong!'

It seems that we live in an area which, because of its isolation, is a favoured haunt of criminals. Of an evening, people in the area fire their rifles or pistols to let the criminals know that they are armed. Our front window opens onto the street, there are no shutters. Simply by lifting the frame, anyone could enter our house at any time of the day or night.

In the evening, when the moon appears or goes behind a cloud, it makes eerie shapes out of the branches of the trees buffeted by the wind, and casts moving shadows onto the calico blinds which serve as our curtains. We are always on the defensive. Lionel is as brave as a lion but Marie especially, and I, have unconquerable fears.

Lionel has taken one of the two rooms as a temporary consulate.[6] Already, a lot of people are coming to see him and all of them give atrocious accounts of the confidence tricks, theft and crimes that take place here, even in broad daylight. A large number of requests for help and repatriation have already been made and we have only been here three days! All these poor people do indeed look wretched. The accounts of their hardships make us unhappy also for we can help them only within the limits of our means—and these are not ample. Lionel says that we must manage our finances to provide for the sick and disabled: as for those who are able-bodied and making a living from begging, he will release them from the sin of laziness.

Marie, who greets those who arrive on consular business, comes to tell Lionel that a man is asking to speak to him.

—I don't know whether he too has come to ask for something but I'm sure he's not bringing anything: he has a very long face. I made him wait in the street for the count's reply.

Given our cramped living space, we use the street as our waiting room. When the weather is fine this is acceptable, but when it rains?

—It's five-thirty, replied Lionel with such seriousness that I could not remain serious myself. Tell him that the consulate closes at four o'clock.

—I would point out to the consul that his consulate is a long way from Melbourne.

—All right, let him in then. The sooner he comes in, the faster I shall be finished with him.

Marie shows him in.

—What do you want? asks Lionel in the abrupt tone that he is obliged to adopt, and which would lead people to believe that he is not the best and most affable of men.

—I would like to be repatriated. I am French, I have just left hospital and I have neither money nor strength.

—Sit down, Lionel says more gently. You said you are French?

—Yes, sir.

—Your name?

—Louis-Edouard Manceau.

—Your age?

—Twenty-six.

—You came here . . . ?

—On an English ship, four months ago. I went straight to the mines and I sold some of my goods. Obliged to come to Melbourne to make some essential purchases for my business, I was stopped by a man in Calinwood [sic] here, near your house, at eight o'clock in the evening. He asked me what money I had in my belt and, before I had time to reply, to put myself on the defensive, I heard several shots and I thought my right arm was going to fall off. Six men were behind me; it seemed that they came out from the trees. I had a bullet in my leg and a broken arm. I felt myself being searched and stripped, but I lost consciousness. When I came to, some men who seemed to have carried me were arguing with the hospital attendant who was no doubt refusing to let me in. After a long quarrel, I was lifted from the floor and carried to a bed where I stayed for three months. I came out two days ago, with no money or food.

—All this is very sad, said Lionel as he struggled to control his emotions, but I don't have the authority to send back to France, at the government's expense, all the emigrants who have come here on their own account to try their luck. The State would not cope with it, given the very high cost of the voyage. As for the captains of our ships, they refuse to make any concessions because the French generally emigrate on English shipping lines. I am going to give you some money and I shall do everything that is within my power to help you, but I can't promise you anything. Would you have any relations who could pay for you on your arrival?

—There is my mother, replied the young man, consoled by a sudden idea. I had not dared to count on her for fear of having to wait too long for her reply but . . .

—But you need a guarantor here. Well then, I shall arrange that as best I can.

—If the count continues like this, said Marie, who could not help but hear the entire conversation through the thin walls of the partition, he soon won't have enough money to buy water.

It costs twenty-five francs a barrel—dearer than wine at home—and it's dirty; you can't use it to wash anything white. The fact is that the Yarra-Yarra is the main sewer of the town. We live a long way from it and the roads are so shocking that, even paying twenty-five francs for it, we can't have as much as we want.

The month of May begins with a wind that lashes our faces and torrential rain that comes in everywhere. Lionel puts his papers in the so-called living-room which he uses as an office; they are drenched and he is forced to place an umbrella above the table to do his correspondence. The wind makes our hut shake, and I have the feeling that it is going to take off like a balloon. To top it all off, it's very cold and wood costs seventy-five francs a small cartload. However, when we have some it lasts a long time: it's red, hard as stone, it turns as black as coal and doesn't burn.

Thefts and crime are increasing. Last night, a poor Irishman was killed for his tools. It happened just 100 yards from our place. I had only been sleeping a little, now I don't sleep at all.

We have just found a small four-roomed brick house. It's barely finished, but here you don't even give the walls time to dry. This house is situated on Victoria heights. From the first-floor windows one can see, on the right, the town of Melbourne; in the distance, on the left, the harbour filled with ships; opposite, a hill where the Chinese emigrants have permission to set up their tents for the first few days after their arrival. At the foot of this hill, the Yarra-Yarra; on the left, in a valley, a huge village called Richemont [*sic*], and behind on the horizon, Mount Alexander.

We have just moved house in torrential rain, the likes of which are seen nowhere else. If we had waited a few hours we would have had to pay for a full week. Besides, I was in a hurry to leave this hut where the rats were fighting each other to eat my shoe.

Our crates have not arrived from Le Havre, so we have to furnish the house in the meantime. A white deal table costs 100 francs, a mattress made of grass (called vegetable horse-hair), seventy-five francs. Fortunately, we have some linen, table cloths, curtains and lots of books. I did some upholstery myself with boards, hay and chintz. Marie does the cooking. There is really no funnier sight than Marie when she returns from the market. She goes into Lionel's office on the ground-floor and, whether there are people there or not, she adds everything up and groans at the expense of it all:

—Eggs, twenty-five sous each, and they are very small; one cauliflower, five francs, idem, very small.

We laugh. Marie is fairly plain-spoken but she amuses us and we need her very much.

Our house is very expensive: 250 francs per week. It was impossible to get it at a cheaper rate. That is almost the same amount as Lionel earns. People here talk only in 100 000 francs. Horses and carriages are starting to crowd the streets. The omnibuses cost three francs a trip and they are always full. Carpenters, builders, locksmiths, painters earn up to fifty francs a day. Everything happens as if by magic: today you see a plain, a week later it's a village.

Civilization will take giant steps forward when everyone finds it worthwhile to protect their rights. It would advance even more rapidly without the heavy domination of the farmers and stock-breeders. They monopolized the country and the land before the discovery of gold, and they did so to such an extent that for twenty-five years they have occupied farms of ten square leagues. Emigrant farmers cannot establish themselves on the land at any price. Yet the gold mines seem to be running dry: they are over-exploited. If this continues, I believe that we shall soon see a flood of miners.

Their camps on the goldfields, which are fortunately a fair distance from Melbourne, are frightful to behold. They are like colonies of moles

digging their holes. The women work like the men, and the children likewise. There is not an idler to be seen: gold obsesses them, fascinates
them. They hope to find tomorrow what they failed to find the day
before. The miners dig such deep holes that accidents often occur. Pits
excavated without any forethought cave in and bury those who built
them.

A man came to ask us for help: he has children, and his wife is in
hospital. He is from the province of Berry, a stonemason by trade. Lionel
had bought a very large stone to have engraved for the Duke d'Esclignac's
tomb. Once the inscription was finished, we went to the cemetery but it
was impossible to find the final resting place of the poor duke. We had
to lay the tombstone down by the entry wall. Lionel's good intentions
were not totally wasted, the stonemason profited from them, but we are
poor enough already without wasting 300 francs.

It has been cold for the whole five months that we have been here.
Several days ago, there was snow on the blue mountains and in the
morning we have white frosts as in France. It's now 18 August 1854. I
can't say that time is flying here. Time is old and it moves slowly.

I hear the cannon being fired, heralding the arrival of a ship. I am
overcome with excitement. This is the only emotion that I feel in this
country, but it is so intense that I cannot describe it. A letter that is
addressed to you, even if it comes from a creditor, gives you immense
pleasure. Even if you are not due to receive any mail, you always hope for
some. And when, at about midday, you see the postman in his red
uniform approaching in the distance, you run out to meet him. When he
indicates that there are no letters, you feel quite downcast as you go back
inside, for it will be another month before he returns.

The *Great Britain*, which arrived from England this morning
is in quarantine because there has been an outbreak of smallpox on
board.

The *Intrépide* has finally entered the harbour. It's the ship which has
transported our goods and furniture. It took 120 days to come from Le
Havre to Melbourne. It has finally arrived and I sincerely hope that it has
made the voyage without incurring any damage, because all that we
possess in goods, furniture and materials is on board.

We can't stay where we are: the rent is decidedly too high. We have
found some land two leagues from the town in the heart of the woods,
near a village called Saint-Kilda. We are going to erect the house that I
bought in Bordeaux on this site.

CHAPTER 6

Céleste the Landowner and Consul's Wife

HERE I am, a landowner in Australia: I have a weatherboard gable with a forest view. I no longer fear anything but fire and water.

Before leaving France, Lionel, in the presence of Mr Titac, a lawyer in Dauphine Square, had a marriage contract drawn up in which he opted for the separate ownership of property, and in which he credited me with twice my actual assets and, in addition, he committed himself, despite my protests, to paying me an allowance of 6000 francs in the event that we should ever separate.

While my house was being unloaded at a great cost, I went with my husband to take a horse-ride around the mines. We stopped in a village of Chinese emigrants and were nearly given a less than warm reception. These miserable souls are exasperated by the English who treat them like harmful animals. Indeed the children of Albion beat them and chase after them on the pretext that they don't spend all that they earn and because they eat rice. One of their interpreters having assured them that they had no reproach to make against the French, they presented me with very pretty handcrafts that they had made.

Upon arriving at Balarate [*sic*], the sight of the mines frightens me: it's like a large cemetery where each person digs his own grave.

It's suggested to me that I go down a mine shaft. If I were alone, I would certainly refuse but everyone is watching me. Lionel is there as I take my place in the trolley. They lower me very carefully, but I am plunged into a sort of pit that is at least eighty feet deep. If Lionel were not at the mouth of the mine, I would not make a half of this aerial trip. I am given a light and I arrive at the bottom, feeling very apprehensive.

A miner does the honours and shows me around his cramped underground passage. He gives me a small pick, a type of American pickaxe, and invites me to search in the earth for a few grains of gold which would be a souvenir of my visit to the mines. I come back up with two small pieces of gold which the gallant miner had no doubt thrown at my feet.

My Lionel was as emotional as I on my return: he embraced me as if I had returned from a long voyage. They all thought me a very brave soul and I came back to Melbourne, delighted with the impression that I had made on the miners.[1]

Events here take place and follow on from on each other in such quick succession that one can't find the time to write about them with any sense of order. We had hardly arrived home when requests for help started again. Marie announced in her provincial accent that a gentleman who looked honest enough had come three times, and that he was walking around the house like a sheepdog guarding its flock.

Someone knocked. She went to open the door, and came back saying: 'It's him.' She started to show him in and said:

—The count is in. Your name, please?

—Jacques Trumeau.

Lionel and I exchanged a look of compassion as we watched this Jacques Trumeau enter the room. Death was written all over his face. He had regular, handsome features but they bore the stamp of such profound suffering that Lionel stood up and offered him a chair. I waited for a sign from my husband to leave, but he did not make one, knowing that my only diversion is sharing in the troubles of my poor compatriots.

—Your name is Jacques Trumeau, Lionel said finally. Are you French?

—Yes, sir. I set sail from England with my wife and child. We had booked our passage on the *Tayleur*.[2] There were 750 passengers on board. We had been at sea for two days when, during the night of the third, a passenger, dreaming that he was being shipwrecked, woke up with a start, went up on deck and pointed to what everyone thought was an imaginary danger. Yet despite the extreme darkness, he was still able to see a mountainous rock which the *Tayleur* was about to hit. He was so convinced that he succeeded in alarming us all; and soon, once our eyes were used to the darkness, we too could clearly make out the land. The man on watch had fallen asleep. By now, everyone could see how dangerous our situation was, but it was too late to avoid it. We heard what sounded like a tremendous explosion down in the hold: the *Tayleur's* keel had just crashed on to a rock. The ship lurched upwards and then fell back heavily onto another reef. Our cries of despair must have reached the heavens, but God did not hear them. However, we were only a few miles from land. The lifeboats could not carry everyone, and while they were arguing and even fighting to get hold of the boats, the *Tayleur* was sinking into the sea. I was prepared to give my life to save my wife and child. Some men lowered a boat on to the water to go and attach a cable to the rock. Time after time, the waves kept pushing back the frail skiff which, after a desperate struggle, finally broke up. Those manning the boat tried to swim ashore. Of twenty men, only two were able to reach it. There were 160 women and sixty small children crying all around me.

They managed to throw a cable which they tied to a projecting rock. With our bodies in the water and our arms above our heads, we were able to go along this cable. One hundred and fifty men grabbed it at the same time. I put my child on my shoulders; he was very frightened and he clung onto my neck with his thin little arms. My wife followed quietly behind me: she was so brave! She had kissed me and my child before we left the ship's deck. Some of the male passengers had seized hold of the rope, after ruthlessly pushing back women and children. I thanked God that I had by my side those dear ones I believed were saved! We were half-way along the cable; my child tightened his grip and my wife was saying words of encouragement when the ship, as it sank into the sand, gave such a strong jerk on the cable that it snapped. I felt myself plunging deep into the sea. My child let go of my neck and I lost consciousness.

I don't know by what miracle I was saved. In my despair I felt such misery that my companions in distress felt sorry for me. Of 750 people on board, only twenty-five had escaped death. I spent two days on my knees, praying for my poor wife and child. A sail was sighted on the horizon; a ship was coming for us. They took me away, and I regained my senses far from the place where I wanted to die.

They brought me here, but since I have lived through so much sorrow, I want to return to France. I still have my mother and a sister who would suffer as much as I am suffering now if they were to learn of my death. That's why I didn't kill myself.

—Do you have any funds?

—No, sir, but I have a profession: I am a mechanical engineer.

—Do you need anything? Lionel asked him quietly.

The young man's cheeks turned bright red.

—You will reimburse me, said Lionel as he handed him a little money. We shall certainly see each other again. I am going to find you employment on board a ship. You can work to pay your way.

That evening, Lionel sent for a dinghy and six crewmen on board a French ship that had just dropped anchor in the open harbour, and the next morning we set out to ask the captain of the *Hirondelle* if we could have lunch.

He welcomed us with much unnecessary ceremony. All the flags were hoisted, and they fired gunshots on our arrival. The members of the crew, decked out in all their finery, deafened us with their joyful cries.

Lionel was forthright in business matters, and so no doubt finding the moment appropriate to make his request, he broached the question.

—Captain, I remembered your kind invitation because I have a favour to ask you.

—Ask for my head if you like, replied the captain, keeping a straight face that made us laugh.

—You make too good use of it, Captain, said Lionel, bowing. Your ship is wonderfully fitted out. Your men are impeccably dressed. Our French army unfortunately possesses few men as distinguished as you.

Our man puffed himself up so much I thought he was going to burst.

—I would like to ask you to give passage to a young man who lost his wife and child when the *Tayleur* was shipwrecked, Lionel went on. When I say give him passage, I mean give him a position which would allow him to repay you. He is a mechanical engineer.

—Well, it's just that . . . , replied the captain, rubbing his chin.

—You don't need him. If it were otherwise, you would not be doing me a favour, and I would not be in your debt.

—You have a point there. Send me your young man, and I promise you I shall treat him well.

—Try to make him earn something during the time you are at sea. Work brings us relief from our sorrows; when we are thinking of what has to be done, we forget what has gone before.

—That's true. You will need to give him a letter of recommendation for the sake of my shipowners.

—I shall give you four of them if it would please you and help him in any way.

As we were leaving, we saw a vessel whose flag was flapping sadly at half-mast. It was a Chinese ship that had just come out of quarantine.[3] There were 200 of them when they entered Hobson Bay. They think there are no more than ten of them now, for no one dares approach them and as they don't have a flag to communicate by signals, no one knows what is happening on board.

The scene here is one of great activity. Not one day goes by without a mishap. I was a little tired after my outing on the bay, but I found it impossible to sleep all night. The alarm sounded. We thought the whole town of Melbourne was on fire: the sky was all red and the stars looked like rubies.

Chinese immigrants are still arriving in large numbers. I can see them from my window, camped on a hillside, where they have been packed in like oysters. At the moment, they are victims of a strange illness from which they die instantly. They have just been sent doctors, but it's like mercy after death. It is said that this disease comes from the salted meat they ate on board the English ships that brought them out.

There is only the Yarra-Yarra that separates us from their camp, and we could perfectly well be affected by the epidemic. Guards have been stationed around the hill, and no one can go near them any more: they are in quarantine. If God does not come to their aid, they are all going to die, for people here are hardly doing anything for them.

I am starting to think that Marie has remained a spinster in spite of herself. For her, a man is a man, and she spends her time feeling pity for the plight of the Chinese.

One Chinese man, having fled the camp, swam across the Yarra-Yarra and wanted to take refuge in our house. Solange was playing on the doorstep and called out to us, more in surprise than fright, but the man, not understanding and thinking she would have him arrested, gave her a strong push. She fell face-down on the ground and let out screams that made us come running. The Chinese had fled.

Cannon fire has again just signalled the arrival of a ship. Tomorrow we shall have news from France.

The cannon rumbled all night. All the inhabitants stayed on their feet, either in the streets or at their windows. Since the Crimean War, which is always on their minds, and because there is not a single warship

Gabriel-Paul-Josselin-Lionel, the Count de Chabrillan, French consul in Melbourne and Céleste's husband (L'Illustration, 30 April 1859, after photograph by Antoine Fauchery)

Melbourne 23.d October 6

To the Honourable Mr Justice Bar[…]

Sir

Will your honour allow—
me to address to you the History of
France by Anquetil, one of our best
Historians.
I should be most happy if this modest
present be accepted by the Public
Library as the expression of my
Sympathy towards the City of Melbourne
from which I have in every circum-
stance received the most courteous
hospitality.
I have the honour to be
Sir
Your most obedient Servant
The Consul for France
Comte […]

Gift of Anquetil's Histoire de France *to the Victorian State Library*
(State Library of Victoria)

Self-portrait of Antoine Fauchery (Sun Pictures, La Trobe Picture Collection, State Library of Victoria)

Caricature of Henri Murger (Collection Nadar, Bibliothèque Nationale)

Alexandre Dumas père, as Céleste would have known him (Collins New Classics)

in the Melbourne harbour, they are always imagining that the Russians are going to attempt an invasion to pillage the gold of the whole of Australia. They walk about in large groups, prepared for battle. The governor has been informed and he arrives from Toorack [*sic*], situated six leagues from Melbourne. They follow him; they run towards the harbour. Lionel does likewise. The sky is red and all the ships in port seem to be on fire. They think they hear cries of distress.

Lionel comes back, drenched with perspiration. He falls onto a chair and laughs so much that he can't say a word to me. It was all a practical joke that the captain of the *Great Britain*, with the help of a few friends, wanted to play on the inhabitants of Melbourne, to get his own back for having been put in quarantine. He had simulated a naval combat well enough organized to trick us all. The scaremongers and alarmists are frightfully annoyed, and the governor did not find the joke at all to his taste.[4] However the *Great Britain* weighed anchor after all the entertainment, and all that will remain of the whole affair are the satires in *Punch*, which are very witty and amusing.

The captain who is giving passage to Jacques Trumeau comes to collect his boarding papers at the consulate. He was so kind as to bring a Chinese doll for Solange who, since her experience, has been terribly frightened of the Chinese. She took hold of it, shook it, turned it all about and then, holding the dolly head-down and without saying a word to us as we talked, ran away as fast as her legs could carry her.

—Where have you been? I asked as I saw her creeping in through a small back door that opens on to the yard.

—I have just drowned him, she replied secretively.

—Drowned him. Who do you mean?

—The nasty Chinaman.

—You drowned him? But where?

—In the Yarra-Yarra. He won't come back, I tied a stone to his neck.

Lionel gives her a very sound scolding, not for having drowned her dolly, but for having gone to the river bank alone.

We have a delivery of at least twenty kilograms of French papers and a large number of letters. I begin with my mother's. She lives in my house in Le Poinçonnet.[5] Her letter is full of complaints and reproaches, and ends with regrets and tears. The poor woman! she has only expressed some of the grief and distress she feels—to the point of tormenting and deeply saddening others—in the hope of easing her own feelings.

Ernest Baroche writes to me:

My dear Countess. The mail is about to leave, so I am sending you these few lines which are to precede a long letter that I intend writing to the count in order to recommend to him one of my good friends who is on his way to Melbourne. Rumour had it in France that the *Croesus* was lost with all hands. All those who know you and love you,—you know that I am amongst them,—were greatly grieved. We very often speak of you as an author. You have your supporters and your enemies. Don't distress yourself about anything; in my opinion, to be talked about gives us proof that we have a relative value. Goodbye for now. Please remember me to the count. Ernest Baroche.

'Talked about!' He should have said 'brutally attacked'. I have just gone through a few papers and I am dismayed at the way in which they interpret my thoughts and my actions. Is it really courageous to damn or nonchalantly insult people at the other end of the world who cannot possibly justify or defend themselves? It seems to me that the certainty of being able to make these insults with impunity ought to inspire more moderate behaviour in those who are indisputably superior minds.

Lionel is suffering, but only on my behalf. He is the one who restores my strength by being especially considerate and loving.

—When we are rich, he says as he embraces me, I shall go and settle my score with all those individuals. Just think about me, the one who loves you. My love will last much longer than the petty spitefulness of the gossips: they have so little to do that they would rather denigrate themselves than have no one to denigrate at all.

The kind of busy life we lead here hardly leaves us time to reflect seriously on the events of the day before. We are constantly receiving visitors, even some women, of whom there is an infinite variety. There was a jolly fat Englishwoman here who insisted that Lionel should restore her husband to her.

—It so happens, she said to him, that I'm a laundress by trade, working at the mines. When I first arrived, there was a villain of a Frenchman there who was spinning a yarn to all the women.

—And with whom you fell in love? laughed Lionel.

—No, who owed me a month's food and laundry. Do you know what he offered me as payment?

—Promises?

—Ah, yes indeed! of his heart and his hand! As he was a hard worker, a solid lad, a good-looking lad even, and as I didn't want to lose what I had paid out, I said yes. He promised me lots of beautiful things. Oh, those rogues of Frenchmen, what liars they are!

Lionel smiles. She goes on:

—I'm not saying that because of you. Believe it or not, mine used to beat me! When an Englishman hits you face on, you can retaliate, but that horror of a man of mine would raise his leg and kick you anywhere. It's a disgrace to your countrymen.

—What are you getting at?

—I was beginning to get used to his fancy ways when he left me in the lurch, leaving me without a penny or a single word. But you being justice for the French, you will get him back for me.

—So you wish to recover your capital?

—No, she replied, changing her tone. I want to find the father of my child.

—Ah! you are a mother?

—It won't be long now . . . and wouldn't it be a mark of your kindness to put me in hospital while I'm waiting.

Lionel took down the particulars of the deserting husband, gave the Englishwoman a letter of recommendation for the head doctor of the hospital, and said to her with a very serious expression on his face:

—I shall return your husband to you as punishment for having insulted my compatriots.

CHAPTER 7

Fights, a Hanging and
Trouble at Ballarat

PEOPLE claim the Spaniards have cruel hearts because they adore bullfights. What would they say if they witnessed the performance here of fights between men (who have nothing human about them) on the streets and in the town squares? They lay bets on the professional boxers, they boo the ones who are beaten (who often die), with total indifference to the state they are in.

As I watched the Englishwoman walking away, very happy at the idea of seeing her boor of a husband again, I saw two men come and stand face to face on the high ground of Victoria-Parade, and without any shouting, without any apparent anger, start to knock each other senseless with such terrible blows that I could hear the sound from here. The onlookers, men and women, remained unmoved until the moment the taller man, who had missed the parry, received a blow which brought blood gushing from his eye and nose. The spectators booed him, the street urchins hooted at him. He stepped back, took a few deep breaths and once again placed himself on guard. The luckier opponent, encouraged by the cheering and his initial success, shouted at him:

—Haven't you had enough yet? Well, I'll punch your other eye in! They were just about to go on with their fight when a man driving a cart shouted: 'Out of the way! Watch out!' to the roaring crowd which made no attempt to move aside.

—You savages! Make way for the dead! the driver cried out as he threatened those closest to him with his whip.

In the bottom of this cart, there was a coffin covered with a length of black woollen cloth. Four people were seated on top of it, wearing hats with black veils covered with white veils to show they were accompanying a woman to her final resting place. The fighters and bystanders moved back from the road. This sad cortege had no doubt come some distance, for the horse looked worn out.

There is no regular organized service for transporting the dead. Everyone takes them for burial by whatever means they like or can afford.

Among the criminals who make up one of the greatest ornaments of the floating population of Melbourne, there are some who become popular celebrities. It was for this reason that people thronged around the door of the Supreme Court yesterday. An interesting criminal was being sentenced: he had killed at least fifteen people. After long and fruitless argument, the chamber deliberated for an hour. When the hearing resumed, the murderer said to the judge:

—You're in too much of a hurry to find me guilty. It's six o'clock, and you're thinking of the dinner that's waiting for you. Come on, hurry up, or the pudding will get cold.

The sentence was read to him. 'Condemned to be hanged in three days!' he repeated, scratching his forehead. I wish you 'bon appétit'. Drink my health with a glass of sherry before I die.

On the 23rd, early in the morning, the crowd gathered in large numbers on the high ground in Victoria Parade in order to see the scaffold on which the guilty man was to be hanged being erected in the Court of Justice.[1]

A doctor friend of ours, Mr Iwan [*sic*], offered me a place at his window. It has a view over the walls and I accepted in spite of my repugnance for this kind of spectacle. I want to familiarize myself with all of life's atrocities. It will make me philosophical and will help me rise above the petty afflictions that beset me constantly.

The condemned man arrives. The crowd is suddenly full of movement like an ant's nest that has just been run over by a carriage wheel. He looks scornfully at the inquisitive throng, all wrapt and open-mouthed, and his eyes seem to say: 'If you were in my place, not one of you would put on such a bold front.' All the preparations for the execution are carried out like a military manoeuvre.

—Don't worry about him! said a frightful-looking man. He'll have the luck of the damned. Everything will go right for him in the next world.

The condemned man moves forward onto the platform and bends his head towards the executioner, smiling as if he were only going to try on a cravat. Then he plunges into space with such force that his body swings for a long time before the boy, whose job it is to cover his face with a kind of bag, can finally manage to do it.

The onlookers, eager for thrills, can comfortably watch the death throes, the contractions and contortions of the condemned man. His eyes become bloodshot, the veins on his forehead and temples swell fit to burst, his mouth gapes open, showing his swollen, distended tongue, as big as an ox's. Soon all that can be seen is a featureless, purple, round mass.

Yesterday, we went to St Kilda to see our future house. Building contractors in this country will begin work on anything you want, but they never finish anything. We come back in the omnibus. The drivers of these carriages usually own them, and they go after passengers and steal them from each other. Ours gets two men loaded down with mining equipment into the coach. The younger of the two is dead drunk. The coachman hauls him by the collar, lifts him up and places him on the seat beside him. He is a happy drunk, singing and laughing uproariously. He has found gold, he is leaving, he is happy with his lot. He looks about twenty-five and has quite a pleasant face. He is not the inveterate drunkard type. After excavating the bowels of the earth, sleeping in the cold at night, being burned to a crisp by the sun during the day, he wanted to have his day of happiness. Hearing him laugh makes the other passengers laugh too. He pays the price of his seat—three francs. That is all that is required of him: he has paid and no one takes any further notice of him.

Suddenly, I see a shadow pass in front of the glass, and I hear cries. The poor miner has fallen off the seat, which is very high. The carriage jolts twice . . . the wheels have run over his body! We get out, they try to lift him up, saying: 'Get up, you boozer, get up!' They hold him under the arms as they try to lift him up. But he groans dreadfully, his eyes fill with tears and he collapses in spite of people's efforts to get him on his feet. He falls to the ground again. Both his legs have been badly crushed.

The coachman realizes that all this could turn out badly for him, as they are forbidden to take drunken passengers on board. He whips up his horses, which gallop off, leaving us in the middle of the road with the unfortunate miner to cope with. Lionel, who knows how these gentlemen behave under such circumstances, has taken down the number of the carriage. He writes it on a page from his notebook and gives it to the people who have agreed to take the wounded man to hospital. He died there a few hours later.

The police are starting to get a little more organized. An energetic and very intelligent chief has just been appointed. He fills a widely-felt need. All the same, as it is in man's nature to be volatile and bellicose, towards and against everyone and everything, the new colonists are restless and discontented, either openly or behind the scenes. They want laws, they want reforms, they assemble. Meetings and banquets follow and increase every day. There is a lot of meaningless talk. All these soap-box orators think they are Mirabeau.[2]

Here is the question of the day: should we or should we not allow convicts to stay here in the colony of Victoria? It has already been decreed that Melbourne would never be a place for deportation. But when gold was discovered, every criminal in Van Diemen's Land arrived here and took the top places. Now that the colony is well populated and powerful, it wants to cast out those who claim to be its founders. This could well lead to shooting. In the meantime, many a punch is thrown in the streets.

A governor has just arrived among us.[3] He was received with all due honours, but there is talk that if he does not agree with the . . . —in France we would call them insurgents—he should be summarily put on board and sent back to the Queen of England, requesting her to kindly send another who, while being her representative, will do absolutely nothing but what is decreed by the Chamber in Melbourne.

All the shops close at two o'clock as if by magic, and a huge, ever-increasing crowd has begun to march on the governor's house to politely request him to agree to all their wishes without the least objection.

The deputations have come back satisfied, so it seems, for in the evening there are celebrations and fireworks. There are even rockets, which set fire to a wooden house. The fire spreads and lasts for part of the night. More than 100 houses go up in flames.

There is a revolt at the mines. Every miner must pay so much per month to have the right to prospect for gold. They call it paying for a licence. The miners have declared that they will not pay one penny more. To avoid further harassment, they have burned down the collectors' houses. They carried out their own kind of justice in the following manner:

At the Balaratte [*sic*] mines, there was a fairly well-run inn, but the master of the establishment was brusque and disagreeable: people did not like him. On finding one of their friends murdered not far from the house, some miners accused the hotel owner of the crime. The police arrested him; he was judged and acquitted. But the miners had condemned him. They knocked down his door, took the man and hanged him from one of the casements in his house.[4]

There is no force capable of opposing these acts of brutality! The miners' numbers are so great that they are masters wherever they are. However, the police have managed to arrest several, one of whom is a French sailor. He has just been taken to the consulate under armed escort. He looks harmless enough, yet he is accused of murder. While defending himself, he killed the man who was trying to arrest him.

—Are you sure the policeman is dead? I wanted to prevent him arresting me, but I didn't want to kill him. My wretched knife is to blame. Its blade is too long.

—Have you still got your knife? Lionel asked him with a sententious look I shall never forget.

—Yes, sir.

—Well, if you are found guilty, which is more than probable, try to have the courage to use it on yourself, and spare me the shame of seeing a Frenchman hanging from the gallows.

The following day, when they came to fetch the prisoner to begin taking evidence, he was dead. But before taking his own life, he had written these few words:

For the French Consul in Melbourne.

Thank you for the good advice you gave me. I am going to give you proof of my courage. I would never have thought of the idea on my own.

I really regret having left my country and deserted my ship. And why on earth did I do it? To chase after that cursed Lady Luck. I've only ever seen the back of her heels, and then from afar. What does it matter! In an hour all my sails will be furled.

Farewell!

Pierre P***

I thought I had seen the last of all these torments that have soured me, fevered my brain and tortured my heart. Yet I find myself constantly involved in events so sad, so tragic that they no longer leave me an hour's peace, nor my mind a minute's tranquillity. I cannot avoid them, and I cannot help but take some interest in them. Nothing but crime, theft and fire. Then there is the stifling heat and with it the return of rats and mosquitoes, and a host of insufferable domestic worries.

Having decided to keep to myself a great deal, I don't know how to fill in my time to take my mind off things. I make dresses, hats, lingerie. With Solange, there is no lack of work to do. But that only occupies my hands and leaves my mind free to wander where it will.

The uprising has calmed down somewhat, but the opposition papers will finish by stirring it up again.

Two young men have just been arrested. They are accused of having deliberately set fire to their warehouse, one of the biggest in Melbourne for storing merchandise and consignments of all kinds. They walk bare-headed, their hands in chains.

It seems they insured their goods for considerable sums of money. However, the companies were suspicious. They held an investigation resulting in the arrest of the two men, whom the escort has great difficulty in protecting from the fury of the people who follow them, hurling insults and even striking them with their walking-sticks. There is no pity for dishonest agents and fraudulent liquidations of stock. Those who are taken down in the market take revenge for the European exporters, who are very often ruined without even receiving a word in reply when they ask for accounts or return of goods. Are the Melchior brothers guilty or not? No one can say for sure. One of the brothers has made some statements, but with no logic or order in his thoughts. They say he went mad when they put the handcuffs on him. The fire destroyed goods worth more than 2 000 000. Six people died in the inferno: there was no way to help them because there was no water.

I had come to Melbourne in the hope of some enjoyment, but I am left with feelings of indignation at having seen these two chained wretches so badly mistreated. It is possible that they are not guilty; even so they are in the hands of the law.

They are macadamizing the roads: everyone who wants to work can find a job as a stone breaker. I have just come across two of them who looked like perfect gentlemen disguised as day labourers. One was smoking a cigar while the other was adjusting his pince-nez to watch me go past. They started singing—out of tune, I might add: 'Gold is nothing but a dream', and then they went back to breaking stones with small iron mallets that sent sparks flying. I find it much more interesting to observe emigrants than the natives.

The rioting has caused some disruption to the miners' work; and gold is diminishing. Discouragement and need force many people to abandon their claims and go in search of work. They say they can do any-thing, but really know nothing at all—at least this applies to most of them. All the same, there is a shortage of manpower and you have to take what you can get.

CHAPTER 8

The Move to St Kilda, Social Life and Speculation

OUR house is finally finished. We had a jeweller build our chimneys, the only ones made out of brick. Lionel says it's a guarantee that they will work well. He is in a delightful mood. He works like a Trojan, is under constant strain, and has far too many worries, but never complains.

They are busy putting up our wallpaper. Our decorators strike me as two real characters. One is about thirty years old, and has a workman's ways. The other one is younger, tall and blond, and he carries himself with style, despite his grey overall and paper hat. He helps his friend, but goes about it so awkwardly that it annoys me. He looks at me and says:

—I am only serving my apprenticeship; this is not my field. Here is my speciality, he added, lightly tapping Lionel's piano; and it would give me great pleasure if you would allow me to play a little. For so long now, I have only seen them in my dreams.

I unlock the piano, taking care to remove the key because of Miss Solange who would ruin me with the expense of having the piano tuned. My wallpaperer has been playing for an hour; he really does have a remarkable talent. Without interrupting his playing, he says to me:

—I've suffered from hunger and thirst, from the heat and from the cold, but my greatest hardship has been not being able to make music. I've always worked and I play for myself. I've never been able to give lessons without having terrible attacks of nerves, and my compositions never brought me in any money. I came to seek my fortune here and, he said as he stood up,—I'm now going to hang your wallpaper.

I ask him to stay longer at the piano, and he does not wait to be asked twice.

—That's good, very good, says Lionel as he comes into the living room. Don't let me disturb you. Then, looking at the musician, he adds:

—Are you the same one who arrived this morning so drunk that I wanted to send you back to Melbourne?

—Drunk? yes, I was this morning, and I probably will be this evening as well. When I'm in my right mind, I suffer, I feel guilty, I'm bored; but when I've been drinking, heaven and earth belong to me. I feel strong enough to move mountains; every living thing seems as small as a fly. Instead of begging the gods for mercy, I give them thanks. When I feel what they call reason starting to return, I grab a bottle and empty it without taking a breath. That has given me the strength to be in turn a miner, a stone breaker, a wallpaperer, I don't care as long as I earn enough to get drunk every day.

—You are out of your mind, and if you are not at present, you soon will be. There's worth in every trade but not in every person. A drunkard easily turns into a brute. Stop drinking. Come and see me now and then in Melbourne. There's a theatre, parties, concerts. I shall try to get you a job somewhere. It takes willpower and a lot of self-control to reach your level of talent. Use that now to overcome a bad habit. At your age, it can't yet be a vice, but even so . . . In the meantime, he added as he looked around himself, the wallpaper is very badly hung.

—That's true. Find me something else to do and I swear I shall follow your good advice.

6 November 1855

The climate is extraordinary. The heat is intolerable. The sun consumes everything and sets it ablaze; fire breaks out in the dry grass. The forests are burning on all sides at once. The wind strengthens and blows so hard that houses are demolished. It comes from the north and stings your face; it's impossible to go out without running the risk of being blinded. Oh! where are you, my dear France! . . .

Our cottage (house) is set in the middle of a lonely wood which was virgin forest before our arrival.[1] Lionel spends all his days in Melbourne, where he pays a very high rent for a very ordinary little place to set up the consulate, which, given the importance of business here, must be in town and close to the port. He sees a lot of people there, and I fear he may be influenced by a few swindlers who always have wonderful speculations in mind when it comes to funding them with other people's money. However, we must try to get on our feet again, for if this continues we will have spent all our money before we get it.

Given the exorbitant prices of basic essentials here, post office workers earn £1000 stg., 25 000 francs per annum. Lionel earns 12 000, and he has three times as many expenses, so that even living very modestly, we have spent 40 000 francs.[2] It's true that I do own a piece of land. I paid two and a half shillings a metre for it, land uncleared. I think it's two French hectares.

Our chalet has five rooms, a kitchen and a verandah, all made of pine with a galvanized-iron roof. Half of our verandah has just been blown off during a squall. As for the chimneys, Lionel was right when he said they would work very well, for one of them has gone out to do a stint in the garden.

There is serious fighting at the mines; there are 1000 soldiers, 500 sailors and six cannons heading towards Ballarat. What can they do against 25 000 insurgents? Fortunately the miners don't know exactly what they want, and their lack of agreement will treble the strength of the regular troops.

A state of siege has been declared. The governor is not altogether reassured. He is a very nice man, from the best society, but that is not enough.

4 December

They are still fighting. The troops have the upper hand. They have lost ten men, while 100 of the insurgents have been killed.

Talks were held with the miners at four o'clock today. All their demands were met, provided they laid down their arms. Peace has been made: they are all fraternizing, embracing, drinking (quite a lot actually). The town is all lit up, and outdoor banquets have been set up. They have overthrown the colonial secretary and the administration and police chiefs; they would topple the moon if they could reach it.

Every day Lionel receives more invitations. When they are addressed to him alone, he invariably replies: 'The countess is indisposed and I am unfortunately unable to accept your kind invitation.'

For instance, he goes to all the functions for men only, and there are a lot of them. They are held in public halls and by subscription, although this does not mean that everyone is admitted.

Other people take a much a greater interest in me than I do in them. A few ladies, having understood my husband's lesson, have invited me by letter at the same time as Lionel. I suspected they were acting in this way out of deference to him, or out of curiosity perhaps, so I urged him to go to these ladies' gatherings on his own, and to thank them on my behalf, giving whatever excuse he felt appropriate for my refusal.

He did not always give in to my request, but when he did, he would come home in a joyful mood. In order to please him, no doubt, they would make very flattering remarks about me; they had seen me at a few charity concerts for the victims of fire and shipwrecks. He would reply, endowing me with qualities I don't possess, so much so that, after having been an object of terror, of repulsion for the people of Melbourne society, who had expressed such great indignation that echoes of it reached me, I became the object of a different kind of persecution. They had to see me and have me at all costs. The most indulgent, the most brazen of them came to St Kilda to invite me personally. My heart softened a little, but my insufferable character did not. I mistrusted appearances, and did not have a good enough education to carry on a long conversation with distinguished people.

I was afraid of not being well enough acquainted with my new role as countess, and afraid that Lionel would have to endure some unwitting clumsiness of mine. As it turned out, my shyness or reserve served me better than too much self-confidence would have done. For some time now, I have been building up relations that I cultivate from a distance, and when I go out with Lionel I am happy, especially for him, when people want to greet me or shake my hand.

Yesterday was Christmas Day. They laid out a race track at the end of our *podaque* [*sic*] (park). At the entrance, they built a wall in the shape of a horseshoe, six feet tall and ten feet wide. They made a fire in this chimney of sorts and then roasted a whole bullock. Everyone cut off a piece of half-raw meat and ate it with or without bread. They started the festivities with pig races, the animals tied in sacks and chased by young children.

A lot of spectators had climbed onto trees, and others had come in carriages or on horseback. Afterwards, there was a cockfight, fights between dogs and rats and finally boxers. These animal and human fights are the favourite pastimes here.

Lionel has invited several people for dinner: Mrs Sivratt, a tall, beautiful blonde woman, a very good musician and the mother of four adorable children; her husband, the deputy director of the Australian Bank; Mrs Catton, a French woman who has been living in the English colonies with her husband for thirty years. Although she is no longer young, she has a very youthful voice. Mistress Mac-Meen [sic], wife of the Chief Justice, who is stylish, elegant and pretty as an English vignette. Her husband is also very good-looking. Recent events have made his work difficult, and he is rather gloomy, but his wife is very cheerful. She is American but looks Spanish. Finally, the captains of two French ships. There were ten of us at the table. Marie put on a first-rate meal.

After dinner we made music, we sang and danced, and when we parted from each other at two o'clock in the morning we promised to meet more often.

This morning I went to the seaside which is about a mile from my place. There were several ladies bathing. The only male bather was a dog, a magnificent dog with long hair and incredibly intelligent eyes, white teeth and a pink mouth which seemed fixed in a permanent grin. He was sent out amongst the bathers, and every time one of them wanted to do a little diving, he promptly brought her back to the surface. When I went into the water, he looked at his master, and as he gave him no indication concerning me, the dog took no interest in me at all.

29 December

It's my birthday today. The elements put on quite a concert for me: a storm had been approaching us for several hours. The clouds seemed to be touching the ground and thunder sounded with a terrible roar, twice breaking the tall flagpole that flies the tricolour, indicating the French Consul's residence. Is this an ill omen? I don't know, but I feel very miserable. The market is so bad in Melbourne at the moment that they can do nothing with the luxury goods we brought from France; we would make no profit at all, and if you wait, storage costs are so high in this wretched country that expenses will send you bankrupt after a few months.

So! Once again my premonitions did not deceive me. We have just received letters from France, and they all tell us of the great to-do in Paris over our marriage. Ernest Baroche writes to Lionel, 'Landerneau is in turmoil.³ They are clamouring for your dismissal. The minister is hesitating, but they are bringing too much influence to bear for him not to end up giving in to the pressure . . . They can't do anything however without referring the matter to the Emperor who, for the moment, has too many other things on his mind to be worried about his consular agents. Stay on your guard, though, and be prepared for anything that might happen, so that they don't catch you unawares, etc . . . '

—I would rather have made the first move, Lionel said after some reflection; but I shall wait for a while yet and turn the time to profit; after all, I go to ten times more trouble than I should to earn what they give me. I'm very happy to be forewarned, as this will put an end to my uncertainty about several things. As French consuls are forbidden to enter into any type of trade, I had refrained from participating in two or three business propositions, put to me by two Frenchmen established here.⁴ One is the son of a shipowner from Bordeaux; the other is from Toulouse and a real braggart, I think, but he is so industrious that he succeeds in everything he undertakes.

—Do they have any money?

—A little, but you don't need any to carry out the idea they put before me yesterday. My personal guarantee is enough.

—I don't understand.

—Flour is going to be scarce in Melbourne; there's certain to be a food shortage. We need to charter one or two ships which would leave immediately to get flour from Chile. What they pay £200 for over there fetches £1000 here. There's a fortune to be made in providing a service to the emigrants, because, let me say it again, they will very soon be going hungry.

—How much can you make?

—A million.

—How much can you lose?

—Nothing, or at least very little.

—Well, about how much?

—Between 15 000 and 20 000 francs each.

—What if the flour is bad when it arrives?

—We shall have it insured.

—Do as you wish.

—I was afraid you would not be sympathetic to our ideas and I dared not speak to you about it before, but things are already off to a good start. I have two captains in harbour who own their ships, and who have put themselves entirely at my disposal. I need only say the word, and they will raise anchor. One of the men is leaving with them, and he's taking what is needed to make the purchases over there, or a share at least.

—They know him then? So why is he sharing with the others? He can act alone, can't he?

—If the freight is paid in cash, the goods can be dispatched on a cash with order basis. In short, you have to risk the lot.

—Do think about it.

—I already have. Nothing ventured, nothing gained! Come now, don't worry. I'm doing it for you, and I shall be careful.

I realized he had allowed himself to become so taken by the idea that all I could do was say amen—besides, the produce trade is the one that offers the most opportunities here. All the grocers make quick fortunes; thick candles have been sold for five francs each!

3 January 1856

An American ship called *New Word* [*New World*] has just arrived. The consulate has become a branch office of the Crown Court.

For several days now, Lionel has been making inquiries about the captain of the *New Word*, who is almost forcing him to take the law into his own hands. I follow him wherever he goes to avoid staying at home alone with the madman. He's a poor wretch who embarked at San Francisco. It seems that he was quite sane when he went on board the American ship which was sailing to Australia but, during the voyage, he completely lost his mind. The captain brought him to us in St Kilda, partly because he is French, but mainly to be rid of him.

Lionel was going to have this unfortunate man taken to hospital, but he noticed he had spells of clear-headedness when he talked of money and valuables he had entrusted to the captain the very day of his departure from San Francisco. Lionel decided to make inquiries. He sent for a member of the crew and asked him:

—How long have you been travelling under Captain G . . . 's orders?

—Three years.

—Is he liked by members of the crew?

—They're afraid of him.

—Does he sometimes ill-treat them?

—Often.

—Ah! . . . And apart from his brutality, has there been any other reason to complain about his honesty?

—Indeed yes! When it comes to his honesty . . .

—Just answer. I'm not asking you these questions for the pleasure of making conversation with you.

—If you're the law, said the sailor after a pause, then question me.

—They say that passenger Maurice D . . . had some money when he set sail.

—I didn't see it.

—But did you hear about it?

—As far as he's concerned, I don't know anything.

—Oh! Do you know something else?

—If you could keep my name out of this, replied the sailor in a low voice, or else find me another job . . .

—Agreed.

—Ten months ago, the captain took on board a man of about forty and a young twelve- to fourteen-year-old child, his son.

—The father died on the way, and the captain set the child ashore on the pretext of repatriating him, but everyone believed the young boy had been abandoned, just left behind . . .

—Why would he do that?

—His father, so they say, had entrusted some valuables to the captain, but as there was no proof, we have never been able to find out.

—Do you know the names of these two passengers?

—The child was called George Peterson. They came from New York and were going to Bombay to set up a commercial firm.

—Very well, you had better go now. I've sent for your captain, and he must not see you. I shall let you know if I need you.

The sailor did not wait to be told twice; he fled.

Captain G . . . has just arrived. He looks like a nasty customer.

—You sent for me? he asked, giving Lionel a shifty look.

—Yes, I need some information.

—About the Frenchman I set ashore in Melbourne, and who you made the mistake of keeping at your place?

—It concerns a boy who was taken on board by a French captain. This captain took on the role of the child's guardian, and promised to have returned to him the small fortune that had been stolen from him. The child does not know the name of the man who robbed him, but he would recognize him.

Captain G . . . gave a start, and looked around.

—He claims his father had more than 100 000 francs.

—One hundred thousand francs! repeated the captain with a smile.

—But he might be exaggerating; George Peterson is barely thirteen years old.

—George Peterson! cried the captain, rising to his feet; he's here?

—Yes, and ready to ask you for an explanation. Oh! your ship is a den where you strip your passengers of all they have. You kept the money of that poor unfortunate Frenchman you brought to me. You would have left him in hospital, had they been prepared to accept him without word from me. You are an out-and-out rogue. How much did he hand over to you when he embarked? If you don't answer, I'm going to send for the sheriff and have you arrested and your ship seized.

—We played dice and I won.

—Played dice with a madman! and how much did you win from him?

—Eighteen thousand francs.

—How long will it take to deposit that money in the bank?

—An hour.

—Then get on your way!

I said to Lionel:

—If I were you, I would have had him arrested, for he's sure to make his escape.

—No, there was not sufficient proof to have him arrested, but he can't leave without having his boarding papers signed, and his consul won't return them to him until he has had word from me. As I'm certain he won't abandon his ship, he'll be back!

He did in fact arrive at the agreed time . . . I am not sorry to be rid of the madman. No one wanted to take him on board when they thought he was poor, but now that he can easily pay his way, everybody is prepared to repatriate him.

CHAPTER 9

Two Near-tragedies

LIONEL introduced me to the Count de Varenne yesterday.[1] He is still a young man, of average build, slim, blond and with fine, regular features. He has refined manners and an elegant bearing, despite his very worn outfit which is similar to those that grooms from good households wear. He is the greatest eccentric imaginable. He comes from a very good family, but having had only a relatively modest fortune, he was far too extravagant. His passion for horses led him in a short time to such total ruin that he set sail for Australia. On board, he fell in love with a young English girl as poor as he, but more responsible, more down-to-earth. She loved him too, but she did not want to give him any advance on his promise of marriage. The Count de Varenne, who has a nature that is hot-headed to the point of violence, and who is used to conducting everything in a great hurry, did not want to wait the two or three months that remained for him to spend at sea, so he asked the captain to marry them. This was done without objection or further ado. The girl was alone on board, without family or friends; she was also going to try her fortune at the other end of the world. Entrusting her to a gentleman who would later find a way to make the members of his family accept this act carried out without their consent would protect her from any seduction.

Three months later they arrived in Melbourne, with no idea of how they would go about earning their living. The countess could no longer pursue her idea of going into domestic service; besides, she was expecting, and her child would claim all her care and attention. They went to the mines, but the count's delicate state of health could not cope with it. Then, his passion for horses dominated him so much that he entered the service of a man who had a very fine-looking specimen to be looked after. The count looked after him very well, but for his own benefit. He took him out all day, deluding the owner into believing the

poor animal was sick and needed rest. But one fine day as he was returning from his office, this gentleman came across them, the count on horseback, practising haute école half-turns.[2] He immediately dismissed him,
having no idea of his noble origins, without even giving him his week's
notice. After he left there, the count started to do a bit of everything, and
achieved nothing worthwhile.

For him, destitution was nothing; but it was too much for him to
see his wife and child suffer. He was advised to go and see his consul.
Lionel welcomed him with open arms, and did his best to help him with
his most pressing needs.

The count has picked up a bad habit here: he takes to drinking
whenever he has the chance, and once he is well away, he forgets to go
home. His wife is very patient and never reproaches him. But then,
Englishwomen accept drunkenness as an entirely natural habit in men.

12 January

Mr de Varenne is altogether part of the family. He is always in the consulate during the day, and my husband often brings him for dinner.
Admittedly, I find his company very pleasant, but it is so expensive to live
here that visitors are a luxury I would happily do without.

And besides, nothing can distract me any more; I feel a general
sense of uneasiness. The climate no doubt has a lot to do with it;—if
they experienced similar weather in Europe, they would think it was the
end of the world! However the population is active nonetheless. You
never see old people because they don't emigrate. And as for children,
they die like flies.

The country's black natives are the worst built and the most frightful
beings I have seen in my life. They look like monkeys with their dis-
proportionately large heads, their frizzy hair standing on end, high,
broad shoulders and spindly legs, arched backs, and their chests sticking
out because they always hold their pointy elbows back. Their only
covering is a wretched, earth-coloured animal skin. When they come
lurking around the villa, they pick out and eat what we have thrown in the
rubbish. They are very fond of sheep shanks, which they gnaw without
cooking or skinning them.

They are so lazy of body and mind that no one has ever been
able to teach a single one of them how to do anything. Their level of

intelligence consists of catching opposums in trees at night, and in searching in tree bark for fat white worms which they swallow whole. It turns your stomach when, by chance, you are forced to witness one of these meals. But anyway, one comes across them less and less often; as towns develop, their numbers diminish, and I think they will soon disappear.

The Count de Varenne is forever telling us of his troubles, but he seems less upset by them than we are. I cannot help but feel more concerned for his wife and child than for him. He is slightly deaf but will not admit it, so the lectures Lionel and I give him are often a complete waste of breath. He replies to everything he thinks he has heard. Sometimes it's amusing, but more often it's tedious. He is always dreaming of an infallible speculation; it all comes down to this: if I had a little money, I would set up a small business, which would enable me to be with my wife. His requests are so direct that Lionel asks my advice as to what he should do. We agree to lend him ten pounds sterling, if he undertakes not to spend it all on drinking outside meals. He promises, even swears this to us, and leaves after having lunch with us at St Kilda.

But man proposes and fate disposes. On his way, de Varenne meets a man thrashing his horse because it had thrown him to the ground. The count stands up for the horse. The miner becomes angry and hits his mare even harder than before, but he is still unable to get back in the saddle. The count calls him a fool, a brute. The mare's owner attacks him. After a donation inter vivos,[3] they start to quarrel again. The count, who prides himself on being a first-rate horseman, claims that if he had this mare, he would make her gentle as a lamb.

—I will sell her to you, exclaims the man; she cost me twenty pounds.

—I shall give you ten, replies the count, without hesitation.

—It's a bargain. I would rather lose ten pounds than break my neck.

The next day, the count rode over to see us on Miss Nelly, and asked us for a little money to feed her, and then added:

—When she's in good condition, I'll get a good price for her. I've got a bargain there, you'll see.

He was so happy to have a horse that we dared not reproach him, and besides, the damage had already been done. We were about to sit down for dinner, so we invited him to join us. He was in very high spirits and could not keep still. He ate a lot and drank very little. Lionel had rationed his wine as a precautionary measure, yet he seemed light-headed; he was intoxicated by his own high spirits.

I had a premonition and said to Lionel:

—Look how dark it is. The forest is in darkness. What if the count were to lose his way?

—Don't worry, Lionel laughed; God looks after people like him.

The count left after thanking us a thousand times over. In spite of his irrational ideas, he is such a charming man that one can't refuse to have anything to do with him or even be angry with him.

It had only just turned eight o'clock when he left us. Nelly was as docile as a lamb as she let herself be mounted. As they were leaving, I noticed a slight twitching of her tail and ears and a shivering of her skin, but the count was such a good rider he put her into a gallop, after farewelling us with a wave of his whip.

At eleven o'clock they brought him back to us on a stretcher made of branches. His poor face was unrecognizable, and it was impossible to pick out the shape of his features. I washed his face with great care. His lips were split open, his nose cracked down the middle, his whole head swollen to such an extent that you could not see his eyes. He must have been thrown against a tree and dragged along by the horse, for the parts of his body that weren't bruised had been burnt by his flesh being dragged over the sand. The blood coming from his nose and mouth was clotting in his throat and was in danger of choking him. The heat was so intense that his blood decomposed instantaneously and filled the air with a fetid smell which attracted flies to his wounds before we could manage to get rid of them.

The doctor we sent for, and who didn't arrive until three hours later, could tell us nothing, except that he thought he was done for. He needed ice but, as it was impossible to get any, he prescribed the use of brandy. He made the patient drink some, making sure to take his own good share. Apart from our great distress, we were in an extremely awkward position. Despite our entreaties, the count had never introduced the countess to us, and we did not even know her address. Yet we had to inform his wife; he was still breathing, but he was inert, not making the slightest movement. He could not hear anything, and we were afraid that at any moment, we would see him pass away without her being beside him when he breathed his last.

Lionel and I wondered why he had given our address rather than his own to the men who had lifted him from the road. For fear of frightening his wife perhaps? We spent one of those nights I shall never forget by the patient's bedside.

Finally, in the morning, when it was scarcely light, we saw a woman arriving in tears. Concerned by her husband's absence, she had overcome her reluctance to come to my house, but upon seeing her husband's virtually unrecognizable face, she lost consciousness and we had a lot of difficulty in reviving her.

When she came round, she knelt down next to the dying man who did not make the slightest movement. She pressed her lips against his ear and said such sweet, loving things that, little by little, he seemed to stir and his lips moved slightly. That was all.

Lionel had sent for a priest at the same time as the doctor. He arrived just as the count was starting to understand what was happening around him. He touched his wife's face, drew her to him, and then gently pushed her back, gesturing to her to move away. All three of us went out of the room. He did not make confession, but he received absolution. The countess agreed to stay with me since she could not do otherwise, but she was worried about her son, entrusted to a neighbour's care. We suggested to her that we send for Mr Napoléon (her child's name), whom she was still feeding.

We have just spent eight days and nights listening to the wails of poor little Napoléon who is no doubt drinking bad milk, to the countess's cries, and the groaning and moaning of the count who is in dreadful pain. The poor woman has lost her head and knows nothing about caring for an invalid, so I am both nurse to one and maid to the other.

The count is finally feeling better; the doctor is not coming back. We shall have to pay for all the visits he has made to our house. What a pity it costs so much here to do good for those who are suffering, and that one is forced to economize with one's limited resources. The worst is over, but we have to think of tomorrow. The count's convalescence is going to be a long one, and he does not have any money or means of support. After a good deal of thought, we had an idea. Miss Nelly had been found, six leagues away, and we decided to raffle her at five francs a ticket.

Despite all my efforts, I still had twenty-five tickets remaining. Nelly's stubbornness was too well known for us to attract a sufficient number of takers. I was the one who won her! I ride her to try and make her more docile so that I can get rid of her, but she is a real menace: she kicks, bucks and jumps in the air, enough to send you flying a hundred paces. It's very good to know a little about everything. Every day I ride her down to the sea and take her in up to her ears. After the twentieth swim, she came home much more quietly. If she does not kill me first, I shall tame her, but she has developed a new trick: she jumps over everything she comes across, even shadows of trees. I am training Nelly in Lionel's absence. If he knew I was riding her, even in our grounds, I think he would kill her. Our patient is convalescing very well. His nose has been stitched up and his lips are healing, but the gratitude he should be showing us has given way to envy. He holds it against us that we have become the lucky owners of Nelly. That really is nothing to be envious about . . .

I received this letter from the count just in time, for I was starting to have a very bad opinion of him and of his wife, who had not even come to thank us:

Dear Madam,

After thanking God for having spared me for my family, there remains a very pleasant duty for me to carry out: that of sending you my most heart-felt thanks for the extraordinary care and kindness you have shown me. I am happy to be able to do this in writing but, do believe me, as soon as I am as strong in body as I am in heart and mind, I shall have the real pleasure of coming to clasp a hand as kind as yours.

Count de Varenne

15 February

I have been dreadfully sick for two days, and they say I have congestion of the liver. It's a nasty illness, if this early stage is any indication.

The woods are on fire every night. The blacks set them alight in retaliation for being driven away. It's a weird sight to see the flames slithering through the air like snakes, leaving their trail, first red, then black. Poor little birds cry out in despair and fly around and around their nests like lost souls.

My adopted daughter is shooting up fast. So far, she won't learn anything, anything at all. Ah well, I actually get something myself from the little lessons I give her.

Mr Fauchery, who was introduced to me on my arrival in Melbourne, went to the mines with his wife.[4] They earned some money there and came back to settle in town. Having taken on a two-storeyed house, they furnished the first floor in simple colonial style and established a café–restaurant on the ground floor. They had a billiard table, which is such a rare thing in Melbourne that in the beginning their takings were quite good.

Fauchery, this charming Parisian known to everyone, this emulator of Murger, a distinguished writer and tireless worker, finding it impossible to live on the earnings from his works in France, emigrated, with his mind made up to give up the poet's lyre for the miner's pickaxe. Now he has just exchanged the miner's pickaxe for the waiter's apron, but as he suffered countless hardships when he arrived here, he is sensitive to the suffering of others. He married his mistress, for which he has been much criticized, because she is rather common in mind and body, but what spirit! what feeling! in that respect, they are certainly worthy of each other. She admires her husband: she scarcely breathes when he is speaking. She cares for him with unfailing tenderness.

As for him, he is a joker at heart and has always been a man who likes good times. His clients took advantage of this and they so often made him come a cropper, as he puts it, that he was totally ruined within a few months, the proprietor threatening him with seizure of his goods.

In one night, Fauchery moved out all his furniture. He unscrewed his billiard table and took it, we don't know where, piece by piece. The proprietor came to the consulate to lodge a complaint of fraud. Lionel wrote to Fauchery: 'I have to speak to you, but as I don't want to make what I have to say in any way official, come and arrange to have dinner with me in St Kilda. Céleste will be delighted to see you.'

Fauchery has just arrived. He says the proprietor is a real penny-pincher, and that if he doesn't leave him alone, he is going to fetch a leg of his billiard table and break it over his head. Lionel advises him to keep all the pieces of the table in one place, and well hidden. Where there is nothing, there is no place for the devil.

We laugh and talk about France before sitting down to eat. Lionel offers him a glass of a precious liqueur that one of our ships' captains gave us. Fauchery tastes it, grimaces, and says: 'It's very good, it smells like turpentine.' Not that it stopped him from emptying most of the bottle,—to get used to it, he told us.

Lionel likes him very much and advises him to try something more suited to his talents. Fauchery says:

—I've got it! I shall become a stone breaker. My wife knows how to cook, wash and iron. Those who made fun of me when I took up with her would be pretty happy to have her if they were in my position!

After some thought, Lionel said:

—No. I have been recommended a young man who intends to set himself up here as a photographer. He can't do anything alone, not knowing a word of English. I am going to put you in contact with him. There is money to be made, and it will keep you amused while conserving your strength. You are not strong enough to do manual work.

—Me? exclaimed Fauchery, beating his chest. I'm as solid as concrete! I'm all muscle!

—You are always sick.

—In mind, but I shall outlive you all.

—We shall see about that, said Lionel as he stood up to drive him home. I am going to make your landlord listen to reason, and ask him for time . . .

—Just for show! Even if I had all the gold in Australia, I wouldn't give him a brass farthing.

—That is all very well as long as you stay here, but you know English law: they have the right to arrest any debtor trying to leave the colony, and my intervention would do you no good at all. From now on, don't wait months without letting me know how you are getting on.

—I shall come and see you tomorrow. The idea of photography quite appeals to me. Do I need to have money?

—No. I promise to find a clientele for you.

—Thank you, laughed Fauchery. I shall forgive you for being noble, but you are the only one. And I shall make up for my weakness towards you by hating the others that much more.

Lionel went out of his way to try and set up the partnership which he had mentioned to Fauchery, but this photographer was very much the gentleman, extremely well-groomed, with studied dress and facial expression, and he could not get used to Fauchery's very odd manners and ideas.

I rode to Melbourne yesterday on Miss Nelly: she wanted to take the left, I the right . . . I adore horses, but I become very harsh when they resist me, and I am sure she won't forget the thrashing I gave her.

A lot of women on their own here do their shopping or pay their visits on horseback.

At the consulate, I met Messrs Weber, two brothers who live twenty miles from here. They invited us to go and visit their station, promising to take us on a good kangaroo hunt. Lionel eagerly accepted, and he is going to ask Fauchery to replace him at the consulate. He comes home with me and spends a good part of the night polishing his shotgun. Poor Lionel! he loves hunting so much he can't go to sleep.

At six o'clock this morning he was ready, and had the whole household up and about. It's the first time I have seen him so genuinely happy since we arrived in this wretched country. The Weber brothers, who had come to Melbourne to buy horses, sent us a very fine specimen. Lionel mounts it, I take Miss Nelly and we set off, feeling bright and happy as schoolchildren about to play truant.

The virgin forests we gallop through are an unusual sight. There are various types of trees, some lovely heather in the undergrowth, and parrots flying about around us, watching us with more surprise than fear.

After taking an hour's rest for lunch, we set off again. There were six of us, Lionel, the two Weber brothers, two other gentlemen and me.

—Don't lose sight of us, said Mr Charles Weber; it's easy to get lost in the forest.

It was a shooting hunt, almost at point-blank range, for the kangaroos are very numerous and they cluster in groups around the trees, showing no fear of the hunters, whom they allow to come quite close before taking flight. The kangaroos bounded along in front of us like hares, but they did not stop and try to escape in the opposite direction; —it was as if they were trying to draw the hunters after them. And that was what happened before we realized it.

Lionel was beside himself with excitement.

—Hold my horse, he said to me as he dismounted; I can't take aim.

Mr Weber did likewise and passed his horse to his brother, saying to us:

—Go on ahead. There's an inn a mile or so away, and we will meet you there.

I thought my companion knew the way, and I followed him without question. Lionel strode into the undergrowth and disappeared, while Mr Weber told me goodness knows what story, for he only knew a few words of English and he spoke them with such a pronounced German accent that it was impossible for me to understand him.

After riding for an hour, I became worried and when I asked my companion a few questions, I realized he was telling me: 'I have lost my way.' My incompetent guide cupped his hands round his mouth and gave some loud calls like a jackal, but alas! there was no response. Night was beginning to fall and I was worn out and dispirited. I had no choice but to dismount. We tethered our horses and went and sat under a tree, as it was impossible to go on. I felt so upset at the thought of how worried Lionel must be that I dissolved into tears. We would have to wait for day-break before setting off again.

Mr Weber made a fire. I leaned back against a tree trunk, quite determined not to sleep a wink. I can't describe everything I felt during that seemingly never-ending night. Mr Weber slept beside his horse. At dawn, I was soaked through by the heavy dew. I shivered. My arms and legs were stiff and for a moment I thought I would not be able to move.

The horses were licking the damp grass. We remounted without having exchanged a word. Our gloom was mournful, our fear silent as death. My eyelids were burning, my throat was dry. I felt such anguish at the thought of Lionel. I thought he must be lost too. Since I could not see him, I felt something awful must have happened to him. I think hunger was starting to give me hallucinations and ringing in the ears, for I kept thinking I could hear a horse galloping or see something in the distance.

After five hours of exhaustion, pain and despair we noticed the traces of ox-cart wheels. We did not take our eyes off them and followed them like bloodhounds, our noses almost touching the ground, for fear of losing sight of them. We walked this way for two hours until, finally, we saw two bark huts.

Mr Weber shouted, while I forgot to thank God and cried out Lionel's name. I don't know if I fell or was lifted off my horse, for I lost consciousness. When I came round, a man who looked like a real bandit was slapping my hands. I was so frightened by him that I nearly fainted again, but then I saw that big stupid German on the other side, eating a piece of bread almost as big as his huge head.

The stranger was about thirty-five years old, tall and slim with delicate features. After speaking for a while with my companion, he said to me in very good English:

—You have strayed a long way from your path, madam, and because I fear you may get lost again, I shall ride your other horse and guide you, if you will excuse my rough clothes.

He jumped lightly into the saddle, adjusted the reins, and handled the animal like a true horseman. He let me go in front when the track was narrow, and rode on my right when it was possible to go two abreast. On the way, he talked to me about London, France, India, and the horses he had owned. I was thoroughly intrigued.

We came in sight of the inn where my husband had arranged to meet me the day before. I had been turning a coin around in my fingers for a long time, but I did not dare give it to my guide, for something told me I would be offending him in return for the favour he had done me. The stranger dismounted, made a deep bow, and disappeared before I could even express my gratitude. In my great happiness at seeing Lionel, I forgot all about my unusual guide.

Our companions had searched for us into the night, calling out and firing shots. It seems that my poor dear Lionel was showing signs of deep despair, but I was just too happy to find a word to say, and I burst into tears. I think he started to scold me for the trouble I had caused him, but I held him so tightly that I did not hear a word, and besides none of it was my fault.

I was worn out by all these emotions and lack of sleep, and we still had four leagues to cover, either on foot or on horseback, to reach the Weber brothers' property. I asked these gentlemen whether they knew the man who had accompanied me.

—Yes, he is a woodcutter in the forest, one of them said. He was rich in England and the captain of a company in India, but he has an irascible temperament, and they say he has killed several men in duels. He can't bear living in towns, as he hates people, and so he has taken refuge at the foot of this mountain. If any neighbours were to arrive, he would go elsewhere.

I can't describe the exhaustion I felt during the trip to the house, where a very hard bed was waiting for me.

When we returned to St Kilda the household was in turmoil, as they had believed us lost. I needed rest above all else, and I was hoping for a good night's sleep, but no one else was.

Our property was so big that we had been forced to take on a man who helped out around the place and looked after Nelly. He was a young Englishman and quite good-looking. He had fallen sick at the mines and gone into hospital. When he came out, he had no means of support and so we took him on until he was in a fit enough state to find himself a job. But he became attached to us, and did not want to leave. He was a good fellow; he didn't drink and never went out. His only company, apart from Marie, was a terrier bitch who chased after rats, which was very useful for us because there were so many of them and they were so big that the cats ran away when they saw them go by. That is what I am told at least, for I have always loathed cats. I like birds but only when they are in the wild, and I adore dogs and horses. I had grown used to Bool's affectionate ways—Bool was the name of Bob's dog. When I went to the stable, she would jump right up to my face, even though she had pups. When I went out on horseback, she would follow me as far as Melbourne. If I stayed away too long, she would go back and feed her pups, get them off to sleep and then come back to meet me, jumping about madly. She had beautiful, clear, intelligent eyes. Her white teeth protruded slightly over her bottom jaw, and it always looked as if she was trying to talk to you.

I had just fallen asleep when I was awoken by a noise which seemed very strange at first. Someone was moaning outside my door. It was a plaintive whimpering that sounded like the voice of a child crying. I called out: 'Who's there?' There was no reply. After a moment's hesitation, I went and opened the door and saw poor Bool, stretched out on her stomach, with her nose resting on her long paws, her big eyes full of tears. Without taking her eyes off me, she dragged herself to the foot of my bed and then began to writhe in pain.

I woke Lionel and called Bob from the window. He came running, took his dog in his arms, and saw immediately that she had been poisoned. The poor animal! She had come to say goodbye to me and then, realizing no doubt that she was going to die, did not want to go back to her young who would have been poisoned by her milk. From what the veterinarian told us, it seems that Bool must have caught and eaten a rat from a neighbouring property where they destroy them with arsenic pellets.

Bob buried his dog somewhere in the wood and he mourned for her deeply. It was really just one of those things, but we were very affected by it. Nelly also had a small share in our sadness, and she looked everywhere for her dog. When I rode her, she looked behind, first to the right then to the left, and led me against my will in pursuit of any dog that looked like Bool.

CHAPTER 10

Two Balls and Danger
on the Bay

THE whole town and countryside are in a state of wild excitement: the governor is to give a ball! . . . Seven hundred invitations have been issued. Lionel has received one, but it's for him alone. As far as I am concerned, it's an affront which would be of no great concern, were it not for friends, especially women friends, who constantly arrive to talk to me about the ball, which should be a splendid affair. They ask me what I intend to wear and how I plan to get there, as the governor lives several miles from Melbourne. Carriages will cost no less than 250 or 300 francs for the evening, so people want to share the hiring expenses. My reply to them all is that I have not been invited. This gives rise to an endless series of sympathetic protests and recriminations.

No one can understand this treatment, which is quite unjustified, because the governor receives a civil list that obliges him to entertain Melbourne society once or twice a year, and at least one third of this society is made up of convicts who have served their term or even escaped from the Sydney penal colony. They are all wealthy and well established, it's true, but those who are particular about the people they mix with, could surely be more indulgent towards foreigners. There are people who are so sorry for you that they end up convincing you that you really should be miserable. And that is exactly what happened: Lionel and I were quite affected by it during the few days that preceded the much-vaunted Governor's Ball.

The Governor's Ball was held yesterday. More than 700 people set out to attend it in foul weather. The rain fell in torrents. All available carriages, even miners' carts, had been pressed into service at exorbitant prices, but nevertheless everyone was looking forward to a wonderful time! . . . They were very soon disappointed. The Toorak rooms were twenty times too small to accommodate the crowd. Many people could not even get in, and had to wait outside or in their carriages. The ladies' outfits were completely ruined. Some protested; others sulked. All the men could think about was the lavish supper to which they intended doing full justice. The much-awaited hour arrived. They did not push; they rushed forward in a crush; they trampled each other underfoot. But what a disappointment was in store for them too! On the sideboard were a few cold meats entirely surrounded by nothing but hams, and the only drink available—a keg of colonial beer! The newspapers have printed scathing articles criticizing the governor. They are of one voice in their complaints, which border on impertinence. If it's true that he is very sensitive to criticism, he must be most unhappy, and bitterly regret holding what they call 'the beer ball'.[1]

Our friend Coulon, brother of the Paris Opera artist, and a performer himself, has just come back from the mines, where I believe he gave some concerts.[2] He made us laugh when he told us about a madman he met when leaving the mines.

    —I was just leaving Ballarat, he told us, when a man flings himself at me, holds me in a grip that practically strangles me and says: 'You look like a reliable man. I'm going to trust you with my secret. Don't betray me, don't leave me, or the others'll kill me. I don't know you, but I know them, they are swindlers! Come with me to the police, so I can get them to give me an escort. I know I'm a bit crazy, but I'm mad with joy. Put yourself in my place: I've found a gold nugget as big as you are. I haven't said anything to the others. They'd have done me in to get it. I've covered it up again with earth. I shall give you a bit if you help me to get it out. Come on, come on! . . .' And, without giving me time to gather my wits or reply, this madman, who was very solidly built by the way, was pulling me in the direction of the escort post.

    There was nothing for it but to follow him, as he had hold of my coat and would have ripped it to pieces. An officer who saw us approaching in the distance thought I was a thief that the poor devil was bringing in by force. My man began his story again. At first they laughed at him, but he started to cry like a baby. They gave him an escort of four men, and I followed them out of curiosity. They dug the earth with picks at the designated spot, and they did indeed find a gold nugget surrounded by smaller ones. There was a fortune that nearly cost the finder his sanity, and me a coat, which would have been rather a blow, as it's the only one I have.

When Mr Coulon is here, he stays with us. He goes out during the day with Lionel; in the evening we make music together. These hours are the most enjoyable ones for us. They are a rest from my studies, which are dry and wearisome. I have just finished a 500-page summary of Anquetil's *History of France*.[3] Learning would be much easier if I did not have to do English translations at the same time. If this continues, I shall end up knowing neither French nor English well. Lionel does not give me the least encouragement to study; in fact he worries about my health and tells me that I know quite enough to run a household. For the present, I agree, but later? As I don't want to cross him, I study in secret. That is not difficult for me, as I spend so much time alone! . . .

I am also learning music, parrot-fashion. I play on the piano everything I've heard played or sung—and quite well, it seems—but I have little taste for this kind of distraction. It can never keep me occupied for a whole hour, while I can write all day without noticing the time passing.

They are starting to hunt out the Chinese again—those ugly creatures who never bring women of their own, but are keen on other men's, so it seems.[4] Some have married Irish women. There are fears that the emerging Australian race might degenerate. They have to pay very high personal taxes. They are beginning to disappear, and they arrive in very small numbers now.

We are definitely not meant to have a peaceful life: Marie's gone quite mad over Bob. I don't know whether the pain he felt losing Bool has made him sensitive to the advances of our maid, but she makes scenes that I can sometimes hear from my bedroom. He's taught her a little English, which she uses to hurl abuse at him for the slightest thing.

Her character has undergone a complete transformation. She does everything the wrong way and with very bad grace. She complains from morn till night. I don't feel that I can leave Solange with her any more. What a pity that her native province of the Berry is so far away! . . . How

I'd love to send her back to her sheep! She is quite aware of the difficult situation she has placed me in, and she takes advantage of it to do just as she pleases! Still, what can I do! . . .

The captain of the *Gertrude* (from Bordeaux) has just called to invite us to have lunch with him tomorrow on board his ship with several of our friends: Mrs Sivratt, her husband, her sister Miss Blanche, Mr Wertemberg, the brother of a Parisian artist. He is a gentle, very well-educated young man. Lionel employs him when he can to work on the consulate ledgers, for the poor boy is very short-sighted and couldn't do anything at the mines. Nine of us set out to board the *Gertrude* early on Sunday morning. The weather was superb—the sea was as smooth as glass. The captain was waiting for us on the pier with a pretty little boat all decked out with flags.

Six of his sailors dressed in their best uniforms held the oars to attention. We took our places in the boat, which departed, gliding gently and smoothly over the sea. All one could hear was the regular sound of the oars which *feathered* as they skimmed over the water. Everyone was in high spirits, delighted to spend a Sunday on board ship. Sundays are always so dismal in the English colonies.

Indeed, the day was so enjoyable that we accepted the invitation to sleep on board, intending to leave early the next morning. Each of the gentlemen had things to do in town; besides, the *Gertrude* was due to depart at six a.m. Pilots are punctual, so it could be guaranteed that we were prepared to keep our word. The captain is an excellent man, but in this instance, he showed very little judgement or presence of mind. At five a.m. the sailors began to rig the ship, i.e. to unfurl the sails.

—Hurry up, they shouted on all sides, the pilot says there's not a moment to lose.

Lionel and I were ready, but Mrs Sivratt and her sister asked us to wait a little while. This nearly cost us our lives. The sky was black, the sea rough, the sails had quickly billowed. The ship began to get underway and we were still on the deck . . . The boat that was to take us back was banging into the side of the *Gertrude* and then being pushed out to sea by the full length of the rope that attached it to the ship.

—Go! For Heaven's sake go, said an officer. In two minutes it'll be too late and you'll have to sail with us.

These words revived the courage of those who were still hesitating to go down the ship's ladder. Lionel went first, Wertemberg second. They caught me in their arms like a parcel, as the wind made the *Gertrude* list to the right and the ladder became too short to reach the boat. Our companions followed, falling in a heap on top of us. Lionel and Wertemberg tried vainly to push us out to sea. A wave caught us, lifted us up and tore away the rudder. Every movement of the *Gertrude* made the boat heave dreadfully. Our little mast became caught up in her ropes.

—Cut down your mast or you'll sink! shouted twenty people at once.

We could see the danger well enough, but it takes more than a penknife to cut down a mast. The boat keeled over, water was coming in on my right, so I threw myself to the left. Everyone did the same. The jolt was so violent that the mast broke off at the base and fell into the sea.

The *Gertrude* pulled away quickly, leaving us on the open sea, without rudder, sails or provisions, and shivering with cold. Terror was written on every face. Mrs Sivratt and her sister were screaming and crying; the men also showed their alarm or cursed the captain who, preoccupied with his command, had exposed us to certain death then abandoned us. Not one of us knew how to handle a boat at sea. The two men who were to take us back to shore scarcely knew more than we did. Their only concern was for their boat, which, they said, was not solid enough to cope with heavy seas.

I can't describe what we felt during the first five hours after we left the *Gertrude*. My two female companions seemed to swoon constantly. The waves rose over us in a white foam which fell on us like fine rain and flooded the boat. Fog concealed every horizon. It was impossible to think of anything but death. We huddled together, not daring to say a word. Lionel held my hands. I had lain my head on his shoulder, to shut everything out.

—Poor Céleste! he said to Wertemberg, poor Céleste!

As if I were the only one in danger.

A sheet of water suddenly fell onto my lap. I thought it was the end . . . Lionel took me in his arms. I think my heart had stopped beating. It turned out to be only a harmless shower after all and my spirits rallied a little. Mr Sivratt and Wertemberg were bailing out the boat with their shoes. The sea became a little calmer; the fog began to lift. What were we hoping for? I really don't know, as we were far out from port.

At last we saw a small boat in the distance and hailed it. Wertemberg carefully wiped his glasses, looked and said: 'It's coming towards us.' After an anxious hour's waiting, we saw it move away. No one had seen us, I suppose.

At last we saw a big ship tacking to enter port. It was signalling to the *flactof* [*sic*] (telegraph).[5] We waved our handkerchiefs. A rowing boat left the stern of the ship and came towards us. It was a whaler, with a crew of two men, who said as they drew alongside:

—We can't take all of you. Two of the gentlemen must stay with your sailors. We shall come back for them when you're back on shore. Here's our anchor and some rope. We piled into the whaler. The two sailors who were carrying out our rescue knew what they were doing: they avoided the waves by cutting across them. They rowed towards shore, but the wind came up again so violently that once more we thought all was lost!

—Come on, Lionel said, there's no escaping one's fate. Poor Céleste, you must resent my exposing you to all this!

—I would resent it if you thought of facing danger without me.

—Oh, I wish it were possible to love you even more than I do!

—Never love me less.

—Before death that surrounds us, before God, I shall love you all my life as I love you now.

There are supreme moments when human words seem sacred. I kissed Lionel and prayed God to save his life.

—Don't anyone move, shouted one of the rowers, the slightest movement could capsize us.

We stayed motionless and almost stopped breathing. That lasted another three or four hours more . . .

At last we reached shore. When we touched ground, we hardly looked human: no one could stand upright. The men who had brought us asked for 250 francs. It was Lionel who paid them, making them promise to go back for the others. They promised, but they did not do it, and the unfortunate souls must have perished, for we never heard of them again.

Awful disasters happen in similar circumstances every day. We can boast of having had a very lucky escape. It's obvious that pleasure outings rarely turn out well for me in this dreadful country that I detest more with every passing day. I was anxious to see little Solange, who had been in my thoughts a lot during those wretched hours at sea.

Lionel, Mr Wertemberg and I took an omnibus to St Kilda. It's strange how quickly one forgets past dangers.

—Heavens! Gracious Heavens! Wertemberg said to us, I'm so glad to have escaped with nothing worse than a fright! What would my tailor have said if his jacket had gone to the bottom of the sea?

In Melbourne there's a certain Mr Ricard, who sometimes comes to see us. He claims to be a man of letters and criticizes everything anyone else does. He says he gives French lessons. I think he should be taking them, rather than giving them. For example, he has a great command of bar-room language. He moves about all the time when he's speaking and is very clumsy in his movement, breaking or treading on everything around him. He hates aristocrats; he dreams of Italy's independence. Why? We've never been able to find out.

He has composed a song dedicated to me. It's about the miners' sinewy arms, the miners' horses, the miners' picks and shovels, the miners' sweat, etc. It's appalling from beginning to end.

17 July

On the twelfth of this month, the *riflemans* [*sic*] held a subscription ball in aid of the wounded in the Crimea.[6] The *riflemans* are voluntary national guardsmen. No one here would be rich enough to hold a ball at his own expense. The exhibition building is therefore hired out to all those who want to organize such entertainment.

The town notables must always figure at the top of the subscription list. They cannot refuse to pay their dues for fear of being ridiculed. That is why we sometimes go to a ball. There one meets the elite of Melbourne society, tradesmen, miners and others. It's a strange mixture of people indeed.

Lionel had the idea of also organizing a subscription ball for our wounded. He named me Grand Master of Ceremonies. I was allotted the Crystal Palace Room for the 16th, which should be quite a new attraction for the ball. I decided to hold a tombola for the ladies.[7] As I am not wealthy enough to buy the prizes, I shall donate some dresses cut out but not made up, which I brought from Paris, two fans, two little gold bracelets, laces and ribbons, music albums, a writing set and a needlework set. There will be twenty-five winning numbers. I am delighted to donate these things, for I know they will tempt the ladies, who only pay ten shillings, but they don't come unaccompanied, and the gentlemen pay two pounds. I would be so happy if we could send several thousand francs to France.

They are fighting to get our ball tickets. They even come down to St Kilda to get them. Oh! *ma belle France*, how easy it is, and how good it feels, to be able to do something for you!

It's an ill wind that blows no one any good. For some time now, everyone seems to want to make me forget the mean, spiteful way the governor treated me on the day of his *beer ball*. They are still talking about it. Epigrams and caricatures are still appearing morning and evening.

On the occasion of the Emperor's name day, my husband was obliged to give a lavish dinner for the town dignitaries. It goes without saying that there were no women present. They never go to these celebrations, which are usually held in a restaurant.

They drank to the health of all the crowned heads of Europe, to France, to our wounded in the Crimea. Then they passed around some small pieces of paper and wrote on them in pencil the names of people who were absent, but who should be toasted. It was requested, as a matter of deference, that Mr Justice Williams's paper should be read out first.[8] He handed it on to be passed around the table until it reached the governor, who read my name aloud. This was greeted with three rousing cheers. Lionel was so delighted that he came home drunk as a lord.

—You have certainly got your own back, he said to me, for all the nastiness from those women that you have had to put up with since you arrived. The dinner I gave was rather expensive, but I have been amply repaid. Mr Justice Williams is a serious, austere man. I shall go and see him tomorrow to thank him, and if ever he needs anything from me, I shall be his to command. I shall never forget the pleasure he gave me.

For my part, I was very touched by it. I too felt immensely grateful. However, I would not have mentioned it, had not all the Melbourne papers reported it the next day. That gave me new heart. Our ball will have to be really lovely. Messrs de Varenne, Wertemberg, Fauchery, Coulon have offered their services for the decorations. Our naval captains have lent us some weapons to put up as displays and flags as trophies. There are leafy branches and flowers everywhere; it's a superb sight. There will be a lavish grand buffet, and absolutely no colonial beer.

Our ball took place on the 16th. The people of Melbourne had never seen anything so fine.[9] My tombola was all the rage. The ladies found my husband the most gallant of men . . . for it goes without saying that my name was never mentioned in connection with the little gifts supplied by me from my cabin trunks; that would have made them lose all their appeal. In spite of our success, my joy was mixed with a good deal of sadness. I spent the night fighting back the tears. They played all our national songs, then these words: France, the French, repeated a hundred times over disturbed me deeply. There is no getting away from it, I'm a Parisian to the core!

Our subscription ball raised about 30 000 francs, which we will send off through the bank. It caused me a good deal of heartache and fatigue, but fatigue is nothing when compared to such a wonderful result.

CHAPTER 11

Lola Montez and the Theatre

TODAY I can laugh about it, but yesterday I had the kind of fright one never forgets. We had an earthquake that stopped the clock and rattled the glasses in the cupboard.[1] In these circumstances it's better to have a wooden house than one made of stone. The unexpected movement did not frighten me at the time, because I did not know what caused it, but it made me feel something akin to seasickness.

Lola Montez arrived here a while ago with her troupe.[2] She is putting on shows at the theatre. She was so frightened last night that she went out into the street in very flimsy night attire . . . She still has the same lovely face and eccentric character . . .

She has written, or has had someone write for her, a play in five acts entitled *My History*. The first act is called *The First Era*. When the curtain goes up, some working-class men are talking about Lola in terms like these: She is a goddess, divine, an angel of purity turned dancer because she has a philanthropic task to accomplish on earth. She gave her ring to one person; she paid ransom for another. The King of Bavaria comes to hear of her, as they say she is very good at diplomacy. He has her kidnapped.

In the second act she is in the king's palace. She deliberates matters of state with him, constantly proving that he has no idea what he is talking about. The Jesuits fear Lola's clear-sightedness and want to poison her. During the performance she falls ill on stage, but this does not stop her giving everyone a piece of her mind, shouting at the top of her voice.

In the third act, there has been a popular uprising. Lola is accused of being the old king's mistress, of having spent a lot of money belonging to the State, and is ordered to leave the town immediately.

She is furious, she protests and fights with her rifle. Her house is set alight and she escapes, letting out blood-curdling screams all the while.

In the fourth act she is a wandering outlaw. Attempts are made on her life, for even from afar she is the light, the soul and the spirit of the king. All her possessions are stolen. In the end, she has only one thing left, or rather two: her conscience and her virtue:

—Let people malign me if they wish, she says, they maligned Joan of Arc, didn't they!

In the fifth act she also makes a speech to the audience. She asks for their support, for their protection. They can prove their goodwill by coming to her plays every day. She blows kisses to everyone.

—Reduce the price of the seats, shouts an Irishman, lording it in the stalls. Lola answers him and they argue back and forth for half an hour. Others call out to her; she replies with remarkable presence of mind. She speaks English very well. They clap and whistle. There is an infernal din.

The play is followed by a ballet composed and danced by Lola! It consists of moving about a lot while frantically shaking the folds of an extremely short gauze skirt. There is a spider hidden between the folds; it's called the spider dance.[3] I don't know why, but all the women walked out before the end of the ballet, although there is nothing improper in it. However the police have banned a second performance.

Lola says that all the nations are rising up against her: they fear her influence, politically speaking, that is. People say she's mad, but she is simply very excitable. She came to see me. I don't really remember what she said to me. She speaks very quickly and her ideas have no logic to them. She was leaving that evening to perform on the goldfields. She promised to come and see me on her return. She's counting on making a fortune here. I hope she does, but I don't think it will happen.

The inhabitants of Melbourne have an insatiable need for entertainment. Miners are encouraged to come to town and to leave as much money here as possible. Bars, cafés, concerts and dances are increasing in number. Everyone requests *the honour of your company* at the same time. That is the way invitations are worded. Because of people's eagerness to attend our ball, we are obliged to subscribe to theirs. We have not a moment to ourselves.

Last night the freemasons held a ball in aid of allied army wounded. Mr Smith, the Mayor of Melbourne, is the leader of Australian free-masonry.[4] He organised the ball which was under his patronage.

A dais had been constructed under a kind of crimson silk canopy held up with golden tassels. Below it *Napoleon III* was spelled out in flowers, and opposite, at the other end, *Victoria*. Floods of light were reflected in the window panes surmounted with eagles and crowned lions drawn on coloured glass. It all had a magic effect, as it always does, either at a ball or the theatre.

When we entered, the musicians played *Leaving for Syria*.[5] Mr Smith came over and offered me his arm to do a round of the ballroom. I wanted to refuse, but Lionel indicated that I should accept. It really did me too much honour. I was very affected by it and became so pale and trembling that for a moment I was afraid I might faint. Everything that would have been a joy for any another woman was a source of apprehension for me.

Mr Smith is a man of wit and his kindness of heart is known to all. He guessed what I was thinking and said, affectionately squeezing my arm:

—Take heart, Madam. You are among friends. For my part, this occasion gives me the opportunity of proving to the inhabitants of Melbourne my deep friendship for the Count de Chabrillan and my respect for his wife.

Here, as in London, the mayor is a prominent person; he has a great deal of power and is nearly always opposed to the government. His wealth is incalculable and he is very charitable to the needy. He paid £500 sterling for his ball ticket.

Supper was served on the first floor in a large gallery, and it was sumptuous. The finest wines and champagne flowed for those on the dance floor. When the moment came to proceed to the supper table, Mr Smith came looking for me. He introduced Mrs Smith and her sister to me. They were charming—gracious and unaffected. I could see that these two dear good people wanted to publicly make up for the affront done to me by the governor. For me this was nothing unusual, but it had offended Lionel. He had no doubt complained, as his affection for me often makes him unjust towards others. Nonetheless, everyone still admires him. *He* is just perfect![6]

The last part of the ball was full of gaiety. Lionel spent the journey home singing the praises of Mr Smith, his wife and her sister. However much he likes them, he will never like them as much as I do.

14 November

The weather is up to its wretched tricks again. What a frightful climate! There are only three tolerable months in the year. Last night the roof nearly came off our house in a wind squall that was so strong it uprooted trees. We could even hear the sea, which sounded like bulls roaring. There was a din like a witches' Sabbath. Several ships were smashed on the reefs. The damage is considerable. Two of our ships went aground on the coast. In these circumstances, the consul has to go aboard to ascertain the damage for the insurance companies.

Marie and her mad behaviour make life so unbearable for me at home that I am there as little as possible; and so I went with the gentlemen to see our poor ships. Around them were more than fifty small boats with men in them waiting for orders to begin salvaging the cargo of merchandise and assets in the hold. It's dangerous and difficult work. Everything that can be saved is put up for sale by auction, with the proceeds going to the insurance company. As for the ships, they are often abandoned when there is too much involved in refloating them, because labour is too expensive.

As neither of us was feeling very cheerful, Lionel and I decided to have dinner in Melbourne, so that we could go to the theatre in the evening to see *Richelieu*[7] played by an English actor called Brook [*sic*],[8] of whom we had heard a good deal. When we entered the theatre, the scene was set in the Orangery at Versailles with Louis XIII moving about in front of the footlights. He wore a wig *à la malcontent* and a moustache.[9] The seams of his stockings were twisted like a corkscrew from his heels to his knees. Brook himself is really remarkable, but the rest of the cast take away from his performance. I can speak reasonable English, but I have difficulty understanding the actors. Like our artists, they have a particular kind of diction, and at times all I can hear is strident shouting.

No matter how good an English actor is, I prefer to see him in comic roles, so I was waiting impatiently for the second play which featured Copping [*sic*].[10] Copping is a fat man, with a belly like a Chinese figurine. He sometimes slaps his stomach as if he were playing a bass drum, which makes the audience roar with laughter. He jumps, turns somersaults, throws punches, gets kicked. The audience adores him and they applaud with all their might. In the intervals he goes down to the bar (in the pub). He's the owner. He keeps his stage costume on while serving his customers. He's director, artist, wine merchant and waiter all in one.

He parodies everyone. He does a caricature of Brook as his main subject, and has just composed a ballet based on Lola Montez—the spider dance. He is dressed as Cupid, only his gauze skirt sits bunched up on his hips like a baker's smock. On his head is a garland of white roses. He blows kisses to the audience, then after much prancing about that makes them die laughing, he throws a stuffed rat on the ground and jumps on it with both feet.

He mops his brow, comes forward to make a speach [*sic*], simpering and imitating Lola's voice exactly. They throw wreaths of hay decorated with vegetables at him; Lola was thrown lots of flowers. He pirouettes while he picks them up and exits, walking into one of the uprights. They call him back, he comes back on stage looking serious and says:

—I'm a poor fugitive. I have enemies everywhere, but I have right on my side and my bar on the ground floor. God protect me! I know who my true friends are when they come and drink with me.

They shout: Encore! He blows more kisses and adds, puffing like a grampus:

—I'm too weak to do the dance again, but till tomorrow, if you'll give me the honour of your company.

He exits not to cries of 'bravo!', but to boos and catcalls. They say that Lola had wanted to horsewhip Copping, but that she had changed her mind once she laid eyes on this colossus who was preparing to receive her with a birch.

As we left the theatre, we heard the alarm bell ringing. Everyone was shouting as they ran: fire! fire! fire! In the distance you could see a great red patch outlined against the sky. The village of Richmond fell prey to the flames. The wooden houses collapsed so quickly that people scarcely had time to get out, and with nothing but the clothes they were wearing.

Good Lord, what a country! I constantly feel the world is coming to an end.

CHAPTER 12

Ill-health and Financial Disaster

TODAY is my name day. I think it's going to be miserable.

I have been suffering a good deal from sharp pains in my side and I'm turning as yellow as a quince. Solange is also affected by the rigours of this awful climate. We don't really take enough precautions to keep in good health. Every day we hear of people dying because they've overtaxed their strength. Dysentery takes a heavy toll of the miners. I really don't want to complain, but there are times when suffering makes me lose heart.

Lionel is depressed. Not only is he much affected by seeing me ill, but I think he also has considerable worries about our business affairs. We sent a large part of the goods that we brought here to a merchant in Calcutta. We have had neither money nor news from our forwarding agent, or if Lionel has received any, it is bad, for he has said nothing to me about it.

I can't sleep. I am so worried that something extraordinary is bound to happen. I don't dare ask, yet I must know what the situation is.

30 November

I was alone in the consulate and I went through accounts and letters kept in a large portfolio. Lionel had left the key in it. Our debtor in Calcutta has gone bankrupt and fled. No one knows where he is. He has taken 40 000 francs of ours, from which we have no hope of recouping even ten per cent.

The ships that had gone to get flour from Chile are in port, but while they were en route, more than a hundred carrying the same cargo have arrived here. Such a significant drop in flour prices has occurred that I fear a real financial disaster on this score too. I can't reproach Lionel; he thought he was doing the right thing . . . but I shudder to think where all this is leading us.

9 January 1856

The year has begun badly from every point of view. The Governor, Sir Charles Hotham, has just died; some say from cholera, others from the distress he felt at seeing himself treated so viciously by the press since his unfortunate 'beer ball'. Not a day has passed without him being criti-cized for it. They have caricatured him for every little thing. When it comes to making fun of people, the English are quite savage. They don't even stop out of respect for the dead. Poor Lady Hotham is in despair. Lionel went to Toorack [*sic*] to present our cards to her. She received him and apologized for the way she had treated us both.

—She is in full mourning, he told me. She was wearing a long, black crepe veil that covered her from head to foot. She was hardly recognizable . . . and tears came to my eyes when I kissed her hand on taking my leave. She should leave Melbourne, but she is putting it off too long. I don't think she will manage it. Poor woman, she is to be pitied, and I personally feel sincerely sorry for her.

I no longer go out; I write a good deal. I have revised a novel about gold robbers a dozen times. I don't know where to hide it in case Lionel should find it. Perhaps he would laugh at me, and anyway he would scold me. This type of painstaking work affects my health, but when I write I'm less conscious of my troubles. I know it's ridiculous, but I fancy that if misfortune strikes, I could manage to earn some money . . . My story reminds me somewhat of Lachambeaudie's delightful little fable, *The Hen that Hatched Pebbles.*[1]

Still I would rather lose everything I am doing than one day have to admit to myself, 'Oh, if only I had persevered more, perhaps I could have achieved something.' If the desire to be the child of one's works is not an empty saying, who knows, in a few years' time, Lionel might be forgiven for having married me. Poor generous-hearted man! He gave himself to me without reckoning with society and the future. When one is happy and independent, that can still be managed; but if it were officially known that we had fallen on hard times, a lot people who have none-theless accepted us would promptly turn their backs on us ...

Yesterday a fine carriage stopped at my door. A servant in mourning gave Bob a black-edged card for me from Lady Hotham who is leaving for London tomorrow.

15 January

There are newspapers at the Bendigat [*sic*] mines and naturally journalists too, if one can use the term for a few down-and-outs who slander every-one in order to get money out of them. Here, instead of paying for ad-vertising, people buy silence from these gentlemen. Lola Montez, not being aware of it, or not wishing to comply with this custom, was grossly insulted.[2] As this had happened often and with impunity in France, she wanted to horsewhip the man who had belittled her. She was wrong to do so, I admit, but she had scarcely made a move before the lout punched her viciously in the face twice. She has been back in Melbourne since yesterday. I went to see her with Lionel and she has two big black eyes which spoil her looks completely.[3]

This hasn't changed her impetuous character one bit. She wants to show herself like that to all the inhabitants of Melbourne, who, ac-cording to her, will rise up in a body and go and declare war on the Bendigo assassins. We try to reason with her, to calm her down, but she won't listen to a word. It's sheer lunacy.

Yesterday evening she gave a performance in a big improvised circus tent, frequented only by drunkards and miners. It seems she made a long speech to the shouts and boos of the crowd. This morning all the news-papers have made fun of her. She responds by having big notices put up in the streets. She complains about everyone in terms that she hasn't chosen carefully enough. There is talk of dragging her out and horse-whipping her in the town square. Lionel wants to save her this grim prac-tical joke. He goes and tells her to leave Melbourne right away. She still resists, but finally gives in. It's high time. Groups were beginning to form around her hotel.

With great difficulty, my husband managed to put her on board a ship leaving for Sydney, which she would never have reached without him. This gave rise to comparisons and innuendos in the press that I found very unpleasant. Lionel understood it all without having to spell things out. Several times already he had approached authors of certain

Le Consul de France

Aux Francais Residant

DANS LA COLONIE DE VICTORIA.

Au milieu des troubles qui agitent les mines de Ballaarat, le Consul de France croit devoir recommander a ses com-patriotes de s'abstenir de toute manifest-ation qui aurait pour but de meconnaitre *l'autorite des representants de la Reine dans la Colonie de Victoria.*

Ils ne doivent pas oublier qu'ils sont dans un pays ami de la France, et que le premier devoir d'un etranger est de respecter l'autorite du pays qui lui donne l'hospitalite.

Si les Français ont des plaintes ou des reclamations a adresser au Gouvernement Colonial ils peuvent les transmettre en toute confiance au Consul de France qui saura leur faire rendre justice.

Fait au Consulat de France, le 3 Decembre, 1854.

COMTE DE MORETON DE CHABRILLON.

BY AUTHORITY JOHN FERRES, GOVERNMENT PRINTER, MELBOURNE.

The Count de Chabrillan's proclamation to French expatriates at Eureka, 3 December 1854 (Sovereign Hill)

The French Camp, Black Hill, by E. von Guerard (La Trobe Picture Collection, State Library of Victoria)

Paris in the 1850s (private collection)

Bourke Street looking west from Spring Street 1857–1858 (Fauchery, Sun Pictures, La Trobe Picture Collection, State Library of Victoria)

articles he thought were directed at him, and had said to them: (it's Fauchery who told me about it, as he was always with him when he went to see these gentlemen.)

—In England, a man who has insulted you like a coward will not fight with you. If I sent you my seconds, you would tell them to go to the courts, where you would be sentenced to a few shillings' damages and interest. I don't accept that kind of reparation. As a consular agent, as a member of the legal profession, you can treat me any way you like. Laugh at me, make fun of me, write anything you please, but as far as my private life is concerned, I *forbid* you to have anything to do with it. It's my right and I shall make sure it's respected with all the means at my disposal. You don't know how to handle a sword, and I cannot box. I shall therefore be forced to put a bullet in your head. I mean what I say, and I swear to you I shall keep my word.

Wretched Fauchery, instead of reasoning with him, of pointing out all the danger in acting like this, backed him up, even encouraged him to rebel, saying that it's the only way to get the better of prejudiced character assassins.

The fact is that we have been left in peace up to now, but when Sir Charles Hotham, the poor martyr, died they had to find other victims.

2 February

There has just been the most frightful commotion in the fowl yard: all the hens started to screech as though someone was trying to strangle them. Cocotte the budgerigar had gone out for its little turn about the garden and has just flown in again at top speed, screeching '*Oh là là! Oh là là!*' more loudly than the cocks and the hens.

The cause of all this panic was an eagle that had come to rest on the roof of our house. Lionel has just shot it down with his gun, but calm has not yet been restored to the hen-house.

12 April

Another awful disaster has struck.

Last night the coastal pilot was notified of a French ship, but it was too late to go out to meet it. This morning there was no sign of it. It has perished with all hands.[4] What happened on board? No one knows. All those unfortunate creatures, who had broken into song yesterday when they caught sight of land, are now at the bottom of the sea forever. We have just had mass said for the repose of the poor souls.

Never free of tragic events like these, my moods change constantly. I am at a loss to explain the cause of the illness that's overtaken me. I ache all over, my breathing is laboured, I feel stiff. Even when I have not exerted myself, I can hardly drag myself about. Like so many others here, I am no doubt suffering from the effect of this awful climate (25 April).

So, it's total disaster. The flour has sold at a loss. Lionel has once again been taken in by being too trusting. The people he was associated with in this business have absolutely nothing to their names but debts. He is left solely responsible. This morning the sheriff came to seize our house and furniture, right down to our personal effects.[5] I could have protested, as our marriage contract gives me ownership of my own property and the documents are in order, but I would have had to go to court. I signed a paper surrendering all I possess here. I don't want to give the slightest sign of regrets or tears. It's by struggling against poverty and adversity that I can show myself worthy of my name.

When Lionel heard what I had done in the belief that it would get him out of his financial difficulties, he reproached me angrily, saying:

—That won't do any good at all. I owe much more than the house is worth. Now we shall still have debts on our hands and nowhere to live. It's an act of absolute madness!

This sudden outburst was so unexpected that I too lost my temper, and for the first time since we were married, we had a very heated argument. He admitted that he had been in the wrong, then kissed me and asked my forgiveness. We both cried and made up.

All we can do now is face up to whatever happens. In this country the law moves quickly. Our house has been put up for auction. The sale will take place in a week's time. We hope that, as a result of these drastic measures, Lionel will find the money to settle his own and the other debts. But there is no way he can possibly do it. I have not been to bed for three days. All my bags are packed, but where are we going? I have not the faintest idea.

C. de C. in Paris owes me 25 000 francs from the sale of my jewels. The income from it was to go to my mother. He will pay neither the capital nor the interest. I have just had a letter from my mother telling me that her health is deteriorating and that if I put off my return to France too much longer, I shall never see her again. The people in Châteauroux tell her all sorts of tales, and it upsets her. Unhappiness pursues me on all sides. There is nothing for it—some changes will have to be made.

Bob has just been told to look for work elsewhere. Poor Marie broke down. Then she asked for an interview with Lionel. She told him that Bob had seduced her, that she was pregnant, and that he must be made to marry her. Lionel could not help laughing. He did not want to do it, so I was the one who had to confront Bob. The poor fellow stood there looking at the floor and twisting his cap in his hands, as he listened to my accusations.

—I will not listen to any objections, I told him. Even if she were old, ugly and unshapely, you saw her before you took her. If you will not marry for her sake, do it for your child.

What would become of them both? The count can't keep them.

Bob allowed himself to be won over, and relented. The marriage is agreed upon. He will go to Ballarat with Marie, who will run a small canteen. She has a little money set aside, but it won't be enough. Yesterday I sold a cashmere shawl to Mrs Sivratt for £20 sterling, which I gave to Marie. She is leaving this evening with her intended. She seems delighted to be leaving me. As far as I am concerned, I certainly will not miss her. What monstrous ingratitude.

Captain Johnson, a charming man we met at the Cape, has just arrived in Melbourne. He is in command of a 2500-ton American ship. It's a real event every time one of these large ships that look like floating islands makes its entrance into Port Phillip harbour. We were the first people the captain visited.

—I have heard about your trouble, he said, shaking our hands with a bone-crushing grip. You must not be put off by one or two failures. I have been ruined ten times, and I have started all over again. Don't give up, and your luck will return. I can't stay on shore because I have to supervise the unloading of my ship, which will take at least three weeks or a month. Come back on board with me, all of you.

—Thank you, Captain, Lionel replied, looking at me with tears in his eyes, but I think a storm is brewing and my wife is not very well.

—All the more reason to take her mind off things. I shall answer for the weather, and anyway, a bit of water will not do any harm. I have a good doctor on board, he added, looking at me more closely. He will tell you what to do to get fit and well again. Having you both down in the dumps is no way to cure the problem. You have done some bad business deals, or had them done to you. It can happen to anyone. Come and spend a few days on board. My wife, who always travels with me, will be very happy to be of service to Madam; Solange can play with my daughter; and your servant can annoy my cook. He's a Mauritian, blacker than the coal in his stove and sillier than his geese.

—Marie has left us, replied Lionel with a smile. She is getting married.

The captain began to laugh and said:

—Things like that only really happen in Australia. Come along. They are expecting me back, and I don't want to leave without you.

—Why not? Lionel said to me. It will chase away our worries.

It took only a few minutes to pack a bag and close the door and windows. My daughter was wild with delight!

We crossed all the part of the forest that lies between us and the main road without saying a word. Our melancholy affected the child. She began walking more quietly, plucking a few wildflowers here and there, then throwing them away without even looking at them.

We were rugged up in heavy overcoats, as there was a fierce north wind that roughly pushed us on. We had reached the beach where the sea was whipped up into waves, some of which broke at our feet, as the firm sand was the best place to walk. Ever since I arrived in this country, I have never caught sight of a ship on the horizon without my heart starting to beat faster. At that moment there were two going out of the Heads. The wind was behind them and they were heading for the open sea with frightening speed.

I had stopped, and I was following their progress with longing eyes and a heavy heart when I heard a loud cry. Solange had stopped to pick up shells and seaweed on the sand. As she had moved forward and was bent right over, a wave struck her on the head, knocked her over and sent her rolling for more than 100 paces into the sea. I can't tell you what I felt seeing her disappear under the water like that, but I ran after the child and caught her in a hole that was at least ten feet deep. The captain and my husband ran up to us. I still don't know whether I was laughing or crying, but I was very shaken and it was Solange who described what had happened. The clothes of both myself and Solange were dripping wet. I wanted to go back to the house, but the captain pointed out that the ship was closer and that Mrs Johnson would provide us with everything we needed.

We arrived at the port, where a boat was waiting for us. Seeing us in the distance, the captain's six sailors had their oars at the ready. Mr Johnson had already got in and was giving me a hand, when one of the port police approached Lionel, said something to him in a low voice, then added more loudly:

—Your wife is free to go where she likes.

I hurriedly got out again and took my husband's arm. He looked so pale that I did not dare ask any questions.

—Sir, he said to the sheriff at last, I am only going to spend a few hours on board my friend Captain Johnson's ship.

—I can't allow you to go, the man replied very politely, lowering his voice, you have debts and I have my orders. You can't leave Melbourne.

—Do you take me for a thief, Lionel asked with such dignity that the policeman hung his head. I give you my word that I will not try to leave. Let me pass.

—You are under arrest, replied the man, tapping him on the shoulder with his short black truncheon.

A shiver went through Lionel. His face was ashen.

—Very well, he said after a moment's pause, I must respect your customs and your laws, but they are quite arbitrary.

—I did not make them, replied the sheriff, still courteous, and however unpleasant it may be, I have to do my duty.

We took our leave of the captain, who had discreetly moved away and hadn't heard any of this. We then made our way back in deep despair.

The rest of the day and the night was spent holding each other's hands and looking at each other without daring to utter a word. But Lionel wept and his tears were almost more than I could bear. By officially becoming involved in a business venture, he had compromised his position as consular agent. Just one word or one complaint to the minister would mean dismissal, and then we would really be left with no resources at all.

I had an idea.

—How much do you owe? I asked as I stood up to get my circulation going again. I had gone numb with fear and cold.

—Two thousand pounds.

—How much did you pledge the house for?

—For one thousand pounds.

—If you promised to pay the money in a few months, would they give you extra time do you think?

—Yes, he replied with a smile full of bitterness, but still looking me in the eye.

—Well, I could go over to France and get that amount for you. Your cousin owes it to me.

—He refused to pay it in court.

—That's because I was not there to defend my interests, but when he knows the situation you are in . . .

—Do you realize what you are saying? It means six months at sea!

—You managed it, didn't you, when you came to fetch me?

—But I'm a man.

—Well, thinking of you will give me some of your courage.

—No! No! I would be worried to death! . . . If they make life impossible for me, I shall blow my brains out . . .

—If I were strong enough, I exclaimed, forcing him to look at me, I would strike you for what you have just said. Your life is no longer yours alone. It belongs to me and it means more to me than my own. Everything will work out in time. And Johnson was right when he said that you should never give up hope on anything. Trust me, I know all about surviving hard times, and if God leaves me my health . . .

Lionel looked at me sadly, and I understood all the anxiety he felt deep inside. I have altered a good deal—everyone tells him so. No doubt it's due to not having any peace of mind. However strong you are, you can't cope with such emotional upheavals for long. But it's no good lingering over such thoughts. You must keep going or you will give way altogether. As long as I have any semblance of strength, I shall use it to support him. It's one of the oddities of my character: basically, I am happy when I can help people.

I must find a way to allay his fears about the thoughts that worry me, a way to put hope back into his poor, sad heart. Otherwise he will do just as he said: he will kill himself in a fit of depression. The awful habit people here have acquired, of always carrying one or two pistols in their pocket, is the cause of suicides and crimes that would occur less often if they had time to think. Before he knew me, Lionel had fought several duels. He is absolutely fearless; the thought of physical pain doesn't worry him in the slightest. Consequently, he is terribly bold when it comes to challenging people to fight. I shudder at the very idea of it, especially when I think of all the attacks that can still be directed at me.

The rate of our correspondence has slowed down. We receive only letters of no importance. Besides, what can we write to each other when it takes six months to exchange our ideas?

I went to spend the day in Melbourne and pay a few visits. Everyone knows the state of our affairs. They are very sorry that we have been associated with unscrupulous people who would never have been creditworthy without Lionel's guarantee. Mrs Sivratt urged us to see Mr Smith and ask him to arrange for us to be given time to sell our house. It's a good idea, as we're being hounded on all sides.

Mrs Sivratt insisted on coming with me. Mr Smith received us very kindly. I told him everything that had happened and he promised to intercede for us with our creditors. He has a lot of influence. I came back to the consulate with Mr Johnson and his doctor, whom I met on the way. The doctor is still a relatively young man, but his hair is snow white, which actually suits him very well. He looks at me closely and asks me questions as if he were giving me a consultation. I am so happy with what Mr Smith has promised to do for me that I feel quite well, but he does not seem to think I am.

I left the men together and went off to buy some shoes for Solange. When I came home, Lionel was reading a large letter that Mr Smith had just had delivered to him. It contained these simple words: 'You have the time you need and the right to go out in a boat as far as you please.' It was very good news, and yet Lionel was very down-cast. He took me in his arms and pressed me tightly to his heart, saying:

—Poor Céleste. It's all my fault and you'll end up hating me.

After a host of questions from me that he did not want to answer, he admitted in the end that the doctor had told him I have a liver disease that's in an advanced stage and almost impossible to cure in this frightful country that causes illnesses, but doesn't relieve them.

—Well then, if there is no cure, we should not waste time worrying about it.

—But there is one that never fails: it's the land of your birth, the waters at Vichy.

—It's rather far to go . . .

—People go there from all over the world.

—If I did go, it would only be to try and settle our affairs and get you a posting somewhere else. The doctor was right, even though he rather exaggerated my situation. This climate has been deadly for many of our friends. You yourself have been affected by it without realizing it, and you are the one I really fear for.

Several days passed without any decision being made. It was a visit from Fauchery that finally made up our minds. His wife had taken ill and, fearing for her life, he seemed in such deep despair that Lionel said to me:

—You must go back to France with Solange, and put her to board in the convent at Ardentes,[6] near Châteauroux. It was partly founded by my mother. The child would be very well cared for there, if I recommended her. She would not learn anything here, and besides, there are only Protestant schools. We shall review the situation when she has made her first communion.

No one in the English colonies was surprised at the news of my impending departure for France. All the women are used to long voyages. They come and go from one end of the globe to the other without causing the slightest astonishment. Merchants' wives whose children are in England go to see them every three or four years. People are so used to these comings and goings that no one attaches any importance to them. As for me, although I did not admit it, I felt I had taken a very big step. At the thought of going away on my own, of leaving Lionel, I began to like this wretched country of Australia. The plants, the trees, my loneliness—I would miss everything!

Such is life, and to think that there is not a thing one can do to change destiny!

Part Three:

Separation—Paris and Melbourne

CHAPTER 13

The Return Journey

28 July 1856

YESTERDAY I visited an American ship being loaded for Liverpool. Thanks to the extra time Lionel has been granted, after being asked to give his word that he wouldn't try to leave the colony, he was able to accompany me on board the ship on which I'm to travel.

We were so sad and so caught up in our own thoughts that we covered the whole distance without noticing how far we had come. When Captain Johnson's boatswain, who had lent us his sailors and his boat, announced that we were alongside the *James Baines*, I threw myself into Lionel's arms, determined not to leave him.[1] His arms tightened around me convulsively. He gazed out at the sea and sky, then went to the back of the boat again to take the tiller, and said:

—You are right. Come! If we have to be miserable, it's better to be miserable together. I shall go back and work in the mines, if I have to . . .

I knew that one setback would inevitably lead to another. If he did not pay his debts, he would lose his position. All this came back to my mind, and at the words 'I shall go back to the mines', all my energy returned. I signalled to the sailors on the *James Baines* to leave the ladder, and without waiting for Lionel's assent, I climbed on board. He followed me automatically, but once on the bridge, he declared that his mind was made up. He did not want me to make a voyage like that alone. The idea of a separation made him lose heart completely.

His weakness gave me strength. I talked seriously about the need to go to Europe; I emphasized my own personal interests. I admit it was a white lie and it did not fool Lionel, for he said to me:

—Your interests? You could deal with them here. Our main concern should be getting you well again.

He had nothing more to say. After inspecting the ship from the hold to the mainmast, we agreed to book a passage the following day.

I find all preparations for departure depressing. It was these feelings no doubt that brought on a bilious attack. I was ill all night.

I have just pawned what jewellery I had left to pay for my ticket. I have the receipt in front of me, but I still can't believe it. The ship on which I have booked my passage has not fixed a departure date yet.

Time passes . . . and more time passes . . . Everyone but me seems to have accepted the idea that I am leaving. People shower me with recommendations and messages. I wish something extraordinary would happen to prevent me from going. I'm suffering terribly! I wish I could die, then everything would be over . . . When I was packing my bags, I wanted to burn everything I had written, but I did not have the heart to do it. I shall take it with me as a reminder of the past, not as a sign of hope for the future.

Saturday, 15 August, on board the *James Baines*

Offshore. I have been on board for a few hours. The planks of the deck shake under my feet, the waves roar around me, the wind whistles in the rigging and I'm still undecided!

Lionel came and settled me in my cabin, then left, waving goodbye. He's coming back. He only went back to shore to get permission from the captain to spend the night on board with me, as I am not at all well.

I stayed in the same place for eight hours, peering in the same direction for the boat that had taken Lionel away and was to bring him back again. It was pitch black and pouring with rain, but I couldn't bring myself to leave the stern of the ship. Everyone told me to go inside. They said that my husband could neither come back, nor get on board in such weather. I took no notice of anyone.

At nine o'clock in the evening I saw a pinpoint of light coming from the general direction of St Kilda, and I cried out: 'There he is!'

—That's just too bad for him, a sailor replied bluntly, there's a heavy swell. If they can't cut through it properly they'll capsize. And anyway, even if they do make it across, they can't get on board. We don't put the ladder down at this time of night.

—He must have orders from the captain, I replied, without losing sight of the precious light.

—I have orders too, and I always carry them out.

—If my husband were down there and you refused to let him come on board, I would throw myself into the sea or I would set fire to your ship!

The man looked at me. He obviously thought I was mad. I gave him ten shillings, and then he took considerable interest in the feeble light that was coming towards us but with great difficulty.

My anxiety was not over quickly. Finally my poor Lionel was there, but Good Lord! what a state he was in. His clothes were soaked, his hair and moustache were dripping wet, his eyelids were red from wind and tears. His legs, which were stiff with cold, could hardly support him.

I took him to my cabin, wrapped him in my shawls and coats. His teeth were chattering, so that he could hardly pronounce a few halting phrases. When he was a little better, he opened his waistcoat and took out a small ivory figure of Christ on an ebony cross.

—There! he said to me after he had kissed it, this crucifix used to belong to my mother. That is all I have left of hers. It will bring you luck. Keep it with you always, do you understand? It's the last sacrifice I can make for you, the last proof of love that I can give you. I wanted to be strong this morning when I left you, but I felt almost immediately that you were taking more than half my life with you. Listen to what I'm saying, —these are solemn words: *I have no regrets, and if you were not my wife I would still marry you.* I have worked. I have done wrong, thinking I was doing the right thing. The only remorse I feel is having involved you in business affairs that have turned against me.

I kissed his hands and protested that I alone was the cause of all his misfortunes, as without me it's likely that his life would have been totally different. The night was spent exchanging promises and words of advice. When day broke, we were so pale and dishevelled that we were both alarmed.

—Come with me, I said to him, I feel it's more than I can bear to leave you. Let's leave all our troubles, all our pain behind in this frightful country.

He kissed me and said:

—I have given my word. Go! and may God keep you, because if I lost you . . .

The pilot had come on board; we had to part. Everyone who had come to see me off was in tears. I felt I had won some people's friendship, and that somewhat eased my bitter regrets. I recommended Lionel to Fauchery, who asked me to do a few things for him and promised to write and give me news of his wife, who was now a little better.

The dreaded signal sounded and the cannon was fired three times to make our farewells to the town. A little steamer took on board all the relations and friends who had stayed with us up to the last minute. They had to drag my poor Lionel away. As for me, all the fine resolutions I had made vanished into thin air. Sorrow, fatigue and emotion completely overcame me. Faint and worn-out, I fell onto a seat. When I came to, I was lying in my cabin and we were fifty miles from Melbourne.

I went up on deck, but no matter how hard I looked, searching the horizon, there was nothing more to be seen, nothing but the vast stretch of the sea—that huge, sad, green expanse that often makes us believe in the end of the world.

We have been travelling now for fourteen days, and I still have doubts about leaving. I have long periods of depression; I can't manage a thing; it's all I can do to think! I would like to shake off this kind of torpor that makes my heart and my limbs feel like lead. Besides, I must give Lionel an account of my life on board. I don't want to make him unhappy. I shall try to bring out the funny side of the things that happen to me and the people around me.

At sea, on board the *James Baines*

My dear Lionel, I don't really want to talk about myself. You know my nature well enough to imagine the intense, heart-rending emotions I felt after we had to part. Looking but not seeing, listening but not hearing, closing my eyes but not sleeping—that's the state I have been in since I saw the shores of Australia disappear.

Firstly, all my thoughts and all my love go to you.

The captain has given me the place of honour at his table. I am on his right and I come in for all the splashes of sauce he sends flying from the plate when he carves the roast. As he's awkward in his movements and clumsy with his hands, he knocks over everything within reach—wine, tea, beer, everything. At the moment we are experiencing a period of dead calm which gets on his nerves. He is not knocking things over now, he is breaking them, and he has a face as long as his mainmast.

Solange looks radiant. She does not want to speak a word of French. I think that I too may have trouble expressing myself properly by the time we arrive.

It's already becoming decidedly cold. We have been shivering for five days now. The layout of the cabins, the general aspect of the saloon, even the passengers' faces are all awfully dismal. When you think that, at the rate we are going, we shall have to spend three months in these wretched surroundings . . . ! We sleep with one eye open. There are several millions in gold dust in the bottom of the hold, and the fear of being robbed makes us see pirate ships in the clouds, the waves or even the whales that break the surface of the water.

As in all ships, there is a curious mixture of passengers, but the emigrants returning to Europe are much more subdued than those rushing to seek their fortune. Many have wasted their time and their youth, lost their illusions and their hopes.

However, nesting activity has begun and there are couples in corners everywhere. They are looking for warmth to raise their spirits . . . so much for the lovers! Those who have nothing to love criticize others. The only thing I pay any attention to is the captain's dog. It's a sweet little bulldog that hunts rats all night. There are so many on board that they would end up eating us if the dog did not eat them first.

The only light my cabin gets comes from a little window high up that gives onto the deck. It's a most annoying arrangement, as I can't even get dressed properly. When a passenger's foot steps on my skylight I am in darkness until the person walking on deck cares to continue on his way. The men are bad enough, but the women's petticoats drive me to distraction.

It's impossible to write during the day, and they will not give us any light in the evening. It's icy cold, without a breath of wind. How long is this journey going to take?

My travelling companions are not a very cheery lot. All of them are coming away, like me, largely very disillusioned with the wonderful dreams they had about Australia. All you hear are complaints and regrets. It would seem that this disappointment is widely felt.

12 September

It's often said that we are never happy with what we get. We asked for wind; well now we have it, but it's a howling gale.

My companions have stomachs like ostriches. They eat all day long. Their main preoccupation is their daily inspection of the provisions to find out how many are left on board. For my part, it's all I can do to nibble a few biscuit crumbs. Yet they say I have put on weight. I think it's more likely to be swelling.

The wind has suddenly dropped completely. You don't dare go anywhere near the captain. He goes around swearing like a trooper, and if this continues, he is sure to hit someone before nightfall.

This morning we saw the strangest thing: it was as though the sky had suddenly merged completely with the sea and we were passing through a cloud so thick that you could not see anyone five paces in front of you. Yet you could hear a muffled, inexplicable sound. We were surrounded by myriads of birds. They hovered, dived and fought to catch a few biscuit crumbs that people were throwing at the rear of the ship.

At midday we saw some glimmers of sunlight, but still through the cloud that surrounds us. Heavens! how I sympathize with people who are blind. It's so awful not being able to see. This white mist is like a huge shroud stretching out into infinity. We must have passed near land, as all our birds have disappeared. What a pity. It's hard to believe how happy one can feel at sea when a fish, a marine plant or a bird comes into view.

On Sunday they brought us two children from third class who came to mass. The little girl is five and the boy about eight.

—Don't cry, he said to his sister who was sitting in front of me, near my daughter. If you cry, they won't bring us here again.

—I want to see mummy, replied the little girl, trying to suppress the sobs that rose from her tight little chest in spite of her efforts. I want to see her!

—You know that's not possible. She died back there with our father under the big tree.

—I want to see her, the child said again, tossing back a mane of curly red hair.

—You promised to be good, but you're making a noise and they'll send us away.

—Let's go, repeated the little girl sliding off the seat on which she had been sitting, let's go and see mummy.

The little boy looked at me and said,

—She's so naughty!

I understood this appeal for help, and sat the little girl down again, promising that if she was good, she could play with Solange's doll. The child gave me a strange look. Her eyes were blue–green like the sea, her lips were crimson red, her complexion very pale, with skin as fine as rice paper and so transparent that you could see the blood circulating in her veins.

—I don't want to play, she said, I want to go!

The man on my left was delivering a sermon. He gave us a look that his wife intercepted. She raised her silver spectacles and made a meaningful gesture to the little girl. The child hung her head and kept quite still.

—Are you hungry? said her brother after a few minutes. Have this piece of biscuit.

—No! she replied, pushing him away with her elbow, I don't want any.

—She won't eat anything, the little boy said to me.

Solange offered the little girl some chocolate and met with the same refusal.

The poor children were ragged and dirty. After the service I stopped the boy. His sister scampered off like a hare making for its lair.

—You have lost your mother, have you? I asked him while Solange persuaded him to share her piece of chocolate.

—Yes, and my father, too.

—Did they die together?

—Yes.

—How did it happen?

—We came from Ireland five months ago to look for gold back there in Australia. We had lots of tools and a tent to live in. My father had put it up against a big tree to make it more secure and give us a bit of shelter from the wind. But it seems that the big tree wasn't solid.

I remembered having heard about these poor children a few days before I left Melbourne. A terrible hurricane had uprooted a tree which fell on a miner's tent, crushing a man and his wife to death. The children were playing in the bush at the time and had escaped certain death. A fund had been set up for the orphans, and they were being sent back to their grandfather. The little boy has more courage than strength, but the little girl is so withdrawn that she will let herself starve to death.

I have just brought her a few of Solange's things. She did not even look at them. She was huddled in the hollow of her canvas bed, curled up tight like a cat. All I could see were her two big eyes gleaming like jewels.

If I were rich, I'd pay for them to travel first class, as third is awful. The sailors are rough, they get drunk and fight, and these poor children are often frightened, cold and hungry. They are not allowed in the first class saloon, so I go to see them every day with Solange. At first she was rather repulsed by them, but now she pops anything she can find into her pocket—biscuits, dried fruit or cakes—to take to these poor little creatures. The little girl looks at us, but she still has not said a word. She will die, but she will not forget.

22 September

The poor little thing died yesterday at four o'clock. She gave me her last smile when I took her an orange.

Death does not sadden or frighten me, for I have never found living as difficult as I do now. Every day there are worries, problems, sorrows, disappointments, useless efforts, wasted time, vanishing youth. My eyes could not summon a tear when they threw that child into the sea: it seemed to me that she was going to a better world. If an angel is crushed to death when it falls to earth, it must surely go back to God. But here you are sent back unceremoniously, tied up like a parcel in a grey canvas sack, with an iron weight on your feet to send you to the bottom, until a shark or some other inhabitant of the deep offers you hospitality in its stomach. Still, as all roads lead to Rome, they must all lead to heaven, and those who depart are less to be pitied than those who remain.

I wanted to be the strong woman who copes with everything, but I have been sick for three days—so sick I almost had visions of the canvas sack. What melancholy thoughts crowd in when you find yourself alone in an awful cabin, without help, light or fresh air! Even the bravest souls give way to it. Why did I leave my Lionel?

I have not brought enough warm clothing; I am feeling the cold and can't sleep.

The captain seems impervious to everything. Our mainmasts bend like reeds and you can hear dreadful creaking noises. You feel as though everything is going to break up. The rigging is coming apart; the sails are tearing; it's unbearably cold.

Well! Everyone else is merry; they laugh and would even get up and dance if it were possible to stay upright. But you can't keep your balance on board and people are constantly falling over, to the great amusement of the crew. Our noses are red as beetroots and the lovers are less affectionate.

Béranger says that 'beggars are happy people',[2] so what would he say about madmen? We have two on board, a man and a woman. They laugh and sing all the time. I follow them and listen to them for hours on end. The young woman has eyes so big and black that I don't dare look her in the face. They say she's about twenty but looks older. Suffering ages people so quickly. She set sail in a ship from Calcutta with all her family about eighteen months ago. There was yellow fever on board, and in the space of eight days she saw her mother, her father and her two sisters die. As she watched the last sister being thrown overboard she began to laugh, and she's been laughing all the time since. She is being sent back to Europe.

The other one is a man of about thirty. He is tall, well built, and quite good-looking. No one knows what drove him mad. He is in third class, but he can be seen walking about all night. It's as if he is waiting for someone. Sometimes he leans over the side and seems to be signalling to something he can see deep in the water. Sometimes he blows kisses to the moon, whispering to it tenderly. He is in love with a shadow—a happy love, since he never feels cold or tired.

As for me, I am worn out. It seems as though time is standing still. The days and nights drag on, never ending. I feel I have lived ten years in the space of just one month. I can't write because of the weather. Last night our ship must have travelled several miles with its keel in the air and its masts in the water. Everything was broken, smashed. I held Solange in my arms and she was so frightened that she hung on to my neck so tightly she nearly strangled me. We were lucky enough to get off with nothing worse than a fright.

I am writing these notes for myself. I don't want to tell Lionel everything I'm suffering, physically and mentally. What good will it do to make him unhappy? He has enough troubles of his own. As he adores playing chess, I am going to try and learn it during the time when I can stay sitting, as I don't get out of bed very often. They say the captain plays fairly well and I'm the only one he's pleasant to. I shall accept his kind offers.

Though the lunatics on board this ship are amusing, those who are sane are rather boring. They get drunk, quarrel and fight. What a contrast with my trip on the *Croesus!* . . .

We are approaching Cape Horn. It's so cold that the blood almost freezes in your veins. The doctor orders alcohol and spices, so the cook puts cloves and red pepper in all the food. Soups, cakes and custards nearly take the roof off your mouth. I can't eat a thing.

What a dismal scene surrounds us! We constantly come across mountains of ice carried along by the current. They are like floating rocks bearing down on us. They must be avoided at all costs. Just one collision, one hit, and that would be the end of us. During the day we can see danger approaching, but at night we don't dare sleep.

There are six men on watch. These unfortunate sailors have to shout out every quarter of an hour that they can see nothing coming. The prospect is so frightening that we listen anxiously for each cry.

Last night at midnight, a man who had drunk some brandy to warm himself up fell asleep and died on the deck. This morning the captain had him thrown overboard like a dog, saying:

—Good riddance! He should not have fallen asleep.

Funeral prayers don't last long here and death leaves no trace of regret in them. If war service counts double, these voyages in ice-laden seas should surely count triple.

My health is getting worse all the time. I have taken all the medicines in the medicine chest; I give up trying to cure myself. Thank goodness Solange is all right. She jumps and runs around all day long. Poor child! what would become of her if she reached our destination without me! . . .

I have been in bed for a fortnight: it seems I was very ill. They assure me that I am much better. That may be so, but I can scarcely tell the difference. I can hardly stand and have to be helped up on deck. My poor Lionel . . . if he could see me now! I certainly did the right thing to leave and spare him the sight of me looking so dreadful. With me gone, perhaps he will regain his freedom, fortune and happiness. I feel like giving up the struggle.

We have rounded Cape Horn at last, but we are still a long way from our destination. Now the sea is calm and clear and we can see fish in the water as though they were in a bowl. I feel better. I shall write to Lionel.

'The crew have been catching huge sharks. It amuses the sailors and takes my mind off things for a while, and what is more, I have an admirer.' There is an old passenger on board who is as ugly as sin. He offers me his arm for a walk around the deck and I accept, because it's neither dangerous nor compromising to be in his company. He sighs so much he could fill our sails as he tells me that he can't sleep a wink if he has not said good evening to me. He went to the canteen for a bottle of salad oil which he uses on his wig, as there is no pommade. Now it shines like a helmet. Oh dear! The human race really doesn't bear close inspection. Silliness and self-indulgence wherever you look. Young or old, handsome or ugly, all men pursue women with the determination of a hunter or the patience of an angler.

Sunday, 14 October

Most conversation is based on the weather. We say good morning and wish each other a fair wind, but the much longed-for breeze still has not arrived and our ship has started taking one step forward and two steps back.

My nerves are in a terrible state. I really can't describe it. The sea! Nothing but the sea! I am sick of the sight of it . . . There is nothing we can do about it! three more weeks to wait, or rather to put up with.

I am forever having to mend Solange's things. She tears everything to shreds. There is a chubby-cheeked Irish boy with whom she is often at war. They start off playing husbands and wives, but after a few minutes, there's a squall in the household and the couple end up fighting like cat and dog. Bobby (that's my son-in-law's name) runs off to show his mother the scratches on the end of his nose. Solange shows me her tattered dress. Bobby gets a thrashing and Solange has to stand in the corner. But an hour later they go looking for each other, and it starts all over again. Bobby is only seven, like Solange, but he is three times her size.

22 October 1856

Seventy-seven days at sea, and everything is in short supply, except sickness and death! In second class there was a young married couple who were known as the ship's turtle doves. One of the turtle doves has just died and the other is dying. The husband was only just twenty-five. He fell ill only three days ago. Poor young things! They were right to love with such urgency, as they were not destined to love each other for long. They had been married for barely four months.

No words can describe the poor young woman's despair as she saw her husband's body thrown into the sea. She succumbed to dreadful fits of hysteria. I had her brought to my cabin, where I did the best I could for her. When she had calmed down a little, I asked her her name, her age and a few details about her family situation, less through curiosity than through interest.

—My name is Jenny, she told me in a trembling voice. I was born in Australia.

—Do you have relatives in England?

—No. We were going to my husband's mother.

—She is sure to receive you with open arms.

—I don't think so. Her son married me without her consent. She hated me without ever having met me. She will hold me responsible for her son's death and she is right, for if it were not for me, he'd have left Australia a year ago. If I ever get to our destination, I will not go to her.

—You are wrong. At your age, and sweet and gentle as you are, everyone loves you.

—When one is independent, the young woman replied after hesitating a moment, but I am poor and quite unskilled for work. Now, a mother who let her son leave because he was a burden to her will do nothing for a stranger.

—Don't give up like that.

—Besides, she continued, looking at me timidly, I have only one desire, one wish—but even if I were rich, very rich, it could never be realized on board ship. I have a feeling that I won't see the end of the voyage.

—What an idea! We must live to cherish the memory of our loved ones.

—Like all women born in the colonies, I had bad taste in my choice of clothes. These bright colours I always preferred look quite unsuitable on me today. I would give everything I have for a black dress.

I understood what she meant, and a few hours later I had improvised a complete mourning outfit for her. I really enjoyed unpicking green ornaments from a cashmere dress, making a collar and a bonnet with a little veil. I must admit that this poor young woman's sad joy made me feel one of the sweetest and deepest emotions of my life.

However, I can't keep this young woman in first class: I am not wealthy enough to pay the difference. What is more, seeing my protegee dressed by me from head to foot, people are already saying I am mad, extravagant. It does not really worry me. I am getting used to people's schemes and intrigues. No matter what you do, when they set themselves up as judge and judged, they approve of themselves and no one else.

Today is our ninety-fifth day at sea. The boat seems to dance forwards then backwards with the waves. It goes three miles forward, three miles back, and then it tacks from north-east to south.

People are as miserable as they can be. The captain beats himself on the head with his fists. I'm playing quite a reasonable game of chess.

15 November

One hundred and five days at sea and a head wind that keeps us stuck in the same spot. The *James Baines* only uses sail. There is no wind in the sails, so we can't even do one mile an hour.

Everyone is jaundiced, and me most of all.

A poor young man has just died. He was the life and soul of the passengers. He had made a lot of money at the mines and was returning home to see his mother and sisters. For three months he had been dreaming of all the wonderful things he would do. Sadly he died within a few hours. As they were fearful of being quarantined on arrival at Liverpool, he was put overboard before his body was even cold.

Liverpool, 24 November 1856

We have reached land at last. Although I stamp on the ground, touch it, look at it, it still doesn't seem real. I am so happy that I don't dare believe this happiness can last.

There is no doubt about it, joy can have a physical effect on you. When I caught sight of the first lighthouse, my heart started beating wildly and I felt faint. Then I started crying for joy. When I saw the pilot come aboard, I examined him from head to foot three times. Goodness! What a lot of shouting and yelling, rush and bustle there is on landing day.

I thought of you, my good, kind Lionel. All my thoughts and memories went back to Australia, where you are and where I wish I was still . . . However! I am sending you this letter. I love you. Don't lose heart or give up hope! . . .

CELESTE

Everyone is rushing hither and thither. We part without saying goodbye. I found myself so isolated in the middle of all this crush that my joy quickly gave way to the sober realization of the situation I was in. With a child and all my luggage, it was impossible to disembark immediately.

As soon as we had landed, I sent off a letter which Lionel had given me for a friend of his who had been living in Liverpool a few years earlier. Was this gentleman still in the country? No one could give me any information on the subject, and I was just about to entrust Solange, myself and all my luggage to a port worker, when the gentleman in question arrived dressed in his very best. He wore a uniform that was embroidered, brocaded and braided all over, and he was obviously very pleased with the impression he was making on the passengers and crew. The English are very impressed by the glamour of a uniform—any uniform at all.

The gentleman very courteously put himself at my disposal. All my bags were carefully unloaded. The customs men did not open my suitcases, which was very kind of them, as the English government collects duty on gold coming from Australia. There is a lot of contraband and the authorities are very wary. Their trust was well placed—more's the pity—as I had absolutely nothing to hide from customs. My cicerone offered me his arm and took me to a fine hotel. I could not really say much, but it was not hard to guess that, as a countess and consul's wife, I was going to be fleeced.

The man who came and offered me his services is called here 'the Five Powers': he is consul of five different nations. This post is less important to foreigners than it is to the French. They don't have special agents. A grocer, a merchant of any kind can perform this role, which is honorary. The posts are, however, much sought after, as they give the incumbent the right to wear a uniform.

The gentleman in question has five coats of arms above his office door, and five on his visiting cards. This passion for heraldry has been the subject of jibes made by his colleagues, who are no doubt jealous to see him represent five important foreign powers: Frankfurt, Bavaria, Saxony, Baden,—I've forgotten the other one. Mr Fleury, the French Consul in Liverpool, a man of great tact, feeling and wit, told me with a smile and without being at all malicious that my cicerone changed uniform five times when he gave a diplomatic dinner. There was a course for each nation and he did the honours for each in national uniform. At first people had laughed heartily, but then, as this eccentric is also a gentleman, they finished up pandering to his odd habit by giving him an ovation and toasting him each time he entered.

Liverpool is a very important town—they say it's beautiful—but we Parisians have been spoiled by Paris. It takes more than shops and rows of houses to captivate us.

Solange is as happy as a lark. She uses one of my hatboxes as her suitcase. I really have to watch her, as she is quite likely to take the hotel towels in her enthusiasm for packing.

We left Liverpool on Tuesday, 24 November. The weather was reasonably good, but the day after our arrival in London there was two feet of snow in the street. There was an awful wind which made boarding very difficult, and it took us ten hours to cross from Boston to Boulogne. It was all I could do to stop myself being seasick.

    —I don't feel very well, Solange said to me, turning pale.

    —Do you want to take something?

    —Yes, I want some fresh air.

I wanted to take her up on deck, but could not manage it. A sailor came to my aid, put the child on his back and took her up. Fifty women were packed into the saloon where even twenty would have been uncomfortable. They were all sick and sprawled over each other in Heaven knows what state. It was pouring with rain. I had put my shawl around Solange's shoulders and I was soaked to the skin.

CHAPTER 14

Paris Regained

29 December

ONCE we arrived in Paris, I rented very modest lodgings at 11 Rue Alger—two rooms on the ground floor. My return to France has started off badly, as I have been in bed for three days. I had not sent word to my mother. I wanted to surprise her, and she certainly was surprised. She looked at me without really seeing me or else did not recognize me, I had changed so much! Finally she kissed me and burst into tears.

Difficulties always seem less difficult to deal with when one is far away. During the fortnight I have been in Paris, I have made twenty approaches to people but no progress at all. I have met up with good friends, but very bad debtors.

I will have to go to court. But where would that lead me?

I went to see my lawyer.

—Have you been to see Mr C. de C. who owes you money? he asked me.

—No, all my attempts to do so have failed.

—You will have to come to some agreement with him.

—But he refuses to see me.

—Make some concessions. Write to him.

—I have already done that.

—Did he reply?

—That he could not pay.

—Do you have his letter? Does he suggest a time for repayment?

—No.

—Is he being dishonest?

—Very, but what can I do? I hate lawsuits and besides, I want to go back straight away.

—You do have confidence in my efforts on your behalf and my commitment to your affairs? Well, in spite of doing everything in my power, I still can't promise anything under six months.

—Six months!

—Mr C. de C. must at least have paid you with notes which your husband has countersigned?

—Yes, he did that to guarantee them.

—If he were here, it would simplify matters so much more.

—You have given me an idea. Nothing ventured, nothing gained!

—What are you going to do?

—Go and see the minister to ask him, beg him to grant my husband some leave. A most important matter depends on it and I'm sure he will grant it for me.

At last, after countless efforts, after having my hopes raised and dashed a hundred times, I obtained six months' leave for Lionel. The very day I sent him the notice, a letter arrived from him—just at the right time to give me fresh heart and renewed strength.

'St Kilda, 29 August

Since your departure, my beloved wife, hours have seemed like centuries. Even though my heart is with you wherever you go, I am still uneasy, I am afraid—yes afraid: the voyage is so long and it must be so awful for you. And then, if you were to forget me . . . Dear Lord, what would I do without you?—you who are my only love, my only happiness! There are moments when I nearly go mad and my heart breaks with grief, for the only idea, the only eventuality that has never crossed my mind is the possibility of leaving you for an instant.

I was so happy sharing every moment of your life. All my sorrows, all my worries quickly disappeared as soon as I saw you. Now that I am alone in this house, every day when I come back from town I can't help looking for you. So every day brings a new sorrow. Everything seems sad without you, and my deepest regret is that I am the cause of it all. But do believe me, my dear Céleste, if I made a mistake, it's because I was trying so hard to do well. I would be so happy if I could give you a pleasant, comfortable life. Everything I want is for you; everything I work for will be for you. You are the one who has given me the happiness I have known over the last three years. Please believe me when I say that the rest of my life will be spent finding ways to thank you for it.

I received your two letters from the *Heads*.[1]

Thank you, thank you for those kind words. Yes Céleste, I do have confidence in you, great confidence, and although my heart is sad to know you are so far away, I feel all the more grateful for such true devotion. We both have our own road to follow. I hope to make yours smooth and happy with all the attention and love I can give you.

Your heart and your intelligence are the surest guarantees of what is most important to me, and I know that you would never jeopardize a position which, though difficult to acquire, has now almost been attained. But come now, I don't want to make you sad.

We play whist every evening with Fauchery and I kill time as best I can.

The garden is bursting with flowers and there is a bunch of violets in front of your portraits every day. My last thought of the day, like the first, is for you; when I get up in the morning, I send you all my love. Everyone who knows you loves you, and you can be sure that I never let a chance go by to talk about you. Fauchery and Varenne worship you, so I am never happier than in their company when the conversation turns to you.

There I go, writing like a lover again, but you see, that's how it is, my darling. I am like an 18-year-old boy when I think of you.

To get back to the people of Melbourne. Old Cotton's eyes were full of tears when I saw him again after you left. I could happily have kissed him. My own eyes stayed red and swollen for such a long time.

Fortunately for me, I am very busy at the moment. One person who has been very kind is Mr Dollon.[2] The poor man came and spent the evening with me the day you left, and did his best to console me. Console me, my darling wife? Can you console a person whose heart is breaking?

This same poor Dollon caught pneumonia and twenty-four hours later he was at death's door. He called me to make his will. However, today there is some hope of saving him.

I am writing up my major work on Australia and hope to send it to you by the first packet boat.[3]

The railway line to St Kilda is more than half completed.[4] It should pass through your land. If they make me a good offer for the house, I shall take it; if not, I shall wait till you come back, since I have plenty of time. But hurry all the same, my darling! That's the only piece of advice I have to give you; the goodness of your heart makes all others unnecessary. You will never hear me speak of duty; I rely always on your affection and your love.

Get your affairs in good order, so that nothing can trouble us for two or three years. I hope that if I work at it during that time, we can be assured of a good financial position for the rest of our lives.

Were you very sick on board? Has your health improved? How did you find your mother? She must have been very surprised to see you.

This is a terribly rambling letter, but I want to keep writing until the last minute before the post closes. My heart is full of good, sweet things to say to you, and if I let it have its way, I would have pages and pages to write. It's ten o'clock at night. The mail for the packet boat closes tomorrow morning, so I shall only just have time to run to the post-office when I get to town.

Let me tell you once again, my dearest Céleste, that you are the light of my life, the joy of my heart, and that all my thoughts, my desires, my wishes and my prayers are for you; that I love you with the same passion, the same love as I did on the first day, and that till I breathe my last, all my thoughts and wishes will be for you.

I send all my kisses and count on your devotion and love to bring you back very soon. I hope Paris will make you miss your quiet existence in St. Kilda. I shall do all I can to keep up and even improve our modest cottage, as I hope we can save it.

If sometimes your thoughts turn to my bad temper, my dearest love, please remember that worry, and above all the frustration of not being able to provide some compensation for your exile, played a large part in my outbursts.

Give Solange a kiss for me. Tell her often that her father the *cat* will always be a good father to her, and that she will always share in my good fortune, if it ever arrives.

Goodbye, my beautiful Countess. Think of me counting the hours and minutes. I embrace you in the same way as I love you—with all my heart.

Lionel

p.s. Wertemberg, who is here at St Kilda this evening, asks me to send you his warmest regards, as does Fauchery, who has just won a shilling from me.'

I have just left Solange to board with Mrs Liétard at Neuilly until I am able to take her to the Berry. I couldn't keep her cooped up like a prisoner in my room, but I feel very sad to see her go.

I suffered so much from the cold going round that beastly Cape Horn, that I can't shake off the effects. I cough night and day. I have been around the world, it's true, but it was not a very pleasant experience. Ah well, if I can get healthy again, it will all be for the best.

Having decided not to go to the theatre or stroll on the boulevards during my stay in Paris, I have no distractions. I am still writing and studying, but I am just like an English schoolgirl doing her French lessons. I still make spelling mistakes which exasperate me.

Back in Australia, Fauchery had asked me to deliver a sealed package to the editor in chief of the *Figaro* newspaper. It was marked 'personal', so I wrote to Mr de Villemessant, asking him to call on me, as I did not want to go the newspaper office.[5] He replied:

Madam,

Laugh if you will—as much as you like—but the idea came to me that you do not really like the editor in chief of the *Figaro*. You invite me to call on you, but I have the feeling that my life or my heart could be at risk. So, if you have some interesting notes to give me, come and see me. I shall be delighted to receive you.

If Marshall Turenne admitted being afraid,[6] Villemessant has the right to do likewise.

Respectfully yours,

H. de Villemessant

This reply came as a great surprise to me. I had no idea what this witty letter from the editor of the *Figaro* meant. When I left, he was a man who called a spade a spade, as they commonly describe those who fear neither God nor the Devil. I knew with what perseverance and energy he had struggled to succeed by his own efforts and keep the name of de Villemessant, which had been disputed in court. If I had unknowingly been the object of attacks in the *Figaro*, it could only concern my writing, for in all conscience, Mr de Villemessant could hardly reproach me with having accepted a title and a noble name that were offered willingly. Before my marriage he had been kind and generous towards me, and on many occasions when he had been asked a favour, I found him obliging and generous. His own inexhaustible mind was so good at unearthing others that he often went along with those he wished to raise to the honoured status of contributor to the *Figaro*. But lending oneself to others is not the same as giving oneself, and if ever they proved ungrateful, he got rid of them even faster than he had promoted them.

Fauchery could not be one of that number. He had a real affection for Villemessant. Whenever anyone spoke ill of him, which happened often in Australia, he said: 'You don't know him. You could not find a better person once you know how to handle him. You say he would kill a friend to make a witty remark? That is the nature of the job, and what is more, no man has been more criticized, more slandered and maligned than he by riff-raff who even started up rags to churn out attacks on him that ceased only when the paper closed down. If you are bitten often enough, you turn savage. He will never do as much harm to others as they have tried to do to him.'

After having read and re-read Mr de Villemessant's letter, I wrote to him in reply:

Dear Sir,

I regret to inform you that I did not laugh in the slightest. Doubtless it was not my day for gaiety and besides, it is hard to accept the idea that one frightens people. I have never felt any antipathy towards the chief editor of the *Figaro*. If he had any reasons for believing so, I was unaware of them, and you know the old saying: Sins you don't know about, don't count. Even if I did not like the editor, I do like the paper. I am not one of those who hold the children responsible for the sins of their fathers.

The package I was asked to give you concerns the *Figaro*. The message I was asked to pass on concerns you. I am not sure that it would have interested you. I have carried out my double commission, so let that be an end of it.

I am not Villemessant and I am not Turenne. The greater the danger, the braver I am.

You know my address. If one day the bravery I knew you possessed ever returns, choose the time, come armed, come in large numbers. You will always be welcome.

Yours sincerely,

COUNTESS LIONEL DE CHABRILLAN

A few days later I met Charles Edmond, who was then in charge of the serials section in the *Press*. I told him I had written some novels and that I would be very pleased if he could place one. He replied that there was a big backlog at the *Press*, but he could put me in contact with Michel Lévy, one of the best publishers in Paris.

He gave me such a glowing recommendation that Michel Lévy bought *The Gold Robbers*.[7] That's how it came about that I owed one of the happiest things that has ever happened to me to Charles Edmond and Michel Lévy. I can't describe everything I felt the day my first novel, *The Gold Robbers*, went on sale. It had to be a success, so that Lionel wouldn't scold me for having gone into this new venture in the public arena without telling him about it—a venture that could do me so much harm. I admit that I acted as I did out of a pressing need for money, and not for any idea of fame.

The big names of the Parisian press were kind to me. I shall include here some of the articles I sent to my dear Lionel. They made me very proud and happy, especially on his account. I shall never forget those who helped me so much to go beyond what I was so that I could rise a little to his level.

'The *Press*, 16 May, 1857

It is to the publisher Michel Lévy that we owe the release of a novel, a history, a study, a document. Call it one or all of these names, and you will be right. It is *The Gold Robbers* by Madam de Chabrillan. Those who do not know the author will read the whole of *The Gold Robbers* with unflagging curiosity.[8] Those who have read her memoirs and who know Madam de Chabrillan should be doubly satisfied: with the book itself and with the worthy aims of the author.

Only a woman's mind could have conceived such an undertaking. Madam de Chabrillan has set the characters of her novel in that distant land Australia, which she has experienced for herself and from whence she has just returned. It is a land where poverty struggles, angry and disillusioned, against uncontrolled and insatiable wealth; where the fierce energy of murder is pitted against the heroism of noble sentiments.

Max is an outlaw of a kind that would not be found even in the oldest traditions of our civilized Europe. He is attractive, wild, helpful, a cut-throat, a thief and a spendthrift; disdaining the tricks of civilized thieves and putting his trust in the new world revolver.

Mélida, his melancholy victim, Emeraude, Dr Ewans [*sic*] and his wife make up a family of an English type that the author has observed very well and depicted in serene colours that maintain a gentle calm through these terrible scenes.

Mélida's death and her funeral on board ship are told with a feeling and emotion that touch the reader. The style is simple and elegant, the narrative is fast-moving and the dialogue lively.

There is no sentimentality, no recourse to that romantic flirtatiousness that is a weakness of so many works written by women. Madam de Chabrillan has lived in contact with this civilization that has its beginnings in greed and violence.

She has known many dangerous situations, but never the slightest feeling of terror. She has sought two titles: that of countess and that of writer. She has won them both.

NESTOR ROQUEPLAN'[9]

'*Figaro*, 17 May 1857

The publisher Michel Lévy is currently offering my readers *The Gold Robbers* by Madam C. de Chabrillan.

Public curiosity aroused by the author's name will be amply satisfied by some of the chapters of this novel. There is an affecting depiction of the miner's life in Australia, some stirring scenes and appealing characters.

Generally speaking, however, the plot is somewhat disjointed and weaknesses of style are not infrequent.

All things considered, in whatever way this child of the imagination may have been conceived, let us not forget these lines by Musset:

'It's a very good effort, just to have produced one.'[10]

J. HUBAN'

'*Monte-Cristo*, 28 May 57

Firstly, *Madame Bovary*, a novel by Flaubert.

Another work of a quite opposite kind, but most extraordinary, has just been published by the same firm.

It is *The Gold Robbers* by Madam de Chabrillan.

She is a courageous soul, Madam de Chabrillan: one of those creatures that God has destined for dedication and struggle.

Her stay in Melbourne was both of these at the same time. During the four years when she was 5000 leagues away from France, by dint of enormous sacrifice and relentless application, she took up her education again, or rather she undertook her whole education from the beginning. Not only did she learn English, but she also relearned French, which was, in our opinion, a far more difficult thing.

In the end, she returned to France with four or five novels, making twelve or fifteen normal-sized volumes.

The first of these novels—if a book so excitingly realistic that you would think the author had witnessed every scene can really be called a novel—the first of these novels has just been published under the title of *The Gold Robbers*. Our praise can be expressed in these two lines: it took us only two nights to devour this volume of 5000 words. For two nights I saw the dawn come up while I was still reading *The Gold Robbers*.

I felt as though I were reading a novel by poor Ferry, *The Trapper* or *Castal the Indian*.[11] The same energy in the characterization, the same life in the characters, the same feverish activity in the plot. Both writers have been eye-witnesses, and being able to see is a tremendous thing when one is a gifted observer.

In the *Gold Robbers* there is an unusual combination of the fearsome and the graceful. There is nothing more fearsome than the characters of the cut-throat and Max, nothing more graceful than the silhouettes of Mélida, Emeraude and Louisa.

The first two women are English vignettes; the third a drawing by Greuze.[12]

In the midst of all this, there is a mare and a dog that become as interesting to the reader as human beings. I nearly forgot a little girl who comes into the world in mid-ocean. She is called Jewel and is worthy of her name, should the name Jewel be translated as *pearl* or *diamond*.

If you are among those who like fast-moving descriptions, deep and soul-searing emotions, read *The Gold Robbers*.

Ah! when women decide to get involved . . . !

ALEXANDRE DUMAS'

'Revue de Paris, 15 August 1857

The Gold Robbers
LAURENT PICHAT

Well! We are not embarrassed to say it. Even though one does not discern a well-trained hand in this book, it betrays some uncertainty— let us be honest—some awkwardness in the means of expression, in the linking of the various episodes, there is in this novel an intelligence, or rather a quite perfect conception of dramatic motivation. The episodes are so fast-moving, so violent, and Australian society—strange, aggressive, wild and yet civilized to the point of corruption—is so well depicted that one can easily excuse a few defects, a few faults due only to inexperience, and give unqualified praise to the imagination and feeling portrayed in this book. Doubtless this volume is no masterpiece, but it will be among the most moving and interesting works published this year.'

'*Almanach de la littérature*, 1858

JULES JANIN[13]

A word if you please about a book entitled *The Gold Robbers*. This is a real book.

It is written in a lively, energetic style that is very simple and very true to life.

It is definitely a book that bears the stamp of that energy and inspiration that women rarely come in contact with, but once they have found it, this eloquence, this driving force are irresistible.

The author of *The Gold Robbers* is indeed a woman. She formerly had two names and these two names were famous. Today she is known as Madam the Countess de Chabrillan, and one would search her second work in vain trying to find a single trace of what she first wrote during her heady, easy-going days. Only a very gifted and intelligent woman can transform herself, redeem herself by her intelligence, give up the free and easy life and win an honourable place among the distinguished women and good writers of her time.'

I received a host of compliments and some affectionate and encouraging letters. In one of them, Alexandre Dumas *fils* gave me a charming analysis of my book to prove that he had read it with interest.[14]

Murger assures me that my lack of erudition will be a great advantage to me. Given the fact that every idea has already been used, a writer who knows the good authors thoroughly always fears being taken for a plagiarizer. He wastes his life searching for something different; he wants to make a name for himself and he becomes obsessed with a single idea.

—I have never got away from *La Bohème*, he added, and I fear I may never be able to.[15] So, dear comrade, don't be upset by it. Having done what you have done, one can do everything!

As I was showing him everything I had written, he took his hat and raised it to me, saying:

—If I had been able to build up as much as that, I would not write another word for the rest of my life.

—Why?

—Because I would have made my fortune.

—But when one has a golden pen like yours . . .

—Many a time I would have exchanged it for a steak and chips. But that's enough, I don't want to put you off the profession. If you ever want an opinion or advice, don't hesitate to ask me. Having absolutely no energy myself, I like and admire those who have as much of it as you.

With all these articles, this encouragement, these kind and affectionate words, I should have been the proudest and happiest of women. Yet I had no illusions about my real worth and I promised myself to increase my willpower and redouble my efforts to be worthy of what I had been given as an advance on my future merit.

Unfortunately, everything I had done was useless. I had to rewrite it all, and usually four times rather than once. I set to and worked night and day. Days, weeks and months passed by unnoticed, which was just as well, as my court case was proceeding desperately slowly.

My health continued to deteriorate, but work won out over any sort of pain. This feverish activity gained me quite a lot of goodwill. Despite the satisfaction that came from my work, I was tormented by not being able to make more progress in our personal affairs, when I received this letter from Lionel.

'Melbourne, 4 September 1856

My darling wife,

I have just learned that a fast ship is leaving on the 14th for Ceylon.

I can't describe to you, my dear Céleste, how sad and how anxious I am, and I constantly have to recall your last words as you left—*You must have confidence!*—to keep despair at bay.

If you knew how full of love my heart is, you would understand what I am suffering. I would have given up the whole world, so that you would love me as I love you. Think of how dreadful it must be for me so far away from you. But enough of that. I don't want to give way to black thoughts.

I am sending you my work on Australia. I think it will serve a useful purpose. Take it to Mr de Girardin, who will tell you what he thinks of it.

My life here is much the same. I spend as little time in town as I can and come back quickly to Saint Kilda.

Marie has a baby who looks like a little monkey. Bob drinks too much and I suspect that he may beat his wife. Well, this is what she wanted, against his wishes and certainly against ours.

I have not gone to bed once without saying a fervent prayer to God for you. I hope He has granted it and that your voyage has been a short and happy one.

In the midst of the Paris whirl, will you sometimes miss your wooden hut in Saint Kilda and the long days of peace you often spent alone?

Through you I have known much happiness, and if it had not been for business worries, our life together here would have been paradise.

It's already almost six weeks since you left!'

'19 September

I am so miserable that I scarcely dare take up my pen for fear of making you miserable too.

I reproach myself bitterly for having let you leave. I am afraid, yes afraid, that the very long voyage you've just made and under such uncomfortable circumstances might make you too apprehensive to come back. I am afraid that this life at the other end of the earth, which pleases me because you seem to belong to me more truly and completely here, may not be enough to make you happy. By letting you leave, I have broken the vow I make to God and to myself not to part from you for a single day of my life. Everything makes me anxious, even my dreams!

For both our sakes, my darling wife, do pay attention to the kind of life you lead in Paris. There are so many people who would be only too glad to cause me pain . . . I do hope that seeing Paris again does not make you regret the task you undertook in marrying me. Everything passes, everything is forgotten, everything fades away, but a love like mine never fades and all it asks is the satisfaction of seeing you happy. Every single thought I have is for you, whether near or far. I swore to God to devote my whole life to you, and my happiness is in keeping that vow.

I don't see anyone and only leave St Kilda to go to the consulate. Time alone can make up for all the harm these wretched business affairs have done me.

Does Solange remember me? Tell her that despite my gruffness, I have and have always had a deep and fatherly affection for her. She will share in a fortune that is uncertain at the moment, but I am optimistic, as there is always the future . . . Poor child! You love her, so doesn't it go without saying that I love her too?

Don't forget to remember me to your mother.

Goodbye, my dearest wife. Think of the man who has dedicated his whole life to you, who only lives through you and for you, and who deserves that you should love him just a little, as he loves you so much! On the 7th January at midday, send me a loving thought: it's our wedding anniversary. At the same time here, I shall send you all my wishes, all my desires and all my thoughts. Don't forget, from 11 o'clock to midday to shut yourself away alone for an hour to think of me. Our thoughts are sure to cross.

Yours until my dying day,

LIONEL'

After reading this letter I just wanted to fly away. For a moment I thought of going back immediately, leaving everything unfinished, but on reflection I realized that it would be folly to have made such a long and arduous voyage only to be faced with the same problems again. However, I could not resign myself to the idea of being separated from Lionel any longer.

I went to visit the Count de Lesseps, the acting minister, and asked him whether the notification of leave granted to my husband had already been sent.[16] The count received me extremely courteously, but told me:

—Your husband has only been in the colonies for three years. You need five years' service to be eligible for leave and even then . . .

—But I had been promised . . . I have told my husband . . .

—That is unfortunate. It was not up to me . . .

I begged him.

—You are making a very difficult request.

—But it's not impossible?

—I shall see. I shall do what I can.

—I am very grateful to you.

—I can't promise anything.

—One can still hope . . .

A few days later I received another letter containing the notification of leave, and this time it was official. My joy knew no bounds. I wrote a long letter to Lionel which I closed with these words: 'Come to me. First of all I need you, and then so do our affairs. I shall be very happy to go back with you!'

My joy was short-lived. A big tear fell on the seal of that letter which would not be answered for five or six months. I really don't know what would have become of me had it not been for my work, in which I immersed myself more and more each day. I felt I was living between two worlds: I had to turn my back on the first, and as the second had turned its back on me, I had cut myself off from it.

My debtor's father has just died, so my financial affairs are taking a different turn. If I could pay off everything we owe, we would still have hope and work, and one can go far with them.

I have received another letter from Lionel, begun on the 8th January 1857. It opens with a host of reproaches, all the more bitter for being unjust. While reading the first three pages, I thought my eyes would dissolve with the flood of tears I shed. He continues his letter on the twelfth.

'My darling wife, forgive me for what you have just read. I am sending it to you anyway, just to show you what my distress would make me do if you ever left me. Thinking you had arrived long ago and having no word from you, I was going out of my mind, yes, quite out of my mind.

At last I received one dated the 29th November and the 2nd December last. It's all clear to me now. Please forgive me! At last my poor heart feels some relief knowing you are in Paris.

As soon as I can see to your interests and your future, I intend to make up for my past failure. I have been unfortunate and wanted to do too much too soon.

My previous letters have all the advice and information I wanted to give you, so there is no need to repeat them today. Do what you can and come back soon.

I shall try, with love and attention, to help you put up with the few years of exile we have to endure.

Here, apart from social and business contacts, I keep very much to myself. I made my official visit to the new governor when he arrived, but have not been to Toorack [*sic*] to see Lady Barthley [*sic*].[17]

Wertemberg remembers you very fondly. He has started to put on a show of ostentatious luxury. Now he only smokes five shilling cigars and wears patent leather shoes.

Cocotte is in fine form. The two dogs have died, and the chickens also. That is about all the news I have to give you. Come back soon, very soon.

If you have the money, take the Indian packet boat, which does the crossing in forty-five days. Don't forget to bring me back a little medallion with your photograph in it. I adore you!

It's very lucky that we did not have to sell the Saint Kilda property. It's increasing in value every day and by next summer it will easily be worth £2000 sterling. That nice allotment opposite us was sold last week for £150 per 100 square metres.

Give Solange a kiss from me and get people to talk to her about me from time to time.

Fond regards to your mother, and tell her again that in three years' time we shall be back to spend some time in France.

I shall write again soon. Come back quickly.

LIONEL'.

Come back quickly! That is easier said than done!

To plead our case against C. de C., I had engaged Maître Liouville. He is a celebrity, the President of the Bar. I had to visit him frequently to spur him into action, as he had been doing very little during the past few years. By now he was nothing but a famous name. Age, fatigue, and pain had worn out his considerable fine faculties, by all appearances at least.

While I was taking enormous pains to explain my affairs to him, he gave his attention to everything but my lawsuit. Before he said, 'Please sit down', he had his dressing gown, slippers and Greek cap brought to him, then a silver saucepan full of warm milk, which he proceeded to sip.

When I left him after the first visit, I went to my solicitor. It was he who had advised me to go to Maître Liouville to plead my case against the publishers La Librairie Nouvelle, to get an annulment of the contract for my *Memoirs*, which a powerful friend had had seized after the fifth volume. All the fears, complaints and recriminations I expressed to my solicitor were in vain. Maître Liouville was a demi-god to him.

—He does not listen to me, I exclaimed.

—He hears everything.

—He does not reply.

—He is saving his words for your defence.

—He is always hoarse.

—No matter. People listen to him with such attention. He is a great man, I tell you.

—Scarcely five feet tall.

—Do you think that genius is measured in feet and inches?

—No. I don't wish to appear disagreeable about your President of the Bar, but you exaggerate his worth. He has Maître Sénard against him.

—Oh! You are acting like a typical woman!

—Why?

—Appearances are everything to you. You have no conception of what a fine mind he has.

—I must admit that as far as I am concerned, it's imperceptible.

—You need fine phrases, high hopes!

—I don't deny it. They help you to be patient. Heaven knows, unhappiness always comes soon enough. You should get me another barrister.

—You can't be serious! Take a file away from Liouville—why, I would not do that for the Emperor.

—But would you do it for me?

—It's impossible. You will regret this lack of confidence in him.

—It's what I want.

A week later my case was heard. Maître Liouville took two little flasks from his pocket. He drank from each alternately several times then pleaded, to the letter, the very opposite case to the one he should have presented.

Maître Sénard won my publishers' suit without having even opened his mouth. As the seizing of my *Memoirs* had been a preventative measure, and on examination, having found that there were no serious reasons to ban them, I was ordered to give the rest of the manuscript to Messrs Jacottet and Bourdilliat, who wanted to bring out a second edition of the eight volumes in four.

—Well? I said to my solicitor as we left the courtroom. He had to agree that his dear master had declined. I confess that, as far as I was concerned, it was a very small consolation. As for Mr Liouville—he was very pleased with himself and received his fee with the aplomb of a man who is sure that it was well earned.

Having no doubt that Lionel would depart as soon as he received his leave notice, I started to look for a place for him to live comfortably for a few months. I decided on a small apartment in the Rue Ventadour, on the first floor, looking onto the courtyard. My great and famous friend, Adolphe Richard, was having me follow a treatment that gave me long hours of rest. I felt I was well on the way to recovery.

On receipt of my final corrected proofs, Michel Lévy has just paid me for the second edition of *The Gold Robbers* and has bought my second novel, *Sappho*.[18]

Father Mullois has come to see me several times. He spoke to me about a certain passage in my *Memoirs* concerning reformatories, which only increase the delinquency of the children sent there, and about the colony at Mettray.[19] This establishment only serves to illustrate my point, and people are taking a considerable interest in it.

I was very surprised to have had someone so pious as a reader. He informed me that it was His Majesty the Emperor who had pointed out to him the passages concerning the reformatories placed under his moral guardianship, and that he had read everything with great interest. He recommended some changes regarding certain admissions that I should only have made to my confessor . . . He urged me not to lose heart and to persevere. He has promised to come back and see me.

I no longer count my existence in years or months. I am well aware that I live from day to day. Let us hope Lionel does not linger too long!

'29 May 1857

My dear Céleste, my darling wife,

You must have received my letter dated 18th of last month, sent on the *Great Britain*, in reply to your four letters which arrived at the same time. Since you have obtained leave for me, I shall depart soon, but, as no one knows what might happen if I go, I shall sell everything except our curios and portraits.

Oh dear! I am being harassed by a group of sea captains who bore me with their affairs and who don't leave me a single moment to write to the person I hold dearest in all the world. So I shall close this letter, which is very short compared to everything in my heart that I'd like to say to you. But you know what is in my heart and that there is no room in it for anything but thoughts and memories of you. From the moment I knew I could be seeing you soon, I have been in a fever and can't sleep.

So goodbye. I shall see you soon, I hope. I love you.

LIONEL'

This letter helped a little to put my mind at rest, but the nervous tension that had kept me going until then suddenly relaxed, and I was forced to keep to my room first of all, and then to my bed.

Friends I had not seen for a long time came to see me and commiserate. Fiorentino was one of the first.

—Michel Lévy told me that you were ill, he said as he approached my bed, taking my hand like a doctor. Is there anything I can do for you, any service I can render? If you were happy and the centre of attention, I would have left you to your courtesans, but since you're alone, I thought you might need a friend, so here I am!

I was very grateful that he had taken the trouble to see me, as he was not usually very forthcoming with affection or thoughtful behaviour. However, the past faded completely from my memory, and I thanked him effusively for the friendship he showed me.

Every unexpected visit revealed my true situation a little more clearly. My illness was rapidly getting worse. The general opinion was that I had worked too hard: I had written an average of twelve to fifteen hours a day, writing then crossing out everything I had already done, only to do it all again. The work had made me feverish, delirious. It was a passion, like love, drink, gambling and it got worse and worse. There was scarcely a quiet moment that I did not use to start working again. My lamp burned all night. I lost sleep, appetite and strength, and could only revive them with large amounts of black coffee. My mind over-heated my blood. But Lionel would soon be arriving. I needed fame, money and heaven knows what else besides. I was mad . . .

In two months I wrote six bad plays, *Miss Pervel* [*sic*] *and the Emigrants*,[20] not to mention *Sappho*, which has just been published. It was on this subject that Michel Lévy came to see me. He looked morose as he said to me:

—Murger is furious with me because of you.

—Why?

—Because you showed him your contracts and I pay you fifteen centimes per volume while I pay him only ten.

—His novels have appeared in newspapers, while mine are unpublished.

—Yes, but his name is Murger.

—Then pay him a franc for them.

Michel began to laugh, saying:

—Just get better and don't show him your contracts.

I did not promise anything, and besides, this request came too late. I was so happy and so proud to have them that all my friends had seen, touched and read them.

Murger had written some affectionate inscriptions for me on his works, and as Lionel composed quite a lot of music, I had asked the author of *Musette* to write me some words for it.[21] He had promised them to me. I did not really think I would get them, but I used this pretext to write to him.

He arrived and began to laugh, saying:

—I haven't done them yet.

—I don't think they will ever be done. Anyway, it's your prose I am worried about, not your verse. What a false friend you are.

—Oh! What rot! he said, sitting down opposite me. (I was seated at the table.) These eggs aren't poisoned by any chance?

—No. I was not expecting you. You can eat some if you like.

—Are you getting better?

—Yes, I can get from my bed to the table. But I am furious with you!

—Oh! and for what reason?

—Because you made some remarks to Michel Lévy. They are quite true, but they could do me some harm and they won't do you any good at all.

—What! He told you ... Ah! men talk too much. We literary people really are a worthless lot. But don't become too sensitive. At the moment you are only in purgatory. One more success and you will be in hell.

—Well then, you must have been there for quite some time ...

—Yes. I loathe the work I have to do. When I look at my table and see the pen and paper I should be using, I feel seasick.

—How funny!

—It's not funny at all. You will see when it happens to you.

—Do write me some words. Your *Musette* is so pretty.

—I promise. You are not still angry with me over Michel Lévy, are you?

—A lot less, and I won't mind at all when I have a song for Lionel. It will give him so much pleasure to set some of your words to music.

—You are bribing me with flattery. Mr de Chabrillan has composed songs to all Musset's poems.

—Musset,[22] Roger de Beauvoir,[23] Théophile Gautier.[24] He needs great poets.

—I shall try. But look after yourself, and above all, take a lot of rest. I want to find you completely well when I come next time.

I admire Murger and I do like him very much, but his despondency worries me. What a contrast with my great friend Alexandre Dumas! . . . Murger makes me feel anxious, suspicious, lethargic. Alexandre Dumas gives me faith in myself, energy, zeal.

Mr de La Palme, C. de C.'s solicitor, has just written to me asking me to call at his office to settle our accounts. That makes me feel stronger again.

Yesterday he gave me 40 000 francs of capital plus interest and costs. I immediately went and paid Morel and Thiebaud, who had sold us the merchandise we lost in Calcutta. I paid off a mortgage on my house in Châteauroux. I shall only have 6000 francs left, but all the debts we owe in France will be paid.

Part Four:

Reunion and Final Parting

CHAPTER 15

Lionel on Leave

AS ONE piece of good luck is always followed by another, the next day I received a telegram from Marseilles:

'I have arrived from Australia. I will be in Paris at 7 tomorrow evening.
Count de Chabrillan'

It's impossible to describe the effect these few lines had on me. Feverish impatience was followed by convulsive nervous trembling, then such a feeling of faintness that I could scarcely think.

Nonetheless, the following day I went to the station, three hours before the train arrived. These three hours seemed an eternity. At last my husband was there, running towards me with his arms open wide and a smile on his lips, but he stopped short and the expression on his face changed.

—How you have changed, he said. Have you been very ill? You did not mention anything about it.

—Yes I have, but now you are here. I shall soon be better.

He obviously did not share my opinion, as he still looked worried and pensive.

In the carriage he asked me if I had any news of his sister Louise, the marquise de C.[1]

—She will give me a very bad reception, he added light-heartedly, but no matter. She has always been my favourite and I am really looking forward to giving her a brotherly kiss in spite of what she has said.

—Of course, I said to him very quietly. You were on your way here and you have not heard.

—Is she ill?

—You have already had so much suffering in your life. You must be strong, my dear Lionel.

—You are making me very apprehensive! I want to go and see her straight away.

—I am afraid you will not see her again in this life!

Lionel hid his face in his hands and tears slid between his fingers.

—She is dead, he sobbed, my Louise is dead, my poor Louise, without saying goodbye, without forgiving me. It's not possible.

I had learned of Madam de C.'s death on 1st February. I knew that far from forgiving her brother for having married me, she had completely disinherited him because of me. My husband's grief was so deep that I did not tell him anything about that, and we entered the Rue Ventadour in silence. He was weeping for a beloved sister and I was weeping to see him suffer so.

For the first time since our marriage, he turned away from my caresses and perhaps regretted having loved me. After a few hours, Lionel became aware of the pain he was causing me. He apologized, but it was too late; he had hurt me dreadfully.

I gave him a full account of everything I'd done regarding our mutual financial affairs and handed him the bills and receipts.

—I sold your house, fully furnished, he said, to Captain Las Cazas. That house is the only profitable business transaction we made in Australia. I have paid off everything back there. I am no longer in any-one's debt, except yours, and one day I shall pay you back everything. I have absolutely nothing left, but I still have my two arms. I shall try to get a better position.

He did not mention my books, but in the bottom of his trunk I found *The Gold Robbers* bound in leather with gold lettering on the spine, also *Sappho* with the pages freshly cut. He had bought it in Marseilles and read it on the way to Paris.

I sent for Solange, and they greeted each other so affectionately and exchanged so many hugs and kisses that I was almost jealous.

Had I continued to look after my health when Lionel arrived, the illness would have been caught in time and therefore been less serious. But far from admitting to being unwell, I took pains to hide the fact. I was so happy to go out with him, to accompany him everywhere!

He had written to his other sister on arrival, asking her permission to see her and embrace her again.[2] As fate would have it, I was the one who received the Marquise's reply, which I opened by mistake.

'I can forgive you, she wrote, but I do not wish to see you ever again. I no longer know you.'

In an instant, the memory of all the efforts and sacrifices I had made came flooding back in spite of myself. I withdrew into myself, dejected, crushed . . . It was my coup de grâce. I took to my bed, hoping never to leave it again!

The doctor who was called in spite of my protestations declared that I had acute bronchitis and general inflammation. I sent for Dr Ducholet, the doctor who attended my grandfather and my mother. He announced to Lionel that if I did not die very soon, I would be ill for a long time. After two months' treatment, having tattooed my chest and shoulders with vesicatories, frictions and castor oil, the doctors, not knowing what else to do, urged me to have a change of scene. It was decided that I should be taken to the Berry. A few days later I was worse. Lionel was distraught.

One night, feeling very ill, I asked him to come close to me and I made my confession to him, as I would have done to a minister of God.

—You are everything to me, I told him. If I have caused you pain, forgive me. I shall die through having tried too hard to do well; forgive me. When I am gone, everyone will hold you in high esteem again. Perhaps your sister will forgive you. But you will always love me, won't you? If they curse my name, you won't banish me from your heart and mind?

I gave him the Marquise's letter. He read it, then screwed it up. A look of anguish came over his face and heavy tears rolled down his cheeks. He kneeled close to my bed and said, clasping my hand:

—As God is my witness at this very moment, my dear Céleste, I have absolutely no regrets. When I learned that I had been disinherited, I felt a secret joy, because acceptance of that situation was another sacrifice I could make for you. The sister who is left does not want to see me. Perhaps one day she'll regret it. I can bear everything if only you are here with me, but if I lost you, you know, I would kill myself. So fight the things that trouble your mind, fight this illness. Your life is my life. Please look at me and talk to me about the future or I shall go out of my mind.

The next day they brought Solange to me and she did not return to the place where she was boarding. They took my furniture and my effects, and then they took me to Châteauroux in a wagon with a bed made up in it for me. Lionel looked as though he was following my funeral procession, and as everyone takes their hats off in the presence of death, the people of Châteauroux who had known me ten years earlier crossed themselves at the sight of this shadow of my former self going by. Madam Edouard Suard, that good, kind creature who had shown me friendship for and against everyone, could not hold back her tears. I realised that I was finished, or at least terminally ill.

When we arrived at Le Poinçonnet, I looked at myself in a mirror and I was frightened by my own image. My eyes were red and sunken in their sockets, my cheeks hollow and my lips had a bluish tinge. I was frightful to behold!

At that moment I became aware of the full extent of the devotion and love of the person who could say to such a sight: 'You are my whole life. I love you!' Then the dreadful idea came to me that it was all a sham, that they would be happy to see me die. I became sceptical, spiteful, full of hate. I clung onto life, and all my physical suffering paled into insignificance before the mental anguish that I could not overcome.

A few days after we had settled in, the parish priest in Le Poinçonnet came to see me. He gently prepared me for the idea of my imminent departure for the next world. During the night I had attacks of vomiting and dreadful pains in my left side. Dr Ruhe, the leading doctor in Châteauroux, said that he could not prescribe anything without first having spoken to the doctor who treated me in Paris. A telegram was sent to Dr Ducholet, who arrived after ten hours. I had only cried out once and the vomiting had not gone away. My face was covered with big yellow blotches. I was given three consecutive applications of leeches—fifty each time.

Lionel spent a fortnight at my bedside, most of it in prayer I can tell you, as his only remaining hope was in God. My mother made him take a little nourishment. If she had not done so, he would have allowed himself to starve to death. Nature worked a miracle for me. My time had not yet come! . . .

When Lionel saw that I was a little better, he said:

—My leave expires in a few days. I shall try to get another posting, somewhere in Europe, for you are in no state to return to Australia.

He left for Paris, where he wrote to me on 10 January 1858:

'My poor dear Céleste,

If I wasn't happy to know that you are now convalescing, I would have been in despair over the result of my applications. I have been refused any extension of my leave. I must go back there without waiting for another post to become vacant; if I don't, I shall have nothing at all. As this post is our only resource from now on, I cannot let it go. I hope to leave for Châteauroux tomorrow evening.

Look after yourself and don't do anything rash, I beg of you. I have spoken to the doctor. Your recovery will take a long time, but the danger is over. However, you will need a great deal of care and a lot of peace and quiet. There's only one proof of your love that I need, and that is for you to look after your health, which is the thing I hold most dear in all the world.

Tuesday, 5 o'clock

I am unable to leave this evening. I have an appointment tomorrow morning at the Ministry. I shall go and see Dr Ducholet this evening.

I love you with all my heart,

Lionel'

I did not understand the meaning of Lionel's letter. I was so weak that I could not really take anything in. I was suffering less, but suffering still, and I was dreadfully afraid of having more of those terrible pains that had tortured me for so long.

Lionel came back from Paris. He was close to me, yet I had scarcely the strength to reach out my hand to him. I heard everything as though in a dream, but without being able to reply. After talking at length about this and that, he finally came to the point and told me that he would have to leave in July, because he only received half-pay during his time in France and he wanted to earn more to cover my needs. He put on a confident air to give me heart; actually he was happy to feel freed a little from having to watch over me. I don't know, but I remember that I was very hurt at his apparent acceptance of the situation. Oh, what a horrible thing it is to have lost control of one's life. I had only one hope left, and that was to die before he left. He guessed what I was thinking, and his smile changed to tears.

—Necessity knows no law . . . , he said leaning towards me. You know very well that I shall leave my life and my heart here with you. Your health was all the fortune and happiness I wanted. You will need time to regain it, but I am certain you will. You must live to be the shining star of my old age! We shall talk of our sufferings and our joys. You know, I nearly went mad during your illness; now I shall leave with an easy mind. You will be joining me soon, or I shall be back before long. I am thinking about engaging in some new business ventures that I hope will be successful this time.

He was by nature eternally optimistic and his worries were fleeting. I had very often seen things from an entirely opposite point of view from him, but I did not like to disillusion him. However, as chance would have it, I was nearly always right. The very name of Melbourne made me shudder. I was haunted by the idea that one of us would never leave there. As in all likelihood it would be me, I said nothing. Besides, he thought my dreams or my visions were madness. However, the fever had caused such cruelly persistent ones that I asked him for pity's sake not to go back to Australia.

—How would we live?, he asked me. It's not in my nature to retire here in the country. I adore you, Céleste, but I like excitement, travel. Besides, here we would be nothing, but over there we are somebody.

He loved the sea as he had loved hunting.

Towards the end of July, I managed to get up and tested my strength by going from one piece of furniture to the next. Lionel started laughing as he said to me:

—There, you are a big girl now, but you have not got your sea legs yet. Never mind, that will come. Lean on my arm, Countess. Come and take a turn about the garden. I have looked after your flowers. Then he added with a kiss: If you had not been so ill, I would pay you a compliment. You are prettier than you have ever been.

I was white as a sheet and nothing but skin and bone. In the end I took several steps, supported by Lionel and my mother. They seemed very pleased. I was the only one who felt a secret despair.

I asked him if he really would have the heart to leave me behind in the Berry.

—You would certainly have the heart to follow me.

—But not enough to leave you. Take me with you anyway.

—You are talking nonsense, my poor love. You have a long convalescence ahead of you; any relapse would be fatal. I don't want you to run the risk of that happening. Your mother and Solange will stay here with you. Now don't insist, Céleste dear. My mind is quite made up on that score. I want you to stay here until you are completely recovered. I don't want to kill you, after all I went through to save you.

My mother begged me not to insist any further. Dr Ducholet had confirmed her opinion that I was not even capable of undertaking a week's voyage. I had to accede to their wishes.

We still had a few more happy evenings to spend together. Lionel was amazed at the way I played chess. He who claimed to be, who indeed was reputed to be, a good player of this very captivating but difficult game that he had learned thoroughly over twenty years could not understand how I could have learned it so well in a few months that he was checkmate three times out of five. He is both a very good and a very bad player. Whenever he lost an important piece, he became angry with himself and with me. He called himself an idiot or me a bad player, and if I had the misfortune to laugh, he got up and went out into the garden in a huff. But that only lasted the time it took to smoke a cigar. He would come in again laughing, kiss me and apologize, then bring me his chessboard, saying:

—I must get my own back. Be prepared—I shall checkmate you in two moves. It was nearly always the opposite that happened.

One thing that may appear strange to others, for I have often been surprised by it myself, is that I learn more asleep than awake. While I am asleep, I work out what I could not understand earlier . . . In spite of my genuine desire to please Lionel by learning chess so that he could play with me, when I arrived in France I was a much weaker player than he. But during my illness, my mind must have been dwelling on it, because I knew moves and rules that no one had ever taught me.

12 July 1858

Alas! the fatal moment has arrived. Lionel has just left Le Poinçonnet. He has gone . . . alone, and I am here with my nose pressed to the window pane, vainly hoping he will turn back. We cried all night! But what use are tears when fate is so firmly set against us? Death must have decided to come between us. Well! Let it take me as soon as possible for I am tired of suffering!

From that moment, any small interest I had in myself ceased to exist. With tears in my eyes, I touched or gazed at every object Lionel possessed. I walked where his feet had trod. He was the subject of all my conversations with my mother. She was very fond of him, but she could not hide the joy she felt at being able to keep me by her side. For me, this was more upsetting than calming. I defended him constantly as though he were seriously under attack.

My mother has a good deal of natural intelligence, but it has had so little cultivation that she often says things that are painful to both Lionel and myself without realizing that she is doing it, because she is obsessed with the idea of preventing me from going back to the other end of the world. But I am going to leave as soon as possible, even if they have to carry me away. I could not live here, I am bored to death. If I have to die, I prefer to be with him when it happens.

Every day I receive more or less interesting letters and two little illustrated newspapers. Lionel had taken out a subscription for me, mainly to please my mother. She understands nothing of other people's politics; she has her own. She is fanatically Parisian. The only people she approves of are those who make her Paris more beautiful. In her opinion, the greatest kings are those who have had the finest monuments built. As for rioters and barricaders, as she calls them, they are *ravagers* whose only aim is to ruin others so that they can get rich themselves. She maintains that all *political writers* are *warmongers*. When the parish priest comes to see us, she plays piquet with him, and while they play she elaborates upon her anti-clerical theories, which don't seem to appal him. But when she has finished, he tries by every possible means to prove her wrong. Whereupon my mother withdraws into her private thoughts.

So all we received were little illustrated newspapers. *The Thief* is her favourite. It's interesting and quite well done. Its editor in chief is Mr de Bragelonne, a very distinguished man, who has never been involved in scandal or blackmail. When I opened his paper I saw written in very fine roundhand on the wrapper:

'To the Countess de Mogador at the Château du Poinçonnet.'

I took the newspaper wrapper, which could have fallen into Lionel's hands, and I sent it to Mr de Bragelonne, accompanied by a letter that made a great impression on him, for he replied by return mail that the sole culprit of this unspeakable blunder was the man who wrapped the papers and that he intended to dismiss him.

I replied that this excuse was sufficient, that I did not wish the death of the sinner and that I requested him to keep his employee, in spite of what he had done.

I had learned that Murger had at last received a decoration. I had written a letter of congratulations to him and he had replied with a charming letter that pleased me greatly. One piece of good fortune follows another as does misfortune. It's very rare that they don't come in twos. I was re-reading Murger's letter, which seemed to me to have overtones of sadness, when Mr Dumas was announced.

—Dumas! Which Dumas? I asked, as I had no idea that it could be my great friend.

—Me, Dumas! said the author of *The Three Musketeers*, pushing the half-open door. Are there any others?

—There is your son, I said running to kiss him. How lovely to see you! I have often thought of you, you know . . . But I have been so ill!

—So I found out, and I have just been told that the *cat* has left (that is the name he called Lionel). I did not come especially to see you, as my daughter lives in the Berry with her . . . her wretched husband, but I took advantage of the occasion. Here you are quite recovered. When are you coming back to Paris? You know that my house, my person and my advice are entirely at your service.

My mother, who was working on a tapestry on a frame near the window, had stopped still, her neck stretched forward. She was gazing at the master of masters with her large staring eyes that gave her a rather mean look.

—Mama? Dumas said to me.

I indicated that he was correct.

—Good day Madam, he said walking over to her and cordially extending his hand. My mother was so flattered by this honour that, in her haste to reply, she knocked over the frame and the basket of tapestry wools onto Alexandre's feet. He gallantly tried to help her pick them up but only got them all in a tangle.

—Ah! You did better work than this the day you had your daughter. I don't know anyone like her . . .

Mother replied:

—You are my favourite author, you . . . Your books are the only ones I really like. I know them all . . . She then proceeded to recite the titles of all his books. I could see the moment coming when she would start to describe them to him.

I invited him to come on a tour of the property with me, and we went and sat in a grove of trees completely covered with clematis planted a few years earlier by my dear Lionel. We talked about all sorts of things. I showed him Murger's letter, then the subject returned to me and what I was going to do. He would not hear of me going back to Australia.

—You should even use all your influence to prevent the *cat* from staying there, he said. Those climates are impossible for energetic, intelligent people, who wear themselves out in only a few years. They are only good for races that do no physical or mental work, who sleep during the day and rest at night, without a sorrow or a care, and even then . . . My poor friend Dillon has just come back here to die after five years of consular hard labour in the colonies. I have seen many others die in the same circumstances.

He realized that he was upsetting me and changed the subject.

—I hope you are not going to bury yourself here, he said, our Berry is about as lively as the catacombs. It's a pity that I didn't know you earlier. We might have loved each other?

—But I don't think anyone could love and admire you more than I.

—Yes, I am aware of that . . . but it's not what I mean . . . I know myself. Still, perhaps at some time in the future . . .

—No, never. Whatever happens . . . and I shall tell you why, if you will permit me to speak frankly without making you angry.

—Me, angry with you? he said, taking my hand. I don't work against my own best interest, and whatever you say to me I shall certainly not deprive myself of the pleasure of looking at you while I listen. All right then! Put me in the dock, he added, stretching out on his iron seat and pressing his hands to his broad chest. If this is going to take you some time, I shall stay for dinner and we can divide the proceedings into two parts. Keep me something nice for the dessert.

—You are a danger to all women, my great friend. They admire you, run after you and love you as you well deserve, but you are capricious, changeable. Many loves have come and gone without leaving very deep impressions on your generous heart. Constant work has been the reason for it, and it's very fortunate for our dear France, as you are and always will be one of her greatest glories. For you, loving means nothing, and being loved very little more. You change mistresses or deceive them with a facility that proves that you don't really care. Each of them must have had the pride to believe she could hold on to you. I would have too, and I would have been mistaken, just as they were. You have a need for diversion, the unknown, to seek new emotional experiences. The number of your conquests provides you with subjects for your conversation and your novels. You think aloud, which makes you dangerously indiscreet for anyone who loves you. Everyone sees you as an ordinary mortal, living exactly as all men do; for me you are a demi-god, and under no circumstances do I want to see my idol in nightcap and underwear . . . You must think all this quite absurd, but it's so firmly fixed in my mind that having known you before, well before my marriage, we would never have been more than good friends—now more than ever.

—It means quite simply that you find me unattractive to the point of repugnance . . .

—It means exactly what I said, and you will hurt me terribly if, in future, you treat me like your usual women friends. I am exceedingly proud of your friendship. I would like people to know that it's honest and disinterested. Then I shall be able to receive you and visit you, without being taken for a sultana in your ever-changing little harem. I am well aware, having often experienced it, that friendship between a man and a woman is very difficult to sustain, but what would be the good of exceptions if we, who are not like everyone else, acted just like them?

—When the devil decides to become a hermit, he said with a laugh, he preaches to all and sundry . . .

—Then I shall see a procession of all your former favourites and I shall say to myself: my reign has been less brilliant but it will last longer, and I am certain to do my utmost to make it withstand the test of time. Does that suit you?

—Yes! and if I stray a little from this plan of action, you must not hold it against me: I am so used to courting women . . . out of politeness . . .

—Rest assured, I shall call you to order.

During dinner we spoke of Lionel, travel, literature, the theatre. The time went very quickly. At ten o'clock he took the carriage to the Hôtel de la Promenade in Châteauroux.

My mother had not dared speak a word to him during dinner, but when he had left she asked me a host of questions.

—He must be very rich, Mr Dumas, she said sitting down opposite me, a sure sign that she wanted to chat, he earns such a lot of money!

—He would be very rich, it's true, if he were not so soft-hearted, but he is more generous than you could ever imagine. People take advantage of it; he would give you anything.

—Is he extravagant?

—I said he was generous, which is not the same thing. Extravagant people waste their money without being of use to anyone, but when one gives away the money one earns to oblige a friend, to help a person in need, that is generosity. He is kind to the point of it becoming a weakness. He never speaks badly of anyone.

—I have been told that he didn't write all his novels himself and that he sometimes copied others.[3]

—Dumas does not need to copy anyone. Sometimes, to oblige a failed writer who would not get ten francs from a rough manuscript, he gives him a few louis; he changes the characters, the language, the plot: he does a beautiful embroidery on a bad canvas, and the work is certainly his own! So much for that. And now I am going to bed. Goodnight, I shall see you in the morning.

CHAPTER 16

Letters from Lionel at Sea

THE next morning I went out into the garden to watch for the postman; I could see him approaching from a long way off. He gave me a letter from Lionel.

'On board the *Wye*, 20 July 1858

There comes a time when pain and sorrow have broken your heart so badly that your whole being falls into a state of emotional exhaustion akin to madness. During the forty-eight hours since we left Marseilles, I have been staring at the long wake trailing behind the ship, and all my memories, all my life's hopes and dreams turn back to you. But enough of that! I don't want to begin by feeling sorry for myself. I love you, I have said it in every possible way, with every beat of my heart.'

'Malta, 21 July 1858

We dropped anchor at Malta yesterday at seven o'clock. We were due to meet the London packet boat there.

I hope you will be happy at Le Poinçonnet and that you will get well again. That is very important. If I knew what would make you happy, I should gladly give my life to get it. For the sake of the love I have for you, do take good care of yourself.

What a lovely voyage this would have been if we were together. I should have been so happy trying to help you feel and appreciate the wonderful natural world of the tropics, so fertile and luxuriant. Ah! the sun, the flowers and the fruit . . . God chose so well when he put the first man in Ceylon!'

'On board the *Colombia*, Friday 23 July 1858

The packet boat from England, the *Colombia*, arrived yesterday during the night. We have only had a few minutes to get up, pack our things and change ships.

Until now, we have had a fair sea, but also stifling heat that I am not accustomed to and that you would never have withstood.

There are only ten passengers bound for Australia. I am delighted. We are very comfortable.

I was looking forward to such a wonderful time with you on this voyage. It was not God's will and I can't tell you how sad and lonely I feel.

I hope you will give me lengthy reports on the state of your health. I shall take pleasure in receiving others, but real happiness in receiving these. Spend a good deal of time in your garden, with your flowers. That is the best thing for you. Don't do anything too strenuously, for you need rest of both body and mind. Life is short enough as it is, without using it up with pointless exertion.

When shall I see you again? I am under no illusion: my task is indeed a difficult one. Oh! Life is awful when one is isolated like this. But enough! Let us not be downhearted, but rather think of the happiness we shall feel when we see each other again.'

'Saturday, 24 July

We are making very good time and will be in Alexandria tomorrow. I long for the moment when we arrive in Melbourne, to be nearer the day when I shall have news of you. Your letters will be my only moments of happiness. I pray God that they will bring me only good news of your health.

If you need money in January, contact Fleury Hérard. He will have some available for you. I don't want you to skimp on anything that can make you more comfortable. For my part, I promise to live like a true bachelor, putting money away shilling by shilling. To begin with, I have decided to cut down on cigars.

We have only two women passengers and I have not spoken to either of them. One is leek-colour and tuberculous, and the other is carrot-coloured and consumptive—both physically ill-favoured and totally without charm or grace. As for the men—they have nothing to recommend them. The company I keep consists of an old man called

Dreutler, a Sydney businessman whom I knew in 1852. Master Dreutler is a nice fellow.

I promised to tell you all about my travel adventures, but that will not amuse you very much at all. Well, your imagination will just have to invent what I can't describe to you.'

'Cairo, 28 July

I spent the whole of the 25th in Alexandria and did not leave for Cairo until five in the evening. We are staying here until we know that the packet boat from Australia has arrived at Suez. It's already two days late. This is annoying because living in the hotel is very expensive, and besides, I don't want to stop in Egypt for so long without being able to visit the places of such historical interest, especially for the French. So, from the morning of my arrival, i.e. the morning of the 26th, I have been going around the town and its environs by donkey.

Yesterday I visited the pyramids and the banks of the Nile. Today I went around the Turkish and Arab bazaars. I did not want to leave them without buying you something, so I am going to leave a little parcel of Turkish slippers for you at the French consulate. I spent the day with the consul, Mr de la Porte. He seems to be on very good terms with the pasha.

My darling wife, how I regret the fact that you are not with me on this voyage. I should have been so happy to be your history teacher in this cradle of the world. Still, I don't give up hope of you coming to Melbourne, and then we can do a full trip which will give us things to talk about in our old age.

The Egyptian donkeys amaze me. There are thousands of them. Everyone has a donkey and they cost up to 2500 francs. There are some very fine Arab horses, but if you pay 1000 francs for a horse, that is a fairly good price. At the door of every hotel, there are fifty or sixty donkeys waiting to take travellers for a ride. It's a very pleasant way of getting about. After the donkeys, come herds of camels, which are plentiful.

You have probably seen in the papers that there is a kind of general war being waged at the moment by the Mohammedans against the Christians. They massacred a large number of them on the shores of the Red Sea. They did the same at Latakia in Turkey.[1]

Here in Cairo the town is full of troops. The Mohammedans

cannot forgive the sultan for his alliance with the English or French Christians.[2] At least, that is what they are all saying.

The French Consul had urged me not to visit the bazaars and the Turkish quarters. I think he wanted to exaggerate the danger, as I went everywhere and I had very pleasant talks with old Muslims, who, it must be admitted, had fought against France. I found one, actually the one from whom I bought the slippers, who was at the battle of Cairo. He showered me with tobacco, snuff, rosewater and coffee, repeating: 'Me real Turk, you good Frenchman.'

I don't want to go into detail about Cairo; I want to keep it a surprise for when we make this voyage together. I have not yet been able to form any idea of oriental women. They all have their faces covered and it's no use them giving you sidelong glances, you can't take the chance of making a mistake. I am speaking in general here; for my part, I am out of the running.

I take cold baths in rooms attached to the hotel which have nothing oriental at all about them.'

'On board the *Australasian*, 5 August 1858

Last Saturday at four o'clock in the morning, the telegraph informed us in Cairo that the packet boat from Australia had arrived at Suez and that we had twenty minutes to get to the railway station.

I suffered so badly from the heat in Cairo that I had not slept a wink for four days and nights, and I hoped to find some cool air on board to help me recover.

The whole of that Saturday was sheer torture, especially during the five hours when we were all crowded in together crossing the desert. At five in the evening I was on board again, on the *Australasian*, a huge ship and a veritable furnace. I have been here for five days and have not yet been able to go down to my cabin.

How aptly named the Red Sea is, as it's fiery red: there is not the slightest little breeze, and the thick fog that covers it at night is a kind of burning mist that dries out your chest. Of a morning I stand under the pump when they are swabbing the decks, for the sea water is warm. I spend every night lying in a corner of the deck.

Do you know, my darling wife, what occupies all the thoughts my mind is capable of? Gazing at the sky I wait, I search for shooting stars, for I like to fancy that if you wish or think something during those few seconds, the shooting star, that soul travelling in space, will take your

Canvas Town, between Prince's Bridge and South Melbourne (De Gruchy & Leigh, La Trobe Picture Collection, State Library of Victoria)

Melbourne in the 1850s: Prince's Bridge, opened 1850 (top);
Old Government House, Toorak (centre); Theatre Royal, Bourke Street (bottom).
(I. Selby, A Pioneer Memorial History*)*

The railway station at St Kilda (Illustrated Journal of Australasia, *March 1858*)

St Kilda beach, 1857 (Newsletter of Australasia, August 1857)

wish under its protection or your thought under its wing and carry it straight to its destination. How many thoughts and fond wishes I have entrusted to them; how many times I have repeated: 'Céleste, I love you! Céleste, be happy!'

I take my courage in both hands—the daylight will appear before the sun has taken away the small amount of moisture that the swabbing of the decks affords us—I hold my handkerchief to mop my brow in one hand and my pen in the other. And so I continue my scribbling which you will have to try to decipher.

Never has my heart has been so full of love for you. You have been my only reason for living.

I must leave you, as I can no longer hold the pen. I can only say: Take care of yourself, think sometimes of me, whose every thought is of you.

By the way! In Cairo I was introduced to two young giraffes—a male and a female—two delightful animals only a few months old. Their owners offered to sell them to me. For a moment I considered that hut in Le Poinçonnet where the boars used to be, but then I thought that as the giraffes are a dozen or so feet tall at eight or ten months, they would not be altogether comfortable there!'

'Aden

Aden is situated in the middle of a kind of peninsula on the Arabian coast at the entrance to the Red Sea. In 1849, on the pretext of establishing a coal depot there, the English bought 100 sq. metres of land at the extreme point of the peninsula from an Arab chief. They put on a sentinel to guard the coal, then built a first fort to guard the guard. Finally, from guard to guard and fort to fort, today the peninsula has become cut off and separated from Arabia by a series of fortifications. Today Aden is a fortified town that can well compare with Gibraltar and Malta.[3]

Aden commands the entrance to the Red Sea and is the key to it. The road that leads from the beach to Aden is a magnificent piece of work. It winds half-way up a mountain of rock, and there the rock has been blasted by mining. You cross this mountain that has been cut through the middle, but with two sides standing twelve to fifteen hundred feet high, and on the other side you go down into a kind of funnel-shaped rocky crater, without a tree or a blade of grass. At the bottom is Aden, a frightful Arab town—they are all equally dirty. I rushed to the nearest bazaar, I asked for a drink as I was choking with thirst, and with great difficulty I obtained a glass of water so stagnant that a dog would have backed away before drinking it.[4]

I inquired whether they could give me a bed for the night. The owner offered me everything, for a price, except spending a night under their roof: that was expressly forbidden by the law of the prophet. I was starting to despair at the idea of going back on board, where the coal got into everything, and where it was impossible to stay in the cabin in such heat, when up comes a man wearing a red skullcap and Egyptian slippers, bowing and scraping, calling me 'monsieur le marquis' every few seconds, and asking how he could be of service to a Chabrillan, a fellow country-man.

He was born at Saint-Valier and has the deepest respect and gratitude for anyone who bears my name. I am saved! I glimpse the possi-bility of finding some sort of a bed. My compatriot is called Cani. He is a former non-commissioned officer who served in Africa. He has been seeking his fortune and believes he has found it in a coal mine on the shores of the Red Sea. That is why he has been exploring this country for the last two years.

My friend Cani tells me that everyone follows the local custom and sleeps on the roof or terrace of the house, as they are the only places where one can breathe, and that he lives at a certain Ernesti's, an agent of Messrs Pastrée of Marseilles, to whom he will introduce me forthwith.

When I heard the name Pastrée, I claimed he was a close friend. This was a frightful lie, but he is on very friendly terms with one of my relatives. I obtained a mattress on the roof of his house where I slept the sleep of the just, thus proving the advantage of being from the Dauphiné and a Chabrillan.

The next morning after a good cup of mocha coffee, while walking in the town, which looks like a quarry site, I noticed a small French plaque on a roof. So, there was a consul or a consular agent here. I went in and found, as representative of France and defender of those poor Christians whose heads are presently being chopped off, a certain Mr L., a former clerk in Sydney and indescribably incompetent. After having read me his dispatches to the minister—and what dispatches!—he said with inimitable self-importance:

—The whole thing, Sir, could have been averted if the government had taken notice of my warnings.

I left hurriedly and wearily set out for the house where I had obtained a glass of water the evening before. I was making my way through the bazaars that are nothing like the fantastic images from oriental tales that the word conjures up in the mind, through all those Arabs sitting on the ground, selling all kinds of tobacco, knick-knacks, dried fish and other malodorous things, when my friend Cani met a little man whom I immediately recognized as French from his Bordeaux accent. He was the captain of a small boat, the *Lucie*, that had just delivered a load of coal.

He invited me to dine on board, which I accepted provided they gave me a mattress so that I could spend the night on the poop deck. I did not want to abuse the terrace hospitality of Mr Ernesti, a charming fellow, but with a great drawback as far as I was concerned: he spoke only his own language, modern Greek, and all I have retained from my Greek studies is the first two lines of Lucien's *Dialogue of the Dead*. What is more, do modern Greeks understand ancient Greek? *That is the question*, and I very much doubt it.

My friend Cani followed me around like my shadow; where I went, he went; when I smoked, he smoked. And so I went to dine on board the *Lucie* where I spent a good night in the fresh air, which I sorely needed as the heat had affected me very badly since Cairo. After dinner Cani asked me whether I would be interested in visiting an Arab village, especially a village made up of different racial types, either Arabian or African. He offered to take me there the next day, in short to be my guide. I accepted with alacrity and invited him to dinner in Aden. It was agreed that we would spend the evening with these blacks of different hues.

Until tomorrow, for there goes the tom-tom that announces that dinner is served on board the *Australasian*. They use neither a bell nor a trumpet to announce meal times, but a Chinese tom-tom, an instrument as unappealing as it is deafening, and of which I had only the vaguest notion before this voyage. The ship's boy has a quite remarkable talent on this instrument. In the beginning it's scarcely a sound, more like a slight murmur that grows in a steady crescendo until it becomes deafening and wild, such a frenzy of noise that you end up by stuffing your fingers or fists in your ears and rolling on the floor.

We are slowly approaching Ceylon. I take up where I left off my notes on Aden. To the north, ten minute's walk away in the same funnel-shaped depression, is a village built of rushes with matting walls. From a certain distance away, it is impossible to imagine that these openwork huts are houses. The furniture in each hut invariably consists of a kind of cane and rush sofa on which one reclines. The hookah in the middle of the table is always alight.

The population is made up of three distinct types: the Indian, the Arabian and the Somali coast African. We went on our expedition at eight o'clock in the evening. At that hour of night, the women were lying at the door of their huts, each in her national costume and all smoking. I shall not tell you about the Indian or Arab women, who are very inferior in type to the Somalian women from the African coast. From the point of view of their physical form and features, they really are extraordinarily beautiful. Then there are also the brilliant colours of their clothes, their necklaces of imitation pearls, the silver jewellery, the long earrings and abundance of silver metal circlets about their arms and heads. All this gives them a fantastic appearance in the light of the lamp hanging from the ceiling.

I asked my friend whether I could look more closely, and having straight away noticed a young Somali woman of a more striking bearing than the others lying on a mat at her doorway, we unceremoniously seated ourselves around her on mats. An old grey-haired, gap-toothed shrew brought me a lighted hookah and placed it at my feet in front of me, fanning me with a *pança* or palm leaf fan. I was absorbed in gazing at my young woman opposite me, when the old woman took it into her head to squeeze my feet. At first I did not understand what was happening and paid little attention to what I thought was a Somalian custom, but after massaging my feet, she began again with my calves, and from there pounced on my arms, massaging away furiously just as François used to do in the Russian baths at Tivoli.

I did not understand what it all meant, and I had finally come to the conclusion that it was some sort of religious purification ordained by Mohammed when the old woman, with renewed determination, finished with my shoulders and lunged at my thighs. I sat up, very apprehensively, looking aghast at the old witch whose intentions seemed quite outrageous, and questioned my friend Cani about it.

He had fallen half asleep while he smoked.

—It's nothing, he told me, she is the mother of the young Somali woman and she hopes that this stimulating, exciting massage will make you want to buy her daughter. Besides, she is very pretty and her mother will sell her to you cheaply. She is not stitched up, or rather she no longer has the stitches.

Putting an end to the old woman's performance I asked for an explanation. Here are the customs of this tribe from Somalia, one of the points of Africa opposite Aden, both of which almost come together to form the entrance of the Red Sea. A female child from Somalia, at eighteen months to two years of age, undergoes an operation that results in her being partially sewn up. A young, pretty Somali girl who is still stitched can fetch up to fifty thalaries. The thalary is worth about five francs. A girl who has never had the operation or who is no longer stitched is worth very little—two to three rupees or five to six francs.

I was listening intently to all these details about their customs, when my attention was diverted by music coming from a pipe, a kind of flageolet played by a young Arab boy. He stopped in front of me and began a sad, unharmonious tune. Yet I noticed that little by little he was becoming more lively. The Somali girl opposite me swayed, lurched from side to side and finally got up and danced around this young boy, clapping her hands, singing and laughing in an extremely lascivious manner. The music was gradually becoming wilder and wilder. The young Arab himself was dancing when a young Arab girl dressed in a very dirty costume consisting only of a long petticoat of grey cloth rushed up to the Somali with grotesque gestures and poses.

That continued until the Arab boy had no more breath left to blow into his pipe and the two young girls had fallen onto their mats with exhaustion. I was told that the young Arab girl who had come and danced in front of the Somali was a virgin seeking a husband.

As the *Australasian* was due to depart during the night, I went back on board under the spell of this phantasmagoria. I concluded from all this that the wary peoples of the African coast are no fonder of being deceived in business than in love. This study of manners is the most remarkable thing that I noted during my voyage. What is more, it is a voyage that should take several weeks if it is done properly, especially if you are going up the Nile, which is the strangest trip one can take in the Orient.

In Cairo I was able to see the pyramids only at a distance, not daring to leave for fear that the boats might arrive in Suez. So, I have only a very vague impression of them.

I was very struck by the extravagant amount of money the Orientals spend on their donkeys. Another thing that intrigued me for a long time is the care people take to collect camel droppings. Finally, my curiosity demanding to be satisfied at the sight of an Arab who had got down from his camel to pick up a few droppings, I asked and found out that in Arabia and in the desert, these dried-out droppings provide the only fuel they have to burn.

Another thing I learned was that the hens don't brood in these parts, and it's only by artificial incubation that they get poultry from eggs. It's an Arab specialty and a fairly lucrative business. You give a hundred eggs to a person who, after a certain amount of time, gives you back fifty or sixty chicks according to the agreement you have already made with him.

The Arabs who live on the shores of the Red Sea are extraordinarily strong swimmers. At Aden our ship was surrounded by almost a hundred blacks swimming and waiting to be thrown a coin that they go after en masse at the bottom of the water. The *Australasian* has a draught of twenty-six feet of water. I have seen twenty-five or thirty dive at a time, swim under the ship, trying to be first to reach the other side—and all that for a penny. The harbour is full of sharks, but they are not partial to the flesh of the blacks.

That is about all I have to relate about my stay in Aden. I arrived on the morning of the 6th and departed on the night of the 9th. I have been suffering from stomach trouble since my departure and can't eat anything. The sea was terrible until the 13th, but on the 14th, as the sea had become much calmer, I took pen in hand to write to you. It's my only consolation on board.

Apart from the captain with whom I have chatted two or three times, I don't know anyone and have not spoken to anyone. There are two women passengers; one is with her husband and the other is going to rejoin hers in Melbourne, where he is a merchant. I have not said a word to them. I have taken a cabin right at the end of the forward section, the opposite end from the saloons and the first class passengers. Last Saturday was the first time I slept in this cabin. Up until then I had slept on deck, sometimes on a seat, sometimes on the ground.

As we were leaving Aden, I had expressed regret at not having been able to buy a pair of little gazelles, a type of small African roe deer, extremely delicate, quite delightful and very easy to tame. Mr Cani brought a couple on board for me, which I gave into the care of the butcher. They are very young and I hope to bring them to Melbourne safe and sound.'

'Ceylon, Wednesday 18 August 1858

My dear Céleste,

Since our departure from Aden I have been battling with frightful stomach cramps. The day before yesterday, as I finished writing, the pains became so intense that I fell to the ground. They carried me to my cabin and the ship's doctor gave me English-style treatment and a glass of ginger essence to drink. All through the night I thought I was going to die. I spent a dreadful day yesterday, but arriving in Ceylon today, I felt a little better. I was so afraid of dying far away from you.

But let us not talk of that! It's improving and two days' rest in Ceylon—which, they say, is the ancient earthly paradise—and I shall be quite well again. It's the winter season here: the temperature is humid and the vegetation even more lush than when I called here six months ago in mid-summer. The flowers and fruit grow luxuriantly.

I have just settled into the hotel where I stayed ten months ago. At that time it was run by a Portuguese, a handsome young man, recently married. The couple were a pleasure to see. It seems the wife died of cholera and fever not long after I was here, and three months later, the husband cut his throat. Life had become too wretched for him to bear. Whether people's skins be white, black, yellow or red, wherever you go in the world, you will find the same passions, the same suffering, the same pain!

I wish I could put my whole heart into this envelope and send it to you with all my thoughts, all my love! . . .'

'Trincomalee (east coast of the island of Ceylon, 25 August 1858)

My dear Céleste, I really do not know how this letter will get to you. I shall give it to the man who will have to cross the whole island of Ceylon to ask for help in Colombo and a ship to get us away from here. Since the long letter I sent you from Galle on the 19th, I have spent miserable days and miserable nights, but all that would have been nothing at all if I had been well.[5] At the end of my last letter, I told you that I was not feeling very well; the fact is that I have not been able to eat anything since Aden. You will certainly know what I have suffered, as I have often seen you with renal colic. Well, since Aden I have had colic severe enough to make me cry mercy and roll on the floor.

The ship's doctor, who has been requested to sleep next door to me, has exhausted his supply of pills both black and white. He claims that it is either gastritis or a chill I caught when sleeping on deck. I am in constant pain and it's all I can do to hold this pen. When the cramps go away, sleep overtakes me. In short, since Aden, all I ask of God is my health and that strength you have always known in me, so that I may see you again. I am afraid, yes, afraid of dying . . . what would become of you if I were not here?

I hope that this letter reaches you before the news of our catastrophe gets into the papers. I am writing to you from a port I did not even know existed and where, thank heavens, we have found refuge. During the crossing from Aden to Galle, we had been very well aware that the pumps had often been used, but no one could have imagined that our ship had sprung such a big leak. We learned, however, on the 19th at Galle, that the *Australasian* was taking on eighteen inches of water per hour in spite of the pumps.

On the 20th a committee of experts was sent on board. They declared that the engine was in good condition and that the ship could get to Melbourne with the help of the pumps. Our fate depended, therefore, on the engine, for if it broke down and if the pumps were no longer operable, it was obvious that we were already doomed. This expert opinion was an infamous collusion between the ship's agents and the experts.

I was so ill that I had reached a state of general prostration. On the 21st I went back on board at four o'clock and at half past four we were beyond the lighthouse; at nine the engine stopped; at ten it started again and finally, at one in the morning, it stopped and I could hear from my bed, where I was in awful pain, that all the pumps were working. The engine had broken down and we were sinking. We were only fifty miles from Galle, but it was impossible to go back there with a headwind and without engine power.

On the 22nd and the 23rd, the wind and the current pushed us into the Gulf of Bengal. They tried to keep the vessel in sight of the coast, but at the same time sufficiently far away to avoid being thrown onto the rocks. Fortunately the breeze was fresh and favourable, besides the pumps were still working and all the lifeboats were ready if the worst should happen. I was in such pain that I paid little heed to all these dangers.

On the 24th we were in sight of a port called Trincomalee, which we entered. However, we do not know how we shall get out again. There are two English frigates in the port, but they have orders for India, and so they refuse to take us to Galle where we would have waited for the next packet boat for Melbourne. There is some talk at the moment of crossing Ceylon on foot. In my present state of health I cannot contemplate it; I would die half-way there. What is to be done?

I fervently hope that this letter reaches you promptly, so that you are not alarmed by the newspaper reports. I asked Mr Duchesne de Bellecourt, whom I met at Galle and who was going to Paris, to get Fleury-Hérard to tell you that he had seen me and that you should not worry. Have you had any news of him? Well, that is enough! Goodbye my darling wife. I will write to you from the first place I can. Pray God to leave me a few years to look after you and love you.

My two little gazelles have died. I have bought you a good-sized ruby, although it is not worth a great deal. I am in the land of pearls and precious stones.

Think only of my good intentions, Céleste my dear. The fact is that in the midst of my greatest suffering I think only of you, I see only you.

Even with the best of luck, I can't reach Melbourne before the middle of October. There is talk of going to Madras, which is two or three days away from here, to try to send out a call for another ship, but nothing will be decided before tomorrow and the express leaves in a moment, taking the news of our catastrophe to Colombo. I shall hand over my letter so that it will leave by the first packet boat.

All my thoughts and all my love.

Lionel'

'Trincomalee, 29 August 1858

I don't wish to alarm you my dear Céleste, but over the last four days my state of health has greatly deteriorated. There are complications of the liver, stomach and intestines. On the evening of the 26th, I was taken with such violent cramps that I asked if the captain could come to my cabin to give him my last instructions for you, the only person that it pains me to leave, the only person I love! Two heavy tears fell on my cheeks as I said your name.

However God took pity on both of us, and I am still alive.

I asked to see the doctor from the English warship that is in the harbour. They put leeches on my right side, and since then I have been swallowing all sorts of pills and medicines. My strength is waning, but I think I am a little better.

Oh! it's frightful to be separated like this, my darling wife. There is no one here to look after you but servants who are drunk most of the time and a doctor stupefied with drink. For the month that I consulted him, his answer was invariably: 'brandy and soda'. And in addition, a dozen or so passengers whose only interest in you is to see that you don't die of cholera, yellow fever or any other illness that would put the ship in quarantine.

Well, I hope that a steamer will soon arrive and take us to Galle, where the packet boat from Australia will pick us up on the 14th or 15th September. If I can get to a temperate climate I shall survive, and shall only have to look after myself to repair the damage to my health that is occurring at the moment.

Whatever happens, my darling wife, whatever the future brings, remember that I love you as much today as I did ten years ago. There is nothing in my heart but love, and if you have caused me any pain or suffering that I should forgive, I shall forgive you wholeheartedly on my deathbed. I have done everything I could to make your life happy, and if I have not always succeeded, it has not been my fault.

I can't write any more today. I am too weak and too ill. I shall continue this letter until I have the opportunity to send it off.'

'2 September

I have not been able to write to you since 29 August. I am still extremely ill, but I want this letter to reach you as quickly as possible and I will not waste the opportunity today.

On 30 August, feeling much better and following the doctor's advice, I decided to take a walk on an island in the bay. It seems that I walked too far or that it was too soon to go out, for I had a relapse yesterday. Luckily my liver is not involved this time, only the intestines.

As I mentioned to you, they are sending a little steamer from Colombo to take both packet boat and passengers and transport them to Galle where, on about 14 or 15 September, they will meet the packet that followed us. On the other hand, given my state of health, it's impossible for me to leave on this little steamer where we would be piled three in a cabin.

I had a long talk with the captain who has given me his word that the leak has been completely repaired, that within a week the engine will be capable of taking the ship to Melbourne, and that even if the engine should break down, the boat would easily finish the trip by sail, as it would no longer be shipping water.

I have a very big cabin, a fine bathroom, the ship's doctor knows the treatment ordered by the doctor from the warship—exactly the same as the one you had to follow, by the way. So all the others can leave and I shall stay on board the *Australasian*.

I have had a long consultation with the doctor who treated me and I hope that I shall make a quick recovery in Australia, however should I suffer a second liver attack, he has ordered me to go back to France. This voyage and this illness will be the ruin of me.

Take good care of your own health; I am taking care of mine for you, my only happiness, the only thing that matters to me in this world.'

'Trincomalee, 8 September 1858

Here I am convalescing. Yesterday the captain took me ashore and arranged a long outing in a small local carriage.

I am not under any illusion, however, and I think that my robust good health has gone forever. All I ask of God is enough time to come back to you. I was afraid that I would never see you again, and if God heard my prayer, it's because He was touched by the depth of my love for you.

Given my state of health, I acted wisely in staying on board the *Australasian*. I am very comfortable here, having the use of all the cabins. The captain is as attentive and as pleasant as he can be. I think finally that I shall reach Melbourne. I long to get there, as I am not at all well.

Trincomalee is certainly one of the hottest places on earth, with that stifling humid heat that I have heard about from people who have been to Java and Batavia. It's one of those climates that fosters cholera and slow fevers that can be fatal. But from the point of view of its fauna and flora, it's magnificent.

The island of Ceylon is the country of pearls, precious stones, ebony, elephants and tigers, flowers with intoxicating perfumes and the subtlest poisons. It's a pity that I have been so sick and have not been able to go out into the jungle. The little I have seen makes me regret it all the more.

I went to a Buddhist religious festival. It was remarkably strange and interesting. I am keeping all these notes for winter evenings by the fire in Le Poinçonnet.

You remember the Latabie account that was sent to Melbourne and was lost on board a ship which was wrecked on its way from Calcutta. It was actually on the Trincomalee coast that this ship (*The Avo*) was lost about five or six miles from here. There was £100 000 sterling in gold on board, of which £70 000 have now been recovered, and they are hopeful of finding the other £30 000.

The diver they used is the same as the one who came to locate the leak in our ship. I watched that operation, which is really quite extraordinary. He wears a type of complete suit made of gutta-percha with a helmet that is screwed onto a breastplate. The air comes into it from a machine operated by two sailors turning a wheel, thus forcing the air into a long pipe joined to the top of the helmet. The diver can see quite clearly through the glass window in his helmet. He can move his hands, and the diver I am talking about stayed in the water for up to eight hours without coming to the surface. He has calculated that, since being employed in salvaging the *Avo*, he has spent more than nine hundred hours under water.

The divers who do this work die young. It's this artificial air that kills them. They are a sorry sight when they come to the surface, so pale and dazed. The man I saw is an ordinary sailor on board the warship, and the only extra pay he gets is a shilling for every hour spent in the water. It's very cheap labour.

There is competition here as everywhere else. Another diver came from Colombo to offer his services, claiming that he could do as well if not better than the man in question. He died after two days.

There is no road linking Trincomalee with Kandy, another town on the island of Ceylon, roughly in the centre. The postal service is carried out by Indians who run through the jungle and who have to cover five miles (nearly two leagues) every half-hour. Every five miles there are houses made of cane and reed with roofs of coconut palm leaves. They are called *bungalows*, where travellers can rest during the hottest part of the day. The name bungalow is used in India for all buildings of the same kind, which are more like sheds than houses. The Indians live in bungalows.

In Trincomalee Bay there is an island called Sober Island (the Island of Sobriety), probably so named because all the English who go there in parties come back drunk. This island does not belong to the colony. The British Admiralty has taken it over, using it as a place of rest and recreation for all the officers of the English warships that come here to take on fresh supplies. So the island belongs to all the officers, who have successively built various bungalows furnished with cane and reed sofas. They have also set out paths which they have planted with flowers. All in all it's a charming island, especially when the bands from the warships play there. It was a walk on this island that inspired some research I did a short time ago.

The jungles (they give the name jungle to the impenetrable thickets and woods where elephants, tigers and other animals take refuge) are filled with magnificent birds, hares by the thousands, deer and stags in herds. Jackals watch strangers pass by without even deviating from their path. The elephants and tigers are more difficult to see, and you need to go four or five leagues into the jungle to come across them at sunrise.

Apart from two *stores* (big shops) owned by the British government and five or six cottages inhabited by government employees, from Trincomalee Bay it's impossible to know that there is a town in Trincomalee. Once on land, however, in the midst of the coconut trees, banana trees and the most exotic plants, you find a host of bungalows surrounded by fences covered with flowers, and intersected by streets and roads that look like paths in English parks. All these bungalows are inhabited by a fine race of Indians—handsome lads, very clean, very active, most speaking English and working perfectly in concert selling pearls, precious stones, ivory, ebony and all manner of curios at very high prices to passing foreigners.

Apart from a few English employees, Europeans are conspicuously few in number. In all there are seven married ladies and a spinster of thirty who is beginning to give up hope.

I went to pray in the Catholic church yesterday and I was happy to see a group of little dark-skinned children reciting their catechism in their native language or reading it on long coconut leaves. I noticed several whom I presumed were children of rajahs or important Ceylonese lords from the number of earrings, toe rings, and silver ankle and wrist bracelets they wore.

On the other side of the bay, on the beachfront, I noticed a very plain tomb, but at one end there was a small post of some kind with a lamp that looked very like a Chinese lantern. I asked for an explanation and learned that a rich native of the island who died a while ago had left his fortune to the queen, on the condition that a lamp should be lit at the head of his tomb every evening. Coconut oil is so cheap that, when she accepted his several million pounds sterling, the queen lost no time in issuing orders for the wishes of the dead man to be fulfilled, and every evening coconut oil sheds its pale light over the shades of our dead Indian in his tomb.

A few days ago there were some rather disturbing scenes between the officers and men from the warships and the Indians. At this time of the year there are Hindu religious festivals, which I witnessed at Galle, as they last a month and have just finished. The drunken English sailors insulted and beat some Buddhist priests, and even tried to burn down the temple by the shore where the festivals are celebrated.

The next day there were reprisals by the Indians. They attacked several officers and men and broke the teeth of several others. Moreover they wrote to the commander to warn him that they intended to kill any sailor or officer found on shore after sunset.

The government agent also complained to the captains, who wanted to appear fairly detached from it all. In the end, the two captains were ordered to set sail immediately for India by the governor of Colombo, who furthermore informed them that once back in England they would have to answer for the troubles, which they should have prevented and which could lead to another Indian war.

The English government is starting to realize that these Indians, whom they have treated like dumb animals for so long, do not easily forget the whippings and canings they have received.

Well, Céleste my dear, what a lot of chitchat, but I am so happy to be able to write to you. I hope I shall have good news of your state of health when I arrive. If the winter and the cold affect you badly, go and spend the bad season in Pau or Hyères.[6]

You can count on some money in January. I shall try to send you some before then. So goodbye my darling wife, think of me now and again. I love you so much.

Lionel'

'11 September 1858

I left Trincomalee this morning at eight o'clock. I thought I would never leave there. Thank you God! Just the thought of leaving this poisonous climate makes me feel better. Perhaps I shall see you again Céleste.'

'12 September 1858

I am in dreadful pain. It was two months ago at six o'clock in the evening that I said goodbye to you at Le Poinçonnet. Will I ever see you again? It's doubtful, for I don't delude myself: the heat will soon kill me.'

'15 September 1858

I have spent an awful night. It's going from bad to worse.
    The ship is travelling slowly. Will I ever get to Melbourne?
    The captain is very kind to me. He often comes to see me in my cabin. As for the ship's doctor, he is a lout who is no more worried about me than if I never existed. The only use he will be to me is to sign my death certificate.'

'16 September 1858

It's clear that my state of health is deteriorating by the day and that this liver infection will kill me in a very short time, all the more so since I shall arrive in Melbourne in the middle of the hot season and I certainly shall not be able to stand it. But then, it's much easier to cope with physical suffering than with mental suffering.'

'18 September 1858

I am feeling better. I prayed to God and I spoke to you from the bottom of my heart. The thing that gives me greatest happiness is to look at daguerreotypes of you.'

'20 September 1858

Please forgive the length of my letters. I should be so happy to read yours in Melbourne!
    What delightful perfume wafts from the letter you receive from the person you love and who loves you! Every word contains an idea that your heart instantly understands! All the thoughts, the desires, the

tenderness seem to rise out of that letter like joyful birds flying from their cage, circling the air, and with their sweet song charming the heart whose only consolation for being alone is the certainty of being loved.'

'26 September 1858

I have had a good night at last. I feel better, although I still have stomach pain and feel the effects of all the pills and medicines.

It's a lovely spring day, a little chilly but with brilliant sunshine. I feel as though I am coming back to life, and my whole being responds to this glorious sky. The spirit rises to God to thank Him, and the heart longs for affection and happiness.'

'28 September 1858

I am nearing the end of the voyage that will be my last. My time has run out and I have only a few days or a few months to live. My Céleste, my darling wife, what will become of you?'

'7 October

For the last week I have been worse than ever. I am horribly ill and it's all I can do to reach Melbourne. I spend my life in bed, shaving and doing my nails. I extend my interest in my appearance to having my hair cut. It's amazing how the hair, the beard and the nails grow when one is ill.

All that is left of me is my bones and my large frame. My wedding ring slips off my finger. I have had to wind thread around it. It's the state I saw you in, Céleste, that has brought me to the state I am in now. At times I saw you fall victim to this frightful illness that has separated us. In my sleep I thought I heard your voice saying to me: 'Lionel, I am going to die, I am dying. Come to me!' . . . And I replied: 'Near or far, we should die together, and my soul will cross the world to join yours.' Then I would give way to the pain so that it would take me sooner.

Now that these bouts of fever have passed, I am fighting back because hope returns. Dr Ducholet has guaranteed that your life is not in danger. He has seen my tears and my despair. I have great confidence in his ability.

Oh! How I long to reach Melbourne! I should find a letter from you there.'

'King George's Sound, 8 October 1858

My dear wife,
We are stopping for a few hours only in King George's Sound to take on coal. As we shall not reach Melbourne before the 18th or 20th and the packet boat from Europe leaves on the 16th, I shall leave a few lines for you here, which the boat will take on its way.

My health is bad, but I hope that it will recover quickly once I am on land and can follow a good diet, the same as you, my poor Céleste. Oh! How right you were! These countries are cursed!

After having suffered horribly from the heat in Egypt, the Red Sea and Ceylon, which brought on this illness, for the last fortnight I have suffered a great deal from the cold, which has complicated the situation.

I long for the moment when we arrive in Melbourne so that I can have news of you. I hope that God, who has sent me such terrible trials, will give me the consolation of knowing that your health has been restored and that you are feeling quite well again.'

'King George's Sound

I hesitated for a long time before sending you the few lines enclosed that I wrote during the brief moments when pain gave me some peace.

We are now separated by the ocean, by the whole world, and soon perhaps by death. Never to see you again . . . Dear God, how hard that is! Have You not sent me enough pain to grant me the favour of allowing me to live, so that I can look after her—she whose courage and devotion have never failed. Dear God! I no longer have the strength to weep. Take pity on me!'

CHAPTER 17

Melbourne and Châteauroux

'Melbourne 17 October 1858

I HAVE just this moment arrived in Melbourne. Since leaving King George's Sound, I have had a third attack, just as severe as the first two. However, God has allowed me to reach the end of my voyage.

I have just sent for my letters. I have read and re-read yours. You are still unwell, but you feel better; that gives me some hope for myself. I will fight with all my strength, because I want to live for your sake.

I have found that everyone here has been very worried about me and is delighted to see me again. Our business affairs look promising, but you should not count on very rapid success.'

'Melbourne 13 November 1858

I have just suffered another terrible bout of illness, and for the fourth time I have been very close to never seeing you again. At last the crisis has passed and I have been up for two days. The doctors give me hope that it will be the last and that I am starting my convalescence, but I shall have to be very patient and careful.

I have found a charming house that looks out on Richmond *pad'dock* (big park) and the river. The air is good, I feel as though I am in the country, and I can be close to the consulate. It's also the most economical option.

When I was at death's door, I had only one thought, one regret, and that was you, Céleste. When tears ran down my cheeks, the people who were caring for me night and day must have thought that I was very afraid of death. Those tears were for you, the wife whom I was leaving, you who are the aim and the centre of my whole life.

[230]

There could not have been more members of the French community inquiring after me during my illness. They all came and left their names, and on my return, I encountered a lot of sympathy within the colony. The governor came to see me in person.

Fauchery often comes to visit me, as does a Mr Kreisser, an associate of the Vial d'Arane company of Sydney with a branch in Melbourne.[1] They are the only ones who are allowed to see me. I am quite determined not to allow myself to be harassed.

I hope I can keep the house I am living in now for the whole of my stay in Melbourne, and I will do it up little by little with my own savings, to create a charming, festive mood to greet you. Now, you must come as soon as possible. This illness would have spared my life in vain: the sorrow of being separated from you would kill me! . . .

On my arrival in Melbourne, a Frenchman named Soirot [*sic*], a former Saint-Cyr cadet, and a captain in the 50th line regiment, was sentenced to be hanged for having killed his mistress, who had been unfaithful to him.[2] I called a carriage, and more dead than alive I dragged myself over to see the governor to beg him to pardon the man.

That evening at eight o'clock I received a letter from the governor granting it. I was so ill and weak that the emotion that overcame me on receiving this good news almost killed me. But I felt in my heart that it was a happy beginning in Melbourne.'

'15 November

The packet boat has not yet arrived from Europe. I have no news of you before this letter leaves, and that makes me sad. This letter should reach you about the 7th January. For me it's a date on which I shall certainly go to church and pray to God. I shall not forget it this year. I have so many things to ask for you, your health and happiness.

I should like to be able to pass on some news, but I don't know anything interesting to write. Consul Tarleton has been recalled.[3] His successor died coming out to replace him, so Tarleton is obliged to wait. His wife came and was quite insistent that I be taken to her house, so that she could look after me.

I don't know whether you remember a man named Copping [*sic*]. Well, Copping, the stage clown, is a member of the Victorian upper house—the Lords' Chamber—and is now the Hon. George Copping.[4]

Well, I must go, Céleste my dear, as I have a large amount of mail to finish. There is no need to tell you I love you, as you must surely know it and believe it. Give Solange a kiss from me, and affectionate greetings to all those around you.

I forgot to tell you that in Melbourne at the moment there is a Prince of Wurtemberg who is a first cousin of King Jérôme.[5] He is travelling incognito under an ordinary name, and when he learned that I was ill, he inquired after me every day.'

'Melbourne, 11 December 1858

I have just this moment received your letter dated the 5th October. It's a sad one, and everything really seems to be weighing down on me at the same time. The only thing that allows me to overcome all my troubles is the desire to secure your well-being, and if your health, which is the most precious and important thing in the world to me, should decline once again, my energy and my will to fight will desert me. If I ever lost you, I would no longer have any reason for living, and I would not try to bargain with death over the days of sadness and suffering that I have left . . .

I am not at all well, but I have already escaped death four times and each time, on the point of death, I have had the strength to take a pencil and write a few lines, so that you would know that my last thoughts and words were for you.'

'13 December

Death is by my side and, like a miser, seems to begrudge me the few days of life I need to die with a more tranquil mind.

I have no regrets, no resentments; I have no more desires. Having spent the whole day in the sunshine, I am watching the sun set and go over to that other hemisphere where you are now, and where it will never again rise for me. I ask it to do you all the good that it has done me.

I am including a few words for Solange.'

'Melbourne, 15 December 1858

My dear Solange,
I received your little note which pleased me so much. I am very happy to know that you are in the convent at Ardentes, where you are learning your

[232]

prayers and your catechism very well. I hope that your first communion will soon be here. It's an important day and a beautiful memory in one's life.

My dear Solange, once you have made your first communion, you will no longer be a child. It's the first step in life. Do it wholeheartedly and God will make your life easy and happy. Pray God for your mother and for me who needs it so badly!

All my love,

Your father,

Lionel'

'Melbourne, 16 December 1858

Céleste my dear, I have read and re-read *The Gold Robbers* ten times over. I have lent it to everyone.

What marvellous organization you have, and what willpower you must have exercised to delight me so much. I have regretted not helping you in your studies, but I was far from suspecting how greatly your mind has been transformed.

I am settled in my stone house and very comfortable.

Many of our friends have died here in Australia in a very short space of time . . .

Ah well! Whatever happens in this world is meant to happen.

Don't forget me. I adore you and dream of you alone.

Lionel'

I can't describe the pain I felt on reading this letter. It was all the keener since I could do nothing to alleviate it at the time. At the first word of Lionel's illness, I had put the house at Le Poinçonnet up for sale. If I had been able to find a buyer, I would have sold it at any price. But nobody arrived, even to inspect it. I resolved to leave anyway and I had already begun my preparations when the letter containing the portrait that Lionel had written about arrived. He was unrecognizable. I burst into tears.

—Illness altered you just as much as that, my mother said, and you are getting better. Come now, be reasonable, and besides, the unhappiness you cause each other will kill you both. You must wait. I am certain that he will come back to France for treatment, for it has done you good.

The truth of the matter was that my mother was convinced that I would arrive too late. Dismayed by my state of mind, my mother persuaded me to go to Paris with her. I saw several people again who received me with open arms. The woman I saw most often because she lived opposite, was Jeanne de Tourbay, a kind, charming woman with a warm heart and such a lively mind. The gentleness of her character was the only thing that could calm the turbulence of mine.

Jeanne, who had read all of Lionel's letters, did not really believe in the hope she tried to inspire in me. But her voice was so gentle, her manner so convincing when she reasoned with me, that she managed to allay my suspicions and I always left her feeling somewhat comforted. She tried above all to reconcile me to the idea of work, that work I had loved so much, but which I no longer wanted to even consider. She introduced me to Mr Marc Fournier, the director of the Porte-Saint-Martin Theatre.[6] He talked to me about my novel *The Gold Robbers*, saying that it would make a fine play and that if I wanted to try writing it, he would read it straight away and perhaps put it on. As I was finding it impossible to sleep, I set to work. I wrote five acts in five nights. Jeanne was patient enough to read them. She thought they were very good, even though at that stage they were very bad indeed. I can't describe the things she made up to ease my pain, but whatever happens, I shall never forget her! . . .

And she was not the only one. Sarah Félix lived near Paris in a charming country house filled with souvenirs of her poor sister Rachel.[7] She had collected these precious relics and had arranged them with exquisite skill and taste. I sometimes went to spend the day with her and we talked about our absent loved ones, for exile and death have a cruel similarity.

—Look, she said trying to smile and hide her tears from me, I have bought back all her furniture, her jewels, and even my dear sister's theatre costumes. But for me, Phèdre's tunic would have been sold for fifty francs! It has taken all the money I have, and as I am determined to keep my treasures, I am really going to work.

—Are you going back to the theatre?

—Oh no! . . . The public changes like the wind: in art and politics they need idols and martyrs. Didn't they want to oust Rachel, one of the glories of the Théâtre Français, in favour of Ristori, a foreigner? Rachel is dead . . . , as for the other one, you never hear of her now.

To dispel her sad moods, Sarah would sit down at the piano. She is a very good musician and sings divinely. When she wants to, she can be very engaging indeed.

One day I went looking for her in her flower-filled garden. She ran up to me exclaiming:

—Eureka! I have it! Guess what I am going to do? I shall give you a hundred guesses, no a thousand . . .

—Well, what ?.

—I am going to farm oysters!

—You must be joking.

—Not in the least. I am going to get an oyster bed, and in a short time you will hear about my little pupils. I shall earn 100 000 francs a year.

—At least, I said with a laugh.

—Yes, at least, she continued quite seriously. It's only small ventures that are difficult and uncertain. Besides, if this one does not live up to expectations, I shall find others. If I had to live with no hope of ever making a fortune one day, given my habits and tastes, I should give up the ghost. I have lived as if I were a young man of means, I have been ruined ten times—some of it for myself and a lot of it for others—but I have hung on. I don't want to have any doubts, because that would mean doubting myself . . .

—If you find yourself alone one day, she added more quietly, come with me to my old mansion by the sea. You will always find a warm welcome, a warm bed and good food there.

Sarah left a few days later. I was really sad to see her go, but alas, a much greater sorrow put that and everything else right out of my head.

CHAPTER 18

Death at the End of the World

A MONTH had gone by since I received Lionel's portrait. I expected a letter from him from one hour to the next, from one minute to the next, but at the same time I was afraid of receiving one.

As my fever had not disappeared, Mr Ducholet, my doctor, came to see me from time to time. A friendly visit, he called it, but he was really coming to check on my state of health, as he had promised Lionel to keep an eye on me and send him reports.

On the 24th March, he arrived a few minutes before my mother who came in looking quite pale, saying:

—I wanted to see you. I have had such a bad dream . . .

The doctor, who was not superstitious, began to laugh.

—Don't laugh, I said to him, my mother and I have unusual natures: we have always had a premonition of any misfortunes that were about to befall us . . .

—You haven't any news, have you? my mother asked with studied indifference.

—No.

—I think the packet boat from Australia has arrived though.

Scarcely had she said these words than the doorbell rang. The doctor was getting ready to leave. He opened the door and was handed a letter.

—From Australia! he said passing it to me. Your premonitions are wrong.

I looked at my mother. She was deathly pale. She had read in the paper what perhaps everyone else knew except me. I looked at the doctor. He was trembling as he spoke:

—This is not the count's handwriting.

I broke the seal. The first envelope contained a second. I did not know the writing of the address either. I turned it over. It had a black seal.

—This letter is not from him, I exclaimed, tearing open the envelope.

It contained his wedding ring and a lock of his hair.

I wanted to scream, but it was as though an iron hand gripped my throat. I could not breathe . . . I felt as if I was suffocating . . . My head spun, my muscles gave way. I thought that everything I lived for had been shattered at the same moment, and I fell heavily to the floor. I heard the sound my head made as it hit the tiled floor, but I felt no pain.

When I regained consciousness, I was half-undressed in an arm-chair. My mother and the doctor were by my side. Mr Ducholet drew his hand across his eyes several times, then read me this letter that he had already glanced through.

'Melbourne, 4 February 1859

Madam,

I hope most sincerely that this letter with its black seal has no more to tell you than you already know. While accepting the painful mission of being the one to pass on a message of bereavement to you, I have made every effort to soften the terrible blow I had to deliver.

The written word is always so blunt in such circumstances, that I thought I should first inform some of your friends, who will no doubt have prepared you for this letter. If these people who were asked to see you have not done what was requested of them, it is because fate has willed it so.

For my part, I have done the best I could. Please do not think too ill of me, Madam, and be strong: your best friend Mr de Chabrillan is dead! . . . You will not believe me, I do not believe it myself. One can never believe that those one has loved very dearly are dead. I have friends in the cemetery, whom I have long expected to return. They do not come back, yet I still keep hoping . . . What more can I say to you? Nothing. Words of condolence can take one's mind off a fleeting sorrow; the sorrow that has befallen you is too deep—it commands respect and above all, silence . . .

To struggle alone against great afflictions until time helps to master them is the only resource reserved for intelligent beings. They usually experience a series of bitter sensations and a kind of elation that is worth more that all the unwelcome visits and the stock epistles.

When you have wept a great deal, Madam, you will read what follows: it is a short report about Mr de Chabrillan's illness, the few details of the last moments of his life, sad details in which you will find but one thought, a thought that remained clear and lucid even as he lay dying and which, until the hour of his death, was for you and with you.

In his letter of the 15th December, Mr de Chabrillan no doubt told you that he felt much better. In fact, since he left the Criterion Hotel to move into his house in Spring Street, his health really seemed to be returning. Although his features had by no means regained all their liveliness, as you yourself were able to judge from the stereoscope that I made of him shortly before his relapse, we were beginning to recognize our consul of old. All of us thought that he was out of danger. There was one thing, however, that worried me, and I always found it a bad sign: Mr de Chabrillan was making plans—all of them too fine and above all too sensible! Living in the closest intimacy with him, being the receiver of all his confidences, I was sorry to see him constructing a whole future life as a wise and moderate man, and I feared one of those unexpected occurrences that too often prove reason wrong.

Alas, my fears were well founded. It was at the moment I least expected it, when no act of imprudence could be alleged, that the illness struck in full force. On Monday afternoon the 20th December, Mr de Chabrillan came as usual to make his tour of inspection of the great photographer's workshops. As I was hurrying to finish some important work, I had scarcely replied to his questions, and accusing me of being like a bear with a sore head, he had gone off into our sitting-room where he talked for at least an hour with my wife about France, that is to say, about Le Poinçonnet—France for him being nowhere else but where you were. I did not see him leave that evening.

He had been complaining of a slight stomach ache. The next day, Tuesday, at five in the morning, he awoke with violent stomach pains and vomiting. He sent his maid to fetch his two doctors, Mr Brownless and Mr Tracy, who immediately applied leeches and gave him mercury pills.[1]

I was only informed of it in the course of the day. I found him very weak. He spoke to me about you who were, he was saying, as ill as he. The next day there was little change, apart from increased physical weakness, but no great pain. On Thursday the 23rd, he spoke of you again at length, and ended by saying that neither you nor I would ever see him on his feet again.

I found it hard to believe that he was in such a critical state; the doctors were confident. I thought he paid too much attention to his illness and I said so to him. Later I remembered the strange way he smiled upon hearing these words, and it was only then that I realized how wrong I was. Mr de Chabrillan was neither weak nor despondent in the face of death; he was sad and resigned, that is all.

On Friday and Saturday there seemed to be no progress one way or the other, but on Sunday it flared up wildly again. On that day, one of those hot winds, whose intensity you yourself have experienced, was raging in Melbourne. When I left Mr de Chabrillan in the morning, he was very agitated and feeling suffocated. At two o'clock his maid ran up to my house in tears to ask me to fetch the doctors, 'as the master was dying'.

I arrived a few minutes before Mr Brownless and Mr Tracy and found Mr de Chabrillan sitting on his bed, his eyes staring, scarcely breathing but hiccoughing violently. He was complaining of a choking sensation. When he saw me he cried out: 'Fauchery, this time I am done for, really done for! Oh! My poor wife!'

Indeed, the doctors arrived and after consultation their gestures did not augur well. There is, in certain professions, a kind of sinister sign language. They withdrew all medication and ordered concentrated chicken broth and brandy diluted with water. This last prescription provoked a strong reaction in the poor dying man, who claimed that brandy would only increase the fire that burned inside him. However, I believe that it was to this strange remedy administered half-hourly, that we owed the slight improvement which resulted. The hiccough ceased and his breathlessness was less severe. The pains in his abdomen and stomach also disappeared, and from the time of that bad attack, partly brought on by the hot wind and a storm which broke during the night, Mr de Chabrillan suffered no more pain, or at least until the last moment, he gave no indication of physical pain.

On the evening of that terrible Sunday, he wanted to make his will. In Melbourne there were only three of us on really intimate terms with him—Frédéric Kresser, Édouard Adet[2] and myself. Unfortunately our friend Kresser, who had been called to Sydney on business, could not be informed in time to be with us. In view of the fact that I was about to leave Australia, I could not commit myself to anything more than staying with him until he was completely recovered. Éd. Adet was therefore the only one who could take on the official duty as executor of the will.

Mr de Chabrillan dictated his last wishes with a perfectly clear mind.[3] As always, you were his only concern, and he requested that after his death we, his only friends present, should not forget the woman who had been his whole happiness in life. Once our secretarial task was finished, Mr de Chabrillan expressed the urgent desire to see a priest. We sent for one who came immediately, heard his confession and administered the sacraments.

All these sad formalities completed, Mr de Chabrillan said to us with a smile that he had nothing further to do than wait for death—death which at that very moment was crossing the threshold of the house. We all awaited it, and yet it took two more days and nights to climb the stairs that separated it from our friend. Two days and two nights! It's a long time, Madam, when all hope is lost and one does not believe in miracles. But even if its progress was slow, it was not painfully impeded by one of those terrible nervous fits that usually precede the last moments. No, even though this cruel visitor never looked back or allowed anything to stand in its way, at least its progress was calm and methodical, without noise, violence or agitation. Two hours before it entered, poor Mr de Chabrillan still recognized me and tried to smile . . .

There is assuredly nothing in all this, Madam, that can bring you immediate consolation. Perhaps, as you read my letter, you may think that I have said too much, that I am cruel to go into too many tragic details, even that I enjoy adding lines that will do nothing to lessen your despair. You will see me in this light, I quite understand that, in one of those first bouts of grief when anything is allowed, and when one refuses to listen to anything or to hear anything. But later you will come back to these details, and only then will you find them less hard to accept, especially if you have ever seen a death.

You know how much people can suffer, how much they struggle, how many regrets there are in the last hours of those who must depart this life, regrets expressed in such tones! You have sometimes heard a person at death's door recounting his life, hurrying to tell you everything, what was in his past and what he dreamed for the future; you have seen all these black shadows finally pass in procession across a black background—and I am only speaking here of mental suffering. You know

how many illnesses torture people for years without sparing them anything on that account. So Madam, just consider that Mr de Chabrillan
took to his bed on the morning of the 21st December; that until the
25th, there seemed to be no sign of danger in his state of health; that
suddenly on Sunday the 26th the doctors decided he would not survive;
and that he then dozed until Wednesday morning the 29th, when he fell
asleep . . . and compare.

Let me repeat that Mr de Chabrillan suffered relatively little. I
scarcely left him during the four last days and I saw him gradually
become weaker, then pass away. The atmosphere of calm around him,
which seemed to be what he wanted most, was never troubled by any of
those awkward moments or careless mistakes sick people too often have
to contend with. As he had given strict instructions to his maid to let no
one near him but myself and anyone I thought should be admitted, I felt
it my duty to be very cautious. Mr de Chabrillan was lucid throughout
and never expressed the desire to see anyone. He talked about you, but
did not ask for you, as he knew only too well that even if you managed
to get here it would be too late. I therefore kept the door firmly shut to
all non-official and unconcerned people. Adet, myself and Sarah, the
maid he had before he left for France, looked after him to the best of our
ability, and right up to the last moment he had friendly faces around him.

At half past nine on Wednesday morning, it was all over and we had
to think about the last duties to be performed for Mr de Chabrillan. In
this case we had to reconcile public opinion and the express wishes of the
departed for the strictest economy. You will be able to judge for yourself,
Madam, if everything was carried out as it should have been, when you
read the accounts of the funeral included. I have translated the article
which appeared in all the newspapers.

Yesterday a service took place in the Catholic church for the unfortunate
Consul of France, the Count Lionel de Moreton de Chabrillan, who died
in his thirty-eighth year.[4] The Governor, the Mayor, the Chief Justice and
all the authorities were present. Then, after the naval officers came the
sailors and two thirds of the garrison. Drums draped with black crepe led
the funeral procession which advanced slowly because of the crowded
streets. The miners had come in such great numbers that they were
obliged to climb up trees or onto roofs of houses to see the cortège.
Ladies waved their handkerchiefs as a sign of farewell; others wept or
threw boughs, flowers, or bouquets under the horses' hooves. Cannon

shots were fired from the harbour; this was followed by martial music. There was really general mourning. We remember how the noble Count, already seriously ill but heeding only his courageous devotion to his compatriots, had been taken almost dying to the Governor, to obtain a pardon for an unfortunate Frenchman who had been condemned to hang. He died as a result of his imprudence. The Count de Chabrillan was a man who lived according to the dictates of his heart, and he died as he had lived. He had a most agreeable character; he held nothing back when he could help someone in need. His friends mourn him and those who knew him, regret his passing.[5]

Today Mr de Chabrillan lies in the new cemetery in a plot reserved for him. We have not, however, taken it upon ourselves to order a headstone or inscription. We thought that we would be overstepping our brief to take this last initiative, which rightly belongs to the Count de Chabrillan's family. You will doubtless wish to advise on this matter, Madam, and make your wishes known to Mr Adet.

Now I have told you everything, Madam. I have the honour to be Your most obedient servant,

A. FAUCHERY

N.B. I am leaving Australia very shortly. If you wish to get in touch with me regarding any information I may have forgotten, please address your correspondence to Antoine Fauchery, poste restante, Manila.[6] I shall always consider it a pleasure and a duty to be entirely at your service.

We have written to no one but you, leaving you the task of communicating to the friends and family of Mr de Chabrillan the news which has been so difficult for us to break to you.'

—There's a letter written by a man of feeling, murmured Mr Ducholet. Come now my child, up to now you have shown great courage throughout all the difficult stages of your life. Try to calm yourself and resign yourself a little. Your health demands it.

—I want to die!

—That will not bring back to life the man whose last thought was of you, and besides, your adopted daughter would be deprived of your support.

—There is nothing in the world I care about now. It's all meaningless.

My mother was crying.

—She is sixty-five years old! the doctor whispered. You are upsetting her dreadfully.

I took to my bed, and for a fortnight I uttered no further complaint, although I went through agonies of both mind and body.

Once again I survived a sorrow that would have killed me, if a person could die of sorrow. Some unknown power behind the scenes loosed its fury against me.

I was called into the Ministry of Foreign Affairs. When he saw me, Mr de Lesseps seemed to feel slightly embarrassed. I was recovering from an illness; I was in full mourning; and I could hardly stand.

He asked me to sit down and tried to soften the blow he was about to deal me with nice words.

—Tell me how, and under what conditions, your . . . marriage was contracted in England. It's impossible for you to keep the title and the name of a family who . . .

—Would like to destroy my marriage! I said, looking him straight in the eye. Lionel had thought of that, Count, for he married me twice and no power on earth has the right or the ability to undo what he did.

—But . . . if you could come to some arrangement.

—Never! It would be disrespectful to his memory. He has given me his name and I will bear it to my dying day. I will make sure that it survives me!

—That is just what we want to avoid, he said, slightly annoyed at my resistance. You must spare yourself the arguments of a lawsuit, which . . .

—Is that all you have to say to me, Sir?, I asked, getting up to take my leave of him.

—Yes, but it's enough to make you reflect that you would be wrong to undertake a course of action that could only do you harm.

—I do not know what the future has in store for me, Sir, but I give you my word that whatever happens to me, I shall keep my husband's name and title. He knew who I was when he gave them to me, and since then I have done, and will continue to do, my utmost to bear them with dignity.

—But you have no means of support.

—And you hope that I shall be forced to give in through poverty, do you? You are quite mistaken about that. One is always rich enough when one asks nothing of others. I am used to battling and suffering; I shall not give in and you will never be strong enough to break me. My only regret, Count, is that your concern for the interests of others has led you to deal with me in the way that you have!

He said nothing in reply and I left, believing myself to be much stronger than I really was.

Having walked straight ahead without knowing where I was going, my mind now took stock of the situation. I had arrived at the Tuileries Gardens. I went in, collapsed onto a seat and began to cry. I cried for some time. I was too fair-minded not to understand the despair that my poor Lionel's family must have been feeling. However I could do nothing about the fait accompli. I had to fight nonetheless, but I could not close my eyes to the fact that this struggle would be like that of the earthenware pot against the iron pot, if no one came to give me moral support. But who would dare to try and reason with my husband's brother to stop him taking me to court, which would only result in one more scandal?[7]

While I was lost in these thoughts, a gentleman passed close by me. He looked at me with some interest, then moved away slowly, like someone trying to recall something. He was still a young man, slim, elegant and very distinguished. He had extremely fine features, and his blue eyes had an expression of both pride and gentleness which struck me, recalling a distant memory to my mind. It did not take me long to realise who he was: Count de Naurois, a friend Lionel had often mentioned to me with great warmth.[8] He liked his fiery, chivalrous spirit.

—He is a valiant knight of the Middle Ages, Lionel said to me one day when our carriage was following his coming back from the races. He has the reputation of being difficult, because he has never compromised in matters of right or honour. He draws his sword like St George, he is as brave as a lion, and if the Devil himself stepped on his toes, he would fight him.

When he applied for membership of the Jockey Club, he was advised that certain members of the circle had spoken up against him without any valid reason, saying: 'We intend to blackball him.' De Naurois called on them—I think they were eight in number—and announced with the utmost courtesy that if he was refused he would hold them all to account, *one after the other*, for a refusal which he considered an undeserved affront. Fortunately he was accepted with a very large majority.

Apart from this brusqueness, which makes him a force to be

reckoned with by his enemies, he is the most sensitive, generous-hearted man you could wish to meet. Some time ago he went to see a female relation whose family did not live in Paris. As he entered the parlour of her boarding house, he noticed a pretty fair-haired little girl who was crying as she looked at a little parcel by her side.

—Now why are you crying? he asked her.

—My Mama has died, Sir. She was all I had in the world. These ladies can't keep me here for nothing, and I have to take my parcel and go to someone who will make me work.

—At ten years old, isn't that rather young? he said with a laugh. Then he added, turning to the mistress of the house who had just entered the room:

—Madam, please keep this child here with you. I shall pay for her board and upkeep until her education is complete.

—Look at him closely, Lionel went on, you would hardly take him for thirty. In July 1815 he was a lieutenant and paid for seventy men at arms to come to the aid of his country. *What is more, when there is a difference of opinion, either hunting, racing or gaming, we choose him as referee. My brother swears by him.*

Chance had just made the bold heart I so desperately needed to plead my cause walk right past me. Alas! I had not recognized him in time and I did not know his address . . . But God was to make him cross my path again one day to save my life twice over.

I went home. My mother was waiting for me anxiously. She passed me two large letters. My heart beat quickly as I unsealed them. I had allowed myself to harbour a hope that was to be cruelly dashed once again. I had thought that I could obtain permission to have my poor Lionel's body brought back to France. I had sold the last of my jewels to pay the costs. I had left no stone unturned: letters, entreaties, requests; I had even made approaches to His Majesty the Emperor. All the replies were benevolent, but all were negative. I was informed that there was not a single captain who would agree to take a coffin on board. Mr Adet also wrote: ' on no account could the body be exhumed in Melbourne because of the heat. There is too much fear of epidemics.'

I therefore had to resign myself to sending funerary ornaments to Australia. I had them done in bronzed iron and included a box of wreaths. I made a rough sketch of what I wanted for the workmen. No one had sought to contribute to this expense; besides, I would not have allowed anyone else to be involved.[9]

I went to Bordeaux to see the captain who was to take this lugubrious present to the man I had loved so much. I gave him all my instructions and came back to Paris. I had sent what was needed for a tomb to be erected to my husband, but that did not seem enough. I would have liked there to be something in France to the memory of this man who was so good, so noble, who died so young and in such unhappy circumstances.

I went to see Mr Paulin, the chief editor of *L'Illustration* to ask him to publish a portrait of Lionel in his paper.[10] He understood how happy this would make me and granted my request with a such a good grace that I shall be grateful to him for the rest of my life. I had at least been able to place his dear picture in a paper that is both historical and French.

I left for the Berry. As it was impossible for me to live at Le Poinçonnet, the superior of the Ardentes convent where Solange was boarding offered me hospitality. I then obtained permission to have two large iron crosses erected at the intersection of the two roads leading from Le Poinçonnet to Châteauroux forest. They were decorated with marble plaques bearing the following inscription in gold lettering: To the memory of Count Lionel de Chabrillan, born in Paris on 3 December 1818, died in Melbourne on 29 December 1858. Pray for him.

Moreover, I did not want him to be forgotten in the region that he had loved so much, and for which he had done so much good in happier times. The good priest I spoke of earlier came to bless the crosses. People from far afield hastened to take part in this moving ceremony, and in the crowd I recognized many people I had seen at the Château du Magny [*sic*] ten years ago. They were all weeping.

I came back to Paris almost completely destitute, as the house at Le Poinçonnet contributed nothing—on the contrary—and there were three of us to support, my mother, Solange and myself. I still had some money owing to me from the publication of the second edition of my *Memoirs*. I went to the Librairie Nouvelle to settle my account. Mr Bourdilliat assured me that knowing I was married, it was somewhat against his better judgment, and under pressure from his ex-associate, that he had published the first edition. That must have been true, as Mr Bourdilliat is a gentleman, highly esteemed by all those who know him. Partly to make peace with me, but mostly to oblige me, he bought my novel *Is He Mad?*[11]

At the front of this volume I wrote:

I dedicate this book to the dear and sad memory of my husband, who was the source of all my strength, joy, hope and courage. There is one less noble-hearted man on earth, but there must be one more star in heaven. Surely Count Lionel de Chabrillan had faith and charity, two virtues that are pleasing to God.

By continuing the work I had undertaken to improve myself a little, to make myself worthy, through hard work at least, of the man who had sacrificed everything for me, I am responding to material need, like the Wandering Jew who answered the ceaseless urging of a voice that cried out to him: Walk on! Walk on!

That is all I could do at the time to honour the memory of my beloved Lionel. I made a vow to myself that I would wear mourning for him for the rest of my life. I have kept my word for eighteen years, just as he had kept his by swearing to love me till his last breath.

THE END

Epilogue

AS CÉLESTE suggests in the last lines of *Death at the End of the World*, after Lionel's death she would have to call on all her reserves of energy and ingenuity to earn a living and carve out a career for herself yet again. These memoirs, however, were not published until twenty years after her return to France in 1857. During the intervening period she did indeed recreate herself once more, becoming well-known for her writing and theatrical productions—several have an Australian theme—and working all the while under her married name and title, which Lionel's family never succeeded in persuading her to relinquish. Nevertheless, her achievements were almost invariably hard-won and, just as during her marriage to Lionel, she was never to shed the notoriety of her past or know real financial security in the fifty years by which she outlived him.

The year 1858 must have been one of the worst years in Céleste's life. Lionel died far away, she was ill for some time, and she also lost a court case to prevent the publication of the second edition of *Farewell to the World* (*Adieux au monde*), the revealing first set of memoirs that was published just before her marriage and departure for Australia in 1854. Not surprisingly, she had remained very bitter about their publication as they had, after all, caused a scandal in France and led to her social ostracism in Australia. Despite her struggle to stop the second edition, she was probably quite grateful for the royalties that the memoirs brought in, for she was still in financial difficulties and the Chabrillans were managing to thwart all her attempts at publication of other works. It is interesting to note that, in this second edition, Céleste includes twenty additional chapters, covering, amongst other things, her life with Lionel before their marriage and the letters he wrote her from Australia in 1852. She also adds a preface in which she justifies her publication of the memoirs, claiming that her motive was to dissuade other young innocent girls from falling into prostitution. The publishers quite possibly allowed this rider as a concession to Céleste, who seems to have been on reasonably good terms with them in spite of all.

The persecution which Céleste suffered at the hands of the Chabrillan family was somewhat counterbalanced by the support she was given by Dumas *père*, who gave a glowing review of her first novel, *The Gold Robbers*. When it was published in 1857, she had a ready audience in the French reading public, with its appetite for stories of travel and adventures in exotic places like the Antipodes. France and the European continent first heard of the Gold Rush in 1852, and the news generated much interest in the Great South Land. Céleste's book was not the first French novel set in Australia, but the handful of works that preceded *The Gold Robbers* were either juvenile fiction or imaginary tales based on second-hand information masquerading as authentic accounts.[1] Céleste's was the first novel to be written by someone who had actually lived here. *The Gold Robbers* is a melodramatic tale of unrequited love, violence and death in Melbourne and on the Ballarat goldfields. There is a rape, twelve murders, a hanging and three natural deaths, but also two births—both illegitimate—and three weddings. While the novel's plot and much of the characterization are unquestionably fictitious, the descriptions of Melbourne, of the diggings at Ballarat, and of life and culture in Australian society, are authentic and for the most part accurate. Many of these unfavourable descriptions are reiterated, in several cases word for word, in *Death at the End of the World* which, although published twenty years later, was presumably written in diary form contemporaneously with *The Gold Robbers*.

Dumas continued to take a keen interest in Céleste's literary career and it was he who encouraged her to dramatize her novel, which she proceeded to do with considerable help from the great man himself. However, her first attempts to stage the play proved futile as theatre directors, presumably under intimidation from the Chabrillans, refused to be involved with it. Not to be outdone, Céleste sold her house in Le Poinçonnet—her only asset—to raise the money to buy a theatre, the Folies-Marigny, off the Champs-Elysées; and there, in 1862, she directed and acted in three of her own one-act pieces under the rather transparent stage name of Madam Lionel. One of these is entitled *In Australia*. The action, which takes place in Melbourne in 1853, ends with a satirical song that exaggerates the deficiencies of life in Australia for theatrical effect:

Cursed Australia,	Maudite Australie,
I'll leave you with no regrets.	Sans regrets je t'ferai mes adieux;
Did you ever see a more dreadful country	Jamais de la vie,
In all your life?	Vit-on un pays plus affreux?
The north wind burns you,	Le vent du nord vous brûle,
The mosquitoes are an absolute plague	Le moustique est un vrai fléau,
And I'll spare you any mention	Et je me tais par scrupule
Of all those things that devour your skin.	Sur tout ce qui vous dévore la peau.
No, no more travelling	Non, plus de voyage
In these miserable faraway lands.	Dans ces tristes pays lointoins;
Let's go back to shore,	Gagnons le rivage (bis)
Repeating this carefree refrain:	En répétant ce gai refrain:
Vive la France!	Vive la France!
Land of happy days,	Pays des beaux jours,
Land of prosperity,	Pays d'abondance,
Land of love.	Pays des amours.[2]

After a short period of success the theatre failed but, with the help of her friend the statesman Léon Gambetta, she finally managed to stage *The Gold Robbers* in 1864 in the working class area of Belleville, where it proved very popular. She then toured Holland and Belgium with the play, again to very enthusiastic audiences.

Céleste wrote two other novels with an Australian setting: *Miss Pewel* in 1859 and *The Two Sisters* (*Les Deux soeurs, émigrantes et déportées*) in 1876. Both combine melodrama with a certain amount of realism in tales of life and adventure on board ship and in far-distant Australia, which had captured the imagination of the French reading public of the time. In *Miss Pewel*, the protagonist and her sister live for many years in Australia. The setting does not feature strongly in the unfolding of events, although one episode that does stand out involves a carriage trip from Victoria to Sydney, where an attack takes place, and Céleste makes some very harsh comments about native Australians. *The Two Sisters* recounts the outward journey to Australia and a shipwreck en route, but only the last eighteen pages are set in Australia itself. Neither book, however, is as interesting as *The Gold Robbers*, with its descriptions of life in Melbourne and Ballarat during the gold rush.

Céleste accumulated enough capital from the 1864 production of *The Gold Robbers* to purchase a property in the rural district of Le Vésinet in the same district as Versailles, just outside Paris. She lived there with her adopted daughter, Solange, and her mother, whose life-long companion, Vincent, had recently died. To Céleste's horror, he was buried in the family vault; she never forgave him the abuse he had inflicted upon her in her youth.

At Le Vésinet she befriended her neighbour, the composer Georges Bizet, who was at that stage unknown and very short of money. The *New Grove Dictionary of Music* states that 'Their exact relationship is obscure; he apparently found her presence an aid to composition ... It has been suggested that she may have served as a model for Carmen.'[3] It was at this stage that she also acquired as a distinguished protector Count de Naurois, the former friend of Lionel's whom she mentions in the final pages of these memoirs. He was ultimately to pay off the mortgage on her house in Le Vésinet, and left her a modest allowance in his will. During the mid-1860s, when royalties from *The Gold Robbers* were providing Céleste with a reasonable income, two of her comedies, *On Guard* and *A Compromised Man*, as well as a musical comedy, *In the Breton Way*, were staged at the Folies-Marigny. But as she was constantly in need of money, and also conscious of keeping her name before the public, she accepted an engagement at a café–concert, a type of establishment where customers took refreshments while listening to popular and often ribald entertainment. This provoked legal action from the Chabrillans, who were furious at seeing their name on all the hoardings advertising Céleste's debut. Once more she stood her ground and gave a season's performance of a type of autobiographical soliloquy with songs and dancing.

She continued to write plays, and in 1869 *Crimes at Sea* was produced at the Belleville Theatre. This melodrama about the adventures of a Breton sailor shipwrecked on the coast of Australia met with almost as much success as the dramatized version of *The Gold Robbers*, performed there five years earlier. *Troubles in Love*, staged at the Théâtre des Nouveautés the following year, ran for the unusually long period of three months; this was followed by *The American Girl*, in which Céleste played the title role.

When France declared war on Prussia in 1870, and theatres, businesses and shops were being closed down, Céleste left her Paris apartment to return to Le Vésinet. With what we know of her restless nature and her need to participate in, rather than observe, events taking place around her, she was doubtless soon frustrated by her inactivity and so set up a women's nursing auxiliary, 'les Soeurs de France', to care for wounded soldiers before their return to the front. She recruited more than 150 women, who tended the sick in houses evacuated by their owners on the outskirts of Paris. After the war, she turned her Le Vésinet property into an orphanage, run by nuns, to house orphan girls from Alsace and Lorraine, the two provinces lost by France to Prussia.

In 1872, Céleste set off for Belgium on a lecture tour. She was billed as Madam Lionel de Chabrillan, but the press resurrected all the scandals of her past, and she was initially met with audiences made up mainly of men who, it would seem, were expecting a typical entertainment from the notorious 'Mogador'. They must have been disappointed, as the subject of her lecture was her life and travels in Australia. What is more, Céleste was by now a 47-year-old woman with snow-white hair, still dressed in the black mourning clothes she had promised to wear after Lionel's death.

Australia was to feature strongly in Céleste's publications in the following years. Eighteen seventy-six saw the appearance of *The Two Sisters*, which may well have been published to revive an interest in Australia and to serve as a precursor to *Death at the End of the World*. In any case, we can be fairly certain that she was already doing her best to ensure a high readership for these Australian memoirs, as she published in this same year a third edition of her *Memoirs of Céleste Mogador*. Given her efforts to stop publication of the first two editions, and her constantly frustrated wish to be rid of her stage-name, it is surprising that she consented to this third edition. She was no doubt encouraged by her publishers and her decision was most likely a pragmatic one: by now she needed money and was struggling to maintain her public popularity. *Death at the End of the World*, subtitled *Continuation of the Memoirs of Céleste Mogador*, was published in 1877 under the name of Countess Lionel de Chabrillan.

Céleste was again living in Paris where several more of her plays were being produced, but without much success. Her mother had died in 1874 and her friend and protector, the Count de Naurois, died four years later. She now found herself quite alone. Her adopted daughter Solange had disappeared during the Franco–Prussian War, by all accounts with a German soldier, and Céleste was never to hear from her again. She had taken a room in the Passage de l'Opéra, where she continued to write plays and to oversee their production, the final one being

Door, please in 1886. She had been a prolific writer, publishing a total of twelve novels, twenty-six plays, seven operettas, twelve poems and seventeen songs, as well as her two sets of memoirs.[4]

With failing health and a dwindling income, Céleste decided to retire, and applied for admission to the home for the aged run by the Society of Dramatic Authors, of which she was a member. While acknowledging her significant literary output and giving her a small pension, the directors refused her entry. Once again, she paid the price of her disreputable past. She finally entered 'La Providence', a home in Montmartre, where she spent the last years of her life—'that absurdity between the cradle and the grave', as she described it—in a pitiful state, no longer caring for her living conditions or her own person.[5] She died in 1909 and was buried, in accordance with her final wishes, in the family vault in the Pré-Saint-Gervais cemetery beside her mother Anne-Victoire and the despised Vincent, with the one word—'Céleste'—on her plaque.

Through her self-revelation, attitudes and observations in *Death at the End of the World*, Céleste emerges as an unusual and complex woman. She was obviously a person of great energy and tenacity, and enduring the difficulties she encountered in the two and a half years she spent in Melbourne must have demanded quite a deal of courage. In addition, her ability to teach herself to write her own language and learn English bears witness to a definite intelligence and a great amount of perseverance.

Another side of Céleste that comes through clearly in her writing is her romantic temperament. She paints a picture of unshakeable commitment between herself and Lionel, with only the occasional mention of conflict. It is almost a fairly-tale love story in which they would have lived happily ever after. However, knowing what we do of their personalities and their volatile relationship before marriage, we may well doubt that their life as a couple was quite so smooth in reality. From the point of view of readership and personal pride in the face of the Chabrillans' constant opposition, it would certainly have been in Céleste's interests to romanticize her marriage with Lionel. Hence the slightly theatrical quality in her conversations with him and in her reactions to what he says and does.

One source of conflict between the two was Céleste's refusal to play a subservient role in relation to her husband. From much earlier in their relationship, Lionel insisted that she conform more to the codes of behaviour acceptable for high-class ladies of the day, but she refused to do so. She often comments on the double standards in society, such as when he chides her for her enthusiasm in taking astronomy lessons from the captain of the *Croesus*. Indeed, through her expressions of determination and independence, it could be said that Céleste creates a feminist sub-text in much of her writing. She was very much her own creation.

She shows herself to be a compassionate woman, caring for the mother bereaved by the loss of her baby on board ship, and taking an active interest in the plight of her struggling compatriots who come to see Lionel. There is predictably some selection in her expressions of concern. She is horrified by the treatment of King Signolo in captivity at the Cape of Good Hope, but reiterates the commonly held opinions of the time in her acerbic comments about the Aborigines and the Chinese. She supports Lionel in his efforts to have the widowed Jacques Trumeau repatriated, yet spares little thought for the forthright English washerwoman who, heavily pregnant, has been deserted by her French husband. Her personal prejudices are sometimes tempered by her husband who, for example, defends the sailors on board the *Croesus* against her criticisms of their appearance and behaviour. She clearly dislikes the English in general, and makes numerous derogatory remarks about them in her account of the outward voyage. There is some contradiction then in her dismay at their willingness to denigrate each other in the face of the seemingly constant danger of life at sea.

Céleste is not without a sense of humour, probably quite an asset during her life in Australia. She and Lionel laughed at the joke played on the inhabitants of Melbourne by the captain of the *Great Britain*, while most people were outraged. Her derision of pompous behaviour and self-important people is often tongue in cheek, and she makes light of some situations, such as the unexpected visit by the Chinese escapee. On the other hand, we often see her taking the high moral ground. In her first set of memoirs, Céleste claims that while she did wrong, she admired all that was good; that while she lived in vice, she loved virtue. In *Death at the End of the World* she shows herself striving to meet these ideals.

Death at the End of the World gives the modern reader a first-hand and very personal account of gold-rush Victoria in the hectic 1850s. We first witness the way of life on board an outward-bound passenger ship, with all its adventures and misadventures; then we discover the rapidly growing town of Melbourne, such a shock to Céleste with her Parisian tastes; we read of life in the colony, its land and goldfields, people and society; and the impressions, feelings and reactions of settlers in the frontier land.

Céleste never disguises her dislike for Victoria and its inhabitants. She prophetically called it her land of exile on arrival, for she was to find herself not only exiled from her beloved France, but also from her husband's society in Melbourne. In her writing, it is not surprising that she expresses her disillusionment and resentment for a country that she feels has little to offer her and refuses what she has to offer it. As she wrote somewhat ruefully in *In Australia*, 'In this country the women are only appreciated when they are as strong as men. They saw wood, split logs, groom horses, and do the washing and cooking for relaxation.'[6] And in *The Two Sisters*, 'Dreamers don't go to Australia; dreamers would not have the time to dream there.'[7] This, however, does not detract from the worthiness of the memoirs as a valid and sincere account of colonial Australia. They are essentially a broadly accurate and comprehensive account of life, delivered from Céleste's personal perspective. Indeed, in autobiography, it is often the feeling and subjectivity that the author expresses in the reporting of events that bring the facts to life. *Death at the End of the World* is the unique testimony of a Frenchwoman who left a sophisticated life in Paris, as something of a celebrity, to experience life of a very different kind in the harsh and heady days of gold-rush Victoria.

Notes

INTRODUCTION

1   C. de Chabrillan, *Un Deuil au bout du monde, suite des mémoires de Céleste Mogador*, Paris, Librairie Nouvelle, 1877.

2   'Victoria shunned French consul's "harlot spouse"', *Daily Mirror* (photocopy undated).

3   C. de Chabrillan, *Les Voleurs d'or*, Paris, Michel Lévy, 1857. Céleste de Chabrillan, *The Gold Robbers*, trans. Lucy and Caroline Moorhead, preface by Professor A. R. Chisholm, Melbourne, Sun Books, 1970. The novel also appeared in serialised form in the *Victorian Review* under the title of *The Gold Seekers*, probably translated by James Smith (L. Stuart, *James Smith . . .*, p. 90). *Les Voleurs d'or*, a drama in five acts, was first performed on 28 May 1864 at the Théâtre de Belleville in Paris.

4   H. de Castella, *Les Squatters australiens*, Paris, Hachette, 1861.

5   In her memoirs, Céleste claims that she lost her father when she was six years old (see *Mémoires de Céleste Mogador*, 2nd edn, 4 vols, Paris, Librairie Nouvelle, 1858, vol. I, p. 2), in what would seem to be an attempt to deny her illegitimacy and give more respectability to her family circumstances. Céleste never revealed her illegitimacy during her mother's lifetime.

6   The biographer Françoise Moser disputes Céleste's claim that her mother was a milliner, asserting that she was, in fact, a laundress. Moser was told this in an oral testimony by an old acquaintance of the mother. (See Moser, p. 17.)

7   The theatres in the Boulevard du Temple at this time were: les Délassements-Comiques, le Cirque Olympique, les Folies-Dramatiques, la Gaïté, les Funambules and le Lazary.

8   C. de Chabrillan, *Mémoires de Céleste Mogador*, vol. I, p. 212.

9   The Berry is a historical region to the south of the Paris Basin which today roughly corresponds to the departments of Indre and Cher. Its capital was Bourges.

10 Châteauroux is the principal town in the Department of Indre and is 263 kilometres from Paris.

11 C. de Chabrillan, *Mémoires de Céleste Mogador*, vol. 3, pp. 305–6.

12 *Adieux au monde, mémoires de Céleste Mogador*, published in five volumes by Locard-Davi et de Vresse in 1854, is the original title of Céleste's first set of memoirs. The two later editions, which appeared in 1858 and 1876, were simply entitled *Mémoires de Céleste Mogador*; however, they contain added material, including a final section concerning Lionel. The second edition has therefore been used for reference rather than the first.

13 *Mémoires de Céleste Mogador*, vol. 4, pp. 262–3.

14 See Appendices IIA and IIB.

15 See Appendix III.

16 The *Argus*, 15 March 1856.

17 See *Sun Pictures of Victoria, the Fauchery–Daintree Collection (1858)*. He recounted his Australian travels in *Lettres d'un mineur en Australie* (1857).

18 See Appendices IVA and IVB.

19 Moser, p. 7.

20 The following obvious mistakes in noting or printing the year in the original text have been corrected for ease of reading: in Chapter 8, 6 November 1855 should be 1854, and 3 January 1856 should be 1855; in Chapter 12, 9 January 1857 should read 1856. Céleste corrects herself from then on, apart from one case in Chapter 14 where there is a transposition—1875 for 1857—in the date of *The Gold Robbers* review in *La Presse*.

21 See the *Argus*, 23 September 1854.

22 See, for example, the *Argus*, 5 April 1854, and the *Express*, 15 April 1854.

23 See, for example, the *Ballarat Times*, 2 September 1854.

24 Thornton-Smith, ... *Checklist* .... See also Clancy & Thornton-Smith, *Analytical Checklist* ....

25 The novel by Thérèse Huber, *Adventures on a Journey to New Holland*, was written in German in 1793, first published in 1801 and translated for Lansdowne Press in 1966 by R. Livingstone. However, Huber had never been to Australia, and based her account on reports of Governor Phillip, Watkin Tench, John Hunter and John White. She was greatly influenced by a book written by her husband Georg Forster, who accompanied Cook on his second world voyage.

The book, ostensibly by Marie Giovanni, *Taïti—Marquises—Californie. Journal de Madame Giovanni*, edited and published by Alexandre Dumas, Paris, Cadot, 1856, 4 vols, is a fabricated narration of a round-the-world trip on her husband's sailing ship, using various first-hand accounts interwoven into a loose plot with fictional anecdotes. It was translated in 1944 by Marguerite Wilbur, who assumed that Madame Giovanni actually existed. The involvement of Dumas is significant.

CHAPTER I

1 Emile de Girardin (1806–81), political journalist and talented polemicist, was founder of *La Presse*. He transformed journalism by lowering the prices of news papers and making them an important medium for advertising.

2 Alexandre Dumas (1802–70), known as '*Dumas père*' (Dumas senior), had great success with his early romantic dramas, but became celebrated for his cloak-and-dagger historical romances, notably *The Count of Monte Cristo* (1844) and *The Three Musketeers* (1844). Dumas's extravagant tastes forced him to maintain a hectic writing pace, and an edition of his complete works containing 301 volumes (Michel Lévy, 1862–89) is irrefutable proof of his unflagging energy. (See also Chapter 15, note 3.) That energy animated his journalistic enterprises, his extensive travels and his adventures, including participation in Garibaldi's campaign in Sicily in 1860. Scandals and financial vicissitudes plagued his last years. He died in the home of his illegitimate son, the playwright and novelist Alexandre Dumas *fils*.

3 Prince Napoléon, Napoléon Joseph Charles Paul (1822–91), known by the nickname of '*Plon-Plon*', was a cousin of the Emperor Napoléon III; they were sons of different brothers of Napoléon Bonaparte. Prince Napoléon was the son of

Jérôme Bonaparte, King of Westphalia. He held several political and military posts, but expressed some enlightened views which often got him into trouble; for example, he was against the French expedition in Mexico and the war with Prussia. He was also a patron of the arts and, for a time, gave fortnightly dinners at the famous restaurant 'Voisin', to which he invited various artists and writers; Céleste and Jeanne Tourbay were among the few female guests. Although unable to help Céleste on this occasion, he had been instrumental in having her name removed from the Paris Police Prefecture's register of prostitutes in 1852, and was again to use his influence on her behalf ten years later in obtaining a licence for her theatre, the Folies-Marigny. Despite the claims of her detractors, including her brother-in-law, the Marquis de Chabrillan, Céleste consistently denied having been Prince Napoléon's mistress.

4 Jean-Jacques Rousseau (1712–78), French philosopher and writer, whose works, including *Du contract social* (1762) and *Emile* (1762), were extremely influential in the second half of the 18th Century. Dumas is referring here to the *Confessions* (1782) in which Rousseau lays bare his life and his soul in an effort to show his own life confirming his theory that the natural goodness in man is warped by society.

5 Henri Murger (1822–61), sometimes written Henry Mürger, novelist and play-wright, known almost exclusively for his *Scènes de la vie de Bohème* in which he included many elements from his life and circle of friends. The poet Théodore de Banville claimed that Murger used Antoine Fauchery as a model for the painter Marcel. (See Chapter 9, note 4.) It was written first as a novel and then as a play, before being made into the famous opera by Puccini.

6 Murger dedicated these lines to her in 1852 to avenge the scornful conduct of her rival, known by the name of Judith, an actress at the Théâtre Français, and to defend Céleste against the extremely negative criticism of her latest role at the Théâtre des Variétés:

To upset the actress	Pour vexer la comédienne
Whose only jewels are imitation,	Qui n'a que des bijoux en toc
Céleste who in Morocco	Céleste qui dans le Maroc
In times past found her namesake,	Jadis a choisi sa marraine
From behind a garden all in flower	Derrière un jardin tout en fleurs
Enters as a haughty princess.	S'avance en princesse hautaine.
In Philoxène's rooms	Dans les salons de Philoxène
There were eighty of us rhymesters.	Nous étions quatre-vingts rimeurs.
On to the marble of her shoulders	Dans le marbre de ses épaules
Golconda has set its caskets of jewels,	Golconde incrusta ses écrins,
Visapur has spread stars upon her hands.	Visapour constella ses mains.
'Tis like a polar night.	On dirait une nuit des pôles.
On seeing all her splendour	En voyant toutes ses splendeurs
Judith will shun Holophernes.	Judith va bouder Holpherne.
In Philoxène's rooms	Dans les salons de Philoxène
There were eighty of us rhymesters.	Nous étions quatre-vingts rimeurs.

7 The Hôtel des Invalides, established by Louis XIV in 1670 as a residence to house and care for disabled officers and soldiers. The church has a large dome which, since 1840, has housed Napoleon's tomb.

8 Lionel was thirty-six, not thirty-two, at the time of his marriage.

⁹ In *Farewell to the World*, Céleste names Solange's mother as her maid Caroline, who died in hospital soon after the birth.

¹⁰ The *Croesus* was the first of the regular steamers to be dispatched by the General Screw Steamship Company from Southampton to Port Phillip and Sydney, the terminal port. The captain was J. V. Hall. In this, its maiden voyage, defects were found in the ship's construction and machinery.

¹¹ Céleste first appeared with Adèle Page in a revue at the Théâtre des Variétés in 1852 (see note 6). They remained friends and, in 1862, Adèle was one of Céleste's many supporters at the opening of her theatre, the Folies-Marigny. Born into a theatrical family, Adèle Page first appeared on the stage at the Vaudeville in 1842. J. Arago pronounced her the prettiest and one of the best Parisian actresses performing in the period 1849 to 1853. Like Céleste she had a long and interesting career in the theatre, at one time touring the provinces in *The Lady of the Camellias*. She died in 1882. Barbey d'Aurevilly wrote an article about her in *Old Age* (*La Vieillesse*), which was later republished in *Old Actresses* (*Les Vieilles actrices*). (*Archives biographiques françaises*: taken from Henry Lyonnet, *Dictionnaire des comédiens français*, Paris, 1902–08.)

CHAPTER 2

¹ Mr Bonard, probably a pseudonym for Barnet, whose name appears on the official passenger list. (See PROV VPRS 3501 Passenger Lists of Immigrants (unassisted) from U.K. 1852–1923, microfilm copy, unit 7.)

² The *Croesus* picked up mail from the *Matilda Wattenbach*, dismasted on 13 December about 110 kilometres from Madeira.

³ Lionel sailed from Southampton on the 700-ton *Chusan*, the first P&O steamship to come to Australia, on 15 May 1852, arriving in Melbourne en route to Sydney on 29 July. This was a crossing of seventy-six days; the *Croesus* took ninety-five, but nonetheless this was still not an inordinately slow trip for a ship of that period.

⁴ The shipwreck of the *Medusa* is the subject of the best-known work of the French romantic painter Théodore Géricault (1791–1824), 'The Raft of the *Medusa*' (1819, Louvre). This enormous picture portrayed a current public scandal: the Medusa's captain, who was a political appointee, had abandoned 135 passengers and crew of his shipwrecked vessel. Géricault turned this event into a monumental historical painting, a heroic scene of ghastly suffering with Michelangelesque nude figures in which realism and idealization are combined in a grandiose composition. The painting caused a sensation at the Salon of 1819 for its political allusions.

⁵ A Voltaire chair is a large chair with wooden armrests and an upholstered seat and high back, rather like a Victorian carver chair.

⁶ Mistress Brook is the name Céleste gives to Mrs Brackenbury, whose name appears on the official list of passengers in first class. Mrs Brackenbury, a French expatriate, went from the *Croesus* to the home of the Andersons, one of Melbourne's leading families, and was later joined there by her husband, a British officer serving as an official on the goldfields. One may surmise that Mrs Brackenbury initially befriended Céleste, believing her to be of aristocratic descent, but later discovered her humble origins and reacted accordingly.

⁷ Robert Macaire, a character from the melodrama *L'Auberge des Adrets* by Benjamin Autier, Saint-Amant and Paulyanthe, made famous by the caricatures of Daumier

and the talents of the actor Frédéric Lemaître (cf the film *Les Enfants du paradis*), was a perverse, daring and impudent rogue, an unashamed thief and murderer.

8 'Lady Gamby', probably Lady Campbell, a passenger in first class. Lady Campbell, née McLeod, kept her title after her second marriage, to a Mr Maule. Jean Uhl (*A Woman of Importance . . .*) points out that there was a Mr H. Maule who was Deputy Assistant Commissioner–General in the Commissariat Dept. in Hobart. Lady Campbell and her husband knew Emily Childers, whose brother, Tom Walker, also came out on the *Croesus*.

CHAPTER 3

1 The *Croesus* arrived at Lisbon on 16 January and left eight days later.

2 Tantalus is a king in Greek mythology, punished in Hades for his misdeeds by having to stand in water that recedes when he tries to drink it, beneath fruit that moves away when he reaches for it.

3 Queen Maria II of Portugal died on 13 November 1853.

4 After anchoring in Table Bay on 28 February, the *Croesus* was delayed by repairs until 10 March.

5 The Hottentot or Khoikhoi are a southern African people who once inhabited the southern part of Namibia and the north-western, southern and south-eastern parts of South Africa. They lived a semi-nomadic pastoral life in large tribes and were hunter–gatherers, each nuclear family within the tribe occupying a separate beehive-shaped hut. Their traditionally simple culture and lifestyle collapsed largely as a result of European colonization.

  The name Kaffir was applied to the Xhosa peoples of southern Africa by early white settlers. Hostilities between the Kaffir people and their colonisers increased after the Cape was ceded by Holland to the British Crown in 1814.

6 King Signolo was no doubt imprisoned during the Kaffir war of 1850–53.

7 The legend of the Wandering Jew: it is said that Jesus, labouring under the weight of the cross, wanted to rest in front of the house of the Jew Ahasuerus, who drove him away. To punish him, the Lord said: 'You will wander the earth until I come.' The Jew immediately began to walk, propelled by an irresistible force, and had to wander without finding any place of rest. The legend became widespread from the twelfth century and was linked to the story of Malk or Mark, who was said to have struck Christ. Eugène Sue wrote a very popular version of it (*Le Juif Errant*, 1845), one of the first serialized stories to be published in France. (*Nouveau Larousse Universel*)

8 The Egyptian Obelisk of Luxur marks the centre of the Place de la Concorde in Paris.

CHAPTER 4

1 D. Charlwood in *The Long Farewell* quotes this passage from Céleste's book on p. 145 with the following comments: 'Of all the crew's activities, it was the work aloft among the trapezes of rigging that overawed the emigrants, especially if the ship was rolling' (p. 144). 'At 60° [. . .] at the other end of the yard, [a sailor] could be dipped into the sea with each roll of the ship—a sight often watched by emigrants with terror' (p. 145).

2 *Robert the Devil* (*Robert le Diable*), a grand opera by Giacomo Meyerbeer, was first performed in Paris in 1831. The action takes place in the thirteenth century and is

full of stage spectacle. Bertram is Robert Duke of Normandy's unknown father and the devil in disguise. Many stage devices are used as Bertram works his evil magic, and in the end he disappears back to hell, no doubt by way of a trapdoor. (*Phaidon Book of the Opera*)

CHAPTER 5

1 The *Croesus* arrived in Port Phillip Bay on 9 April 1854.

2 The newspaper articles concerning the late arrival of the *Croesus* were not as pessimistic as Céleste describes. For example, the *Argus* notes, five days before the ship's arrival: 'Considerable apprehensions have been expressed as regards this vessel, but it is highly probable that one of the many minor accidents to which steamers are especially liable, has occurred.' (the *Argus*, 5 April 1854); and later: 'The arrival of the *Croesus*, yesterday morning, after expectations had been some time on tip-toe about her, and some uneasiness had been felt [. . .] was hailed with something akin to enthusiasm' (10 April 1854). No mention is made of Céleste and the first mention of Lionel is ten days later when the *Argus* quotes the *Government Gazette* in announcing the appointment of the Count de Chabrillan to the position of French consular agent in Melbourne (20 April 1854).

3 The desertion of sailors to the goldfields was so common that at one time nearly 100 vessels were unable to sail for Europe for lack of hands, though as much as £70 was offered to each sailor for the run home. (Adcock, *The Gold Rushes . . .*)

4 Ernest Baroche was the intelligent and energetic son of an important conservative Minister of State under Napoléon III. He led a hectic and sometimes scandalous social life, while working in several ministries and industry. When the Franco–Prussian War broke out in 1870, he was elected head of a battalion, and died in action. Victor Hugo remarked that 'On that day, the death of the son made one forget the life of the father.' (*Dictionnaire de biographie française*)

5 There is no official record of the Duke d'Esclignac's death in Melbourne, nor does his name appear on the Melbourne General Cemetery's list of burials—anomalies that can be explained if he died in poverty and possibly anonymously. Horace Viel-Castel, a contemporary of Céleste, also makes mention of the premature death of the Duke d'Esclignac, stating that d'Esclignac, also known as the Duke de Fimarcon, died in poverty in Australia in July 1853, his appeals for help having been ignored by his father. When he was a child, his father, it seems, had already ignored him to such a degree that he grew up almost illiterate. Although Viel-Castel's writings lack impartiality, we can assume his comments on the duke's death at least are well grounded. (See Viel-Castel, *Mémoires . . .*, vol. 2, pp. 274–6.)

6 In early 1854, before Lionel took up his post as the new consul, France was represented by the well-known Melbourne identity Jacob Montefiore. This makeshift office was the first consulate. The address changed annually during Lionel's incumbency: 1855 at Collins Place; 1856 at 87 Collins Street East; 1857 at 23 Stephen Street; 1858 at 42 Russell Street.

CHAPTER 6

1 There is no record in the newspapers of the Chabrillans' visit to the Ballarat goldfields. It is interesting to note that, during this same period, the governor, Sir Charles Hotham, and his wife made an official tour of the goldfields and that Lady

Hotham was widely praised for her courage and kindness. (See the *Ballarat Times*, 2 September 1854 and the *Argus*, 4 September 1854.)

2 The 2200-ton *Tayleur* set sail from Liverpool for Melbourne on 19 January 1854, and sank off Lambay Island in the Irish Sea two days later. Of an estimated 705 people on board (passengers and crew), approximately 250 survived. (See the *Biddle Registers*, vol. 15.) The name Jacques Trumeau (probably a fictitious name) appears neither on the passenger list nor on the list of survivors. (See the *Argus*, 4 May 1854)

3 Of 214 Chinese passengers on board the *Onyx*, which sailed from Hong Kong on 3 May 1854, twenty-four died en route to Melbourne and at least forty-one died within twelve days of their landing. Their deaths were attributed to a form of scurvy induced by their long voyage, insufficient accommodation and a diet of rice, water and inedible rotten fish. The immigrants arrived on 22 August and were immediately quarantined in an encampment beyond Prince's Bridge. (See the *Argus*, 25 August and 8 September 1854.)

4 A similar description of the simulated attack by the *Great Britain* and public reaction to it appeared in the *Argus*, 8 September 1854.

5 Céleste bought the Le Poinçonnet property *La Croix Rouge* in August 1850. Le Poinçonnet is a hamlet near Châteauroux. The Chabrillan castle, the Château du Magnet, was in the same area, and the family was not at all pleased to have Céleste in the neighbourhood.

CHAPTER 7

1 Although there are some inconsistencies in the official records that cover capital punishment during the 1850s, we can assume that, if Céleste did witness a hanging, it was that of John Hughes, found guilty of the murder of at least fifteen people, on 22 September 1854. Céleste gives 23 August as the date of the hanging, but she was often haphazard in her notation of dates and, during this period, was often mistaken by several weeks or more in the recording of events. (See PROV VPRS 5136 Criminal Record Books, microfilm copy, reel 1, 1854–67; and the *Argus*, 23 September 1854.)

Céleste gives a similar account of a hanging in her first Australian novel, *The Gold Robbers*, in which one of the central characters, the younger daughter of a Dr Iwans [*sic*], witnesses the hanging of a mass murderer—also her attacker—from a window of the family home which overlooks the courtyard of the Supreme Court.

It is interesting that Antoine Fauchery, in his *Letters from a Miner in Australia* (*Lettres d'un mineur en Australie*, p. 23), describes a hanging which he witnessed the day after his arrival in Australia, and that he was similarly repulsed by this form of capital punishment.

2 Honoré Gabriel Riqueti, Count de Mirabeau (1749–91) was a French Revolutionary politician and its most eminent speaker.

3 Sir Charles Hotham (1806–55), born in Suffolk, England, was a naval officer until his appointment as Lieutenant–Governor of Victoria in 1853. He soon appreciated the need to increase revenue, strengthen administration and allay goldfields discontent by extending political privileges and improving the licence system, but he totally misunderstood his position as governor of a sizeable Crown colony. He courted the working population, especially miners, while remaining clearly authoritarian. He nonetheless upset the firmest supporters of authority, the

propertied and official classes, by his declarations of 'democratic' principles and his unwillingness to meet with the Executive Council. Despite the weight of public opinion against the mining licence fee, he proved unwilling to abandon it. Thus, in the Eureka crisis, he could depend on little help from his officials; by mid-January 1855 his fragile popularity and support had collapsed. He died at the end of that year. (*ADB*)

4 Céleste is mistaken in her account of the fate of the hotel owner, Bentley. He fled to the government encampment when the miners set fire to his establishment. During the Eureka Stockade, the Count de Chabrillan published a proclamation to French expatriates residing in Victoria, advising them to dissociate themselves from the agitation on the Ballarat goldfields. (This proclamation is reproduced facing p. 148.)

CHAPTER 8

1 It has not been possible to locate the exact position of the Chabrillans' house in St Kilda, but it was probably north of Fitzroy Street, as it was some distance from the village and Lionel reports that the railway line was to go through part of their land.

2 12 000 francs was the equivalent of £480 stg. This can be compared with the annual salary of £700 earned by the goldfield commissioners Joseph Panton and Walter Brackenbury. (See 'Despatches from Victoria', no. 42, 7 December 1854, p. 1451, Mitchell Library, NSW; details supplied by C. B. Thornton-Smith.)

3 Landerneau, a small French town on the Elorn estuary in Brittany, whose name is used in expressions to convey news that is of little importance but likely to arouse public curiosity; for example, 'They'll be talking about that in Landerneau.'

4 Lionel's official position differed from that of a number of other consular agents working in Australia, who were often involved in business. Some countries appointed merchants working in the country to the position, which they then carried out in a part-time capacity. (See J. Smith (ed.), *The Cyclopedia of Victoria*, pp. 289–94.)

CHAPTER 9

1 Little is known of the Count de Varenne, apart from the fact that he lived in St Kilda, not far from the Chabrillans' house.

2 *Haute école*, the classical equestrian style.

3 A 'donation inter-vivos' is a legal term meaning a gift bequeathed from one person to another before the death of the donor. Céleste is presumably using the expression humorously to mean an exchange of blows.

4 Antoine Julien Fauchery (1823–61), a high-spirited writer, artist and photographer with a love of adventure, left the bohemian life in Paris in 1848 with the photographer Nadar, supposedly to defend Poland, but was imprisoned for a time in Magdeburg. In 1852 he sailed for Melbourne in the *Emily*; from there he went to Ballarat where he worked for two years on the goldfields. In 1854–55 he spent several months in Melbourne and founded the Café-Estaminet Français, which was well patronized by non-British residents of the town. Melbourne Commercial Directories list him as owner/proprietor of a billiard room at 76 Little Bourke Street East. He returned to the goldfields and for some months was a storekeeper at the Jim Crow (Daylesford) diggings. When this venture failed, he returned to France where, in 1857, he published his eight *Letters from a Miner in Australia*, initially in serial form in *Le Moniteur Universel*, subsequently as a volume by Poulet-Malassis & de

Broise. These *Letters* are his chief claim to interest as a writer, and they paint a vivid picture of life in early Melbourne and on the goldfields. With a grant from the French Government for an official photographic mission to India, Australia and China, Fauchery returned to Melbourne with his wife and worked throughout 1858 in a studio in Collins Street, publishing *Sun Pictures of Victoria* with his partner Richard Daintree. He sailed to Manila in 1859, after which he followed the French military expedition to China as photographer and journalist. He wrote a series of *Letters from China* (*Lettres de Chine*), but became ill there and died in Japan in 1861. (*ADB*)

Fauchery does not mention Céleste in his *Letters*. He makes one reference to Lionel when describing the diverse clientele of his Little Bourke Street café: 'Count Moreton de Chabrillant [*sic*] and I were on very good terms, but he refused to visit my famous café on the pretext that I entertained too many sailors who had jumped ship' (p. 230).

CHAPTER 10

[1] Newspaper reports confirm Céleste's account of the 'beer ball'. See, for example, the *Argus*, 29 May 1855, and the *Melbourne Punch*, January–July edition, 1855.

[2] The *Argus* of 25 and 27 January 1855 reviews Coulon's performances in very laudatory terms.

[3] Louis Pierre Anquetil's *Histoire de France* was first published in 1805 in 14 volumes. Although the *Dictionnaire de biographie française* called it 'mediocre', it was reprinted and re-edited many times. Anquetil's work must have been part of the official bequest of books given to the Public Library by Lionel as French Consul, as it bears the inscription and is still part of the collection.

[4] The Goldfields Commission, inquiring into the Eureka affair, recommended legislation to check the Chinese influx; in June 1855 a tax of £10 per head was imposed on every arrival, and a limit imposed of one Chinaman to every ten tons of shipping. (Crowley, *A Documentary History* . . . .)

[5] This is either a misreading or a misspelling of *flagstaff*. There had been an elaborate system for sending signals between incoming ships, the Harbour Master's office at Williamstown and a station on Flagstaff Hill since 1840. In 1849 a high flagstaff fitted with a time-ball and an iron semaphore telegraph was erected above the new lighthouse at Williamstown. The first telegraph service in the Australian colonies opened between Melbourne and Williamstown in 1854, ten years after the world's first morse telegraph system. (M. Cannon, *Old Melbourne Town* . . .; *Australians: A Historical Dictionary*.)

[6] Céleste is referring to the Rifle Ball in aid of the Victorian Volunteer Rifle Corps. Volunteer rifle forces were formed in Victoria in 1854 during the Crimean War, when the fear of Russian invasion reported by Céleste was widespread in the colonies.

[7] A tombola is a type of lottery held especially at fêtes, fairs or social gatherings. The winning tickets are usually drawn from a turning, drum-like container. On the morning of the French Ball, 16 August 1855, the *Argus* described how it was arranged, giving all the credit to Lionel, as all the accounts do. 'Every lady, on entering the ball-room, will be handed a programme of the dances, bearing also a number. One hundred of these numbers will correspond with others attached to various trinkets and elegant nick-nacks of various kinds, and which are the prizes,

the residue being blanks. The introduction of so novel and pleasing a feature at a ball is attributable to the ingenuity of M. De Chabrillan, and we have no doubt that it will considerably add to the entertainment of the company.'

Emily Childers' husband Hugh, in his capacity as Collector of Customs, went to the Emperor's Name Day Dinner (see p. 139 and note 8) and they both attended the ball. Emily writes: 'A Tombola after supper. Thanks to Mr. Hammond, I got 12 pairs of gloves. Enjoyed the evening very much tho' I did not dance' (p. 186). She was pregnant at the time.

8 Sir Edward Eyre Williams (1813–80). Born and educated in England, the barrister Edward Williams came to the Port Phillip district in 1842, and was active in community affairs in the 1840s. In 1852 he was appointed Solicitor General and then Puisne Judge of the Supreme Court. Justice Williams was an influential man in questions affecting public welfare.

The *Argus*, 16 August 1855, makes mention of the toast, listed as the last for the evening, made to Céleste by Justice Williams at the official dinner given by Lionel to celebrate the Emperor's name day. See Appendix I for this report.

9 The *Argus*, 18 August 1855, gives a full and flattering report of the French Ball. See Appendix IIA for this report and Appendix IIB for a more whimsical account, partly in fractured French, published in the *Melbourne Punch*, January–July 1855.

CHAPTER 11

1 Melbourne experienced this mild earthquake on 17 September 1855.

2 Lola Montez (1818–61), christened Marie Dolores Eliza Rosanna Gilbert, was born in Ireland, the daughter of Ensign Edward Gilbert who died when she was a child. When her young mother married again, she was sent to boarding schools in England and France. Joseph Panton, in his *Autobiography* (MS La Trobe Library, Melbourne), notes that for a time she boarded in London in the care of the Rev. Brackenbury, father-in-law of 'Mistress Brook', the woman Céleste disliked so much on board the *Croesus*. Lola eloped at nineteen, was left, then trained as a dancer in Spain, taking the name Lola Montez. She performed dances considered erotic in England and Europe, her seductive beauty attracting many lovers, including Franz Liszt and Alexandre Dumas *père*. The most extraordinary period in her extraordinary life took place in Bavaria where King Ludwig I gave her titles and power that eventually caused riots in 1848, leading to her banishment and his abdication. Two bigamous marriages and two tours later, Lola and her current lover arrived first in Sydney, then opened a show in Melbourne in September 1855. (*ADB*)

3 Lola Montez's notorious 'Spider Dance', first performed by her in San Francisco during the gold rush. In Melbourne, she had begun adding this description of it to the bills: 'A young Spanish Girl while amusing herself by dancing is stung by a Spider or Tarantula, which fastens itself upon her person, and as the poison gradually disperses itself through her frame, she becomes faint and exhausted, falls upon the stage, or reels off distracted.' Press reports, however, relate that she usually ended by finding the spider, throwing it on the ground and crushing it underfoot in a final dance of triumph.

'The Spider Dance' was parodied by both George Coppin and Joseph Chambers. Opinions about it were mixed, but reactions were mostly scandalized. The *Sydney Morning Herald* called it 'the most libertinish and indelicate performance that could ever be given on the public stage', but *Bell's Life in Sydney* found 'nothing in her beautiful saltation beyond descriptive, coquettish eccentricities' (*Entertaining Australia*, p. 56). It so outraged the good citizens of Melbourne that Mayor Smith was asked to arrest her, but he declined to do so.

4 John Thomas Smith (1816–79), landowner, publican and later politician, was elected to the first Melbourne Town Council in 1842 and was mayor seven times from 1851 to 1864. In 1845 Smith built the Queen's Theatre Royal, Melbourne's first theatre and the first home of George Coppin's company. He was often lampooned and criticized by the press, and although politically conservative, he was also personally generous.

5 *Partant pour la Syrie* was composed in 1810 and became the official march for public ceremonies during the Second Empire.

6 The *Argus* (15 March 1856), in an article entitled 'Consular Dignity', published an unfavourable account of the Count de Chabrillan (see Appendix III).

7 *Richelieu*, by Edward Bulwer-Lytton, was a popular play in the Australian repertoire of Irish Shakespearian actor Gustavus Vaughan Brooke.

8 Brooke was brought out to Australia by Coppin on his return in 1854. He had a declamatory style, but was very versatile. As well as Shakespeare, Brooke played in domestic drama, tragedy, comedy and farce. Coppin ordered a prefabricated theatre of cast-iron, corrugated iron, timber and glass to be made in England and erected on the corner of Lonsdale and Stephen Streets to house his performances. The Olympic Theatre opened in June 1855. The Chabrillans would have seen him there or at the Queen's Theatre Royal. Like all actors in Australia at that time, Brooke often had to act on an improvised stage, and the article on him in *Entertaining Australia* contains a report that he once performed on a billiard table.

9 A wig or hairstyle 'à la malcontent' was closely cropped hair, as worn by the members of the Malcontents party formed around the Duke d'Alençon, who planned with other nobles to succeed his brother Charles IX. The plot was discovered and the ring-leaders arrested.

10 George Selth Coppin (1819–1906), comic actor and important theatre entrepreneur, came to Australia in 1843. He acted in the major cities, dabbled in various kinds of business and opened or renovated many theatres. When Coppin opened the White Horse Cellar at Port Adelaide in 1850, his adjoining theatre met opposition on moral grounds. His fortunes fluctuated, but he made money entertaining miners in Geelong, toured in Australia and England, and in 1863 brought out Charles Kean and his wife. From 1858 onwards, he was in and out of politics, but his involvement with the theatre was a life-long passion. Conservatives did not always appreciate Coppin's innovations in scenery design or methods of advertising, but he was a major figure in the development of theatre in Australia. (*ADB*)

   In the program at the Olympic Theatre, Coppin not only parodied Lola Montez's movements in the Spider Dance; he also made fun of Lola's own description of the dance with his first sentence: 'The young and buxom god, while amusing himself by dancing, swallows a Brandy Spider, which takes immediate effect upon him' (Seymour, . . . *Montez* . . ., pp. 339–40.) Press reports relate that when he extracted 'an enormous animal resembling a spider' from his skimpy skirt and chased it across the stage, the audience 'literally rolled out of their seats with laughter.' (A. Bagot, *Coppin the Great*, p. 202.)

CHAPTER 12

[1] Pierre Lachambeaudie (1806–72), writer of fables and satirical songs. His contemporaries found his *Popular Fables* appealing and elegantly written.

[2] Lola Montez appeared principally in a dramatic presentation of her adventures entitled 'Lola Montez in Bavaria', followed by the 'Spider Dance', when audiences began to dwindle. In Victoria she toured several country towns, including Ballarat in February 1856, when the famous horse-whipping of the local newspaper editor took place. However, it was the wife of her impresario on the goldfields who inflicted the injuries described by Céleste. In spite of attacking Harry Seekamp of the *Ballarat Times* with a horsewhip for commenting on her private life, Lola Montez was very popular on her goldfields tour. She then sailed for America, where her health and fortunes began to decline. She died there of syphilis in 1861. (*ADB*)

[3] Michael Cannon, in *Lola Montès, the Tragic Story of a 'Liberated Woman'*, notes that the Chabrillans went to visit Lola in the Grand Imperial Hotel at the corner of Elizabeth and Little Collins Streets.

[4] There is no record of a French shipwreck on that date.

[5] There is no official record of the Chabrillans' bankruptcy.

[6] Ardentes, a town in the Department of Indre, in the Châteauroux district.

CHAPTER 13

[1] The *James Baines* was built by Donald McKay in Boston and named after the founder of the Black Ball Line of Liverpool. It carried 620 steerage passengers and 80 in other accommodation.

[2] Pierre-Jean de Béranger (1780–1857), a patriotic and political writer of songs and poetry, acclaimed as the national poet of France during his lifetime.

CHAPTER 14

[1] Lionel is referring to the letter Céleste wrote at the beginning of her journey as the ship was leaving the bay through the Heads.

[2] Count Alinant de Dollon became a well-known Hawthorn identity, arriving in the area in 1859. He had a large vineyard and pasture in Tooronga Road West and also a 'restaurant' wine saloon in Swanston Street. His fortunes must have fluctuated as his name appeared on a list of insolvents in October 1868. Nonetheless, in 1872 he won a gold medal for raising £2300 in an appeal for the French wounded in the Franco–Prussian war. De Dollon left in about 1874. (McWilliam, *Hawthorn Peppercorns*; Dunstan, . . . *Pommard* . . .)

[3] There is no trace of the 'great work' on Australia that Lionel says he completed in his letter of 4 September 1856, nor is there any mention of it by his executor Adet after his death. Lionel was no scholar or writer, and it is possible that Céleste was paving the way for some future project which she could publish under his name.

[4] The St Kilda railway, which boasted a chandelier in the station waiting room, opened in 1857.

[5] H. de Villemessant founded *Le Figaro* as a satirical newspaper in 1854. Today it is the leading conservative, political and literary daily newspaper in Paris.

[6] Henri de la Tour d'Auvergne, Viscount de Turenne (1611–75), Marshall of France, Commander of the French Army in the War of Devolution 1667 and the war with

Holland 1672, conqueror of Alsace in 1675. He was a simple, modest man who claimed that his military brilliance was based on 'calculation and reflexion'.

7   C. de Chabrillan, . . . *Voleurs* . . . .

8   Céleste has deliberately misquoted this sentence from the review in *La Presse*. It should read 'Those who have not read Céleste Mogador's very unusual memoirs and who do not know the author will read the whole of *The Gold Robbers* with unflagging curiosity.' The beginning of the sentence was no doubt omitted to avoid any mention of her stage name and the notorious memoirs written under it.

9   Louis-Victor-Nestor Roqueplan (1804–70) was a writer and theatre director, known for his witty observations of social and theatrical life.

10   This line cannot be traced to any published work by Alfred de Musset. Céleste has correctly transcribed the line from the *Figaro* article. Therefore, assuming that the line is attributed to the correct author, it is possibly a misquotation or reworking by Huban.

11   Gabriel Ferry (Eugène-Louis-Gabriel de Bellemarre, 1809–52), traveller and writer of very popular adventure novels. He travelled extensively in Mexico and was best known for his novels *Castal l'Indien* and *Le Coureur des bois*.

12   Jean-Baptiste Greuze (1725–1805), a fashionable painter of anecdotal genre scenes and charming portraits during the late eighteenth century.

13   Jules Janin (1804–74) was perhaps the most influential literary and drama critic of his day. Céleste must have been very pleased to receive a good review from him. Janin was also a novelist and a theatre historian.

14   Alexandre Dumas *fils* (1824–95), not as famous as his father, but popular as a writer of novels and plays. Best known for *La Dame aux camélias*, he was elected to the Academy in 1874.

15   Henri Murger drew on many of his own experiences for *Scènes de la vie de Bohème*. It was staged as a play with songs under the title of *La Vie de Bohème* in 1849, then published in book form with the expanded title in 1851. Editions continued to appear well into the next century. Although he wrote other things, Murger's name was always synonymous with this work.

16   Ferdinand-Marie, Viscount de Lesseps (1805–94), was a diplomat, famous for his work on the Suez Canal (1869) and the Panama Canal. Member of the French Academy.

17   Lady Barthley [*sic*]. Lionel is referring to visiting Lady Barkly, the wife of the new governor of Victoria, at Government House in Toorak. Sir Henry Barkly arrived in Melbourne to take up his post on Christmas Eve, 1856.

18   The novel *La Sappho* was published by Michel Lévy in 1858.

19   Situated in Indre-et-Loire, Mettray was once known for its agricultural reformatory for juvenile offenders.

20   The novel Céleste refers to, misprinted as *Miss Pervel* [sic] *et les émigrants*, was published by A. Bourdilliat in 1859 under the title *Miss Pewel*.

21   Murger's Musette is a character in *Scènes de la vie de Bohème*, the subject and singer of a popular song in the stage version.

22   Alfred de Musset (1815–57), major dramatist, novelist and poet. Céleste names him in her scandalous memoirs, *Farewell to the World*, as one of her literary acquaintances and, more importantly, a regular client.

23   Roger de Beauvoir (Roger de Bully, 1809–66), writer of minor romantic literature, especially novels.

[24] Théophile Gautier (1811–72), famous art critic, writer of romantic novels, and poet of the Parnassian School. Many of his early, more romantic poems were set to music by various composers, from Berlioz to Duparc.

CHAPTER 15

[1] Lionel had been cut off by his family when they learned of his marriage. His sister was the marquise de Colbert-Maulevrier.

[2] According to Moser, this must have been his younger sister, married to Louis-François-Alphonse, Count de Motholon-Sémouville. She would therefore be a countess and not, as Céleste calls her, a marquise.

[3] Dumas *père* had the reputation of boosting his enormous output by cannabalizing the work of minor writers. His friend Céleste, who benefited greatly from his support, was happy to try to contradict or at least explain this. Dumas was indeed at that time running a kind of literary industry, using and adapting material from a variety of sources. In the Australian context, he would make maximum use of authentic accounts by Félix Maynard, a whaling ship's doctor, firstly by adding fictional episodes to *Les Baleiniers* (*The Whalers*), as well as probably using more of Maynard's Australian material in the fictitious [. . .] *Journal de Madame Giovanni*, published at about the same time. (See Maynard, *Les Baleiniers* . . . . For the *Journal de Madame Giovanni*, see Introduction, note 25.)

CHAPTER 16

[1] Latakia or Al Ladhiqiyah, a large town on the Syrian coast.

[2] The French originally occupied Cairo in 1798 to counteract the strength of British trade, but had to evacuate the Valley of the Nile in 1801. The Treaty of London in 1841, while nominally allowing the sovereignty of the Porte to remain, in fact made the government of the pashalik of Egypt hereditary in Mohammed Ali's family, but still subject to certain Anglo–French restrictions. Mohammed Ali died in 1849 after impoverishing the country. The ruler at the time when Lionel de Chabrillan visited Cairo was Said Pasha, who was very much under French influence and was persuaded to grant Ferdinand de Lesseps a concession to build the Suez canal in 1856. Lord Palmerston, who also received concessions but objected to the French project, delayed ratification by the Porte for two years. Said Pasha died in 1863. (*Encyclopaedia Brittanica*)

[3] The old town of Aden is also known as Crater, as it is built in the crater of an extinct volcano surrounded on three sides by steep crags. The colony consists of two peninsulas of volcanic rock, the town and port being on the eastern peninsula. Aden very early became an important entrepôt for trade between Europe and the East, and was captured many times. It was little more than a fishing village when it was taken by the British East India Company in 1839, after an Indian ship had been plundered off the coast. A coaling station was set up and trade renewed, developing enormously after the opening of the Suez Canal in 1869. (*Encyclopaedia Britannica*)

[4] This contaminated water was probably the cause of Lionel's fatal illness.

[5] Galle is near the south-west tip of Sri Lanka (Ceylon).

[6] Pau (Basses-Pyrénées) and Hyères (Toulon) are French winter resorts.

CHAPTER 17

[1] Frédéric Kresser, whose name is spelt 'Kreisser' in this chapter and 'Kresser' in chapter 18, was a wine merchant living in Melbourne at this time.

[2] Désiré Soiron was tried for the murder of his mistress, Sarah Chester, and given the death penalty on 23 October 1858. This was commuted to ten years' imprisonment with hard labour on 27 October by the governor, Sir Henry Barkly, acting upon the recommendation of the prisoner's lawyer. There is no record of correspondence between Lionel de Chabrillan and the governor in the official registers. If the consul did play a part in the prisoner's commutation, it must have been in an unofficial or secondary role. (See the *Ballarat Times*, 23 and 25 October 1858.)

[3] J. W. Tarleton was the American Consul.

[4] Coppin entered politics in 1858, although he was still involved in theatre management. At different times he served in both the Legislative Council and the Legislative Assembly.

[5] King Jérôme, who became King of Westphalia, was Napoléon Bonaparte's brother and father of Céleste's friend Prince Napoléon ('*Plon-Plon*').

[6] Porte-Saint-Martin Theatre presented popular plays, many of them with music like *In Australia*. Australia is the setting for a large part of Jules Verne's novel *Les Enfants du capitaine Grant*, which was also presented in a dramatized version at this theatre in 1878.

[7] Sarah Félix was the sister of the famous dramatic actress Rachel (Elisabeth-Rachel Felix, 1821–58). Born into a Jewish family, both sisters began by singing in cafés, where Rachel was discovered by Choron, one of the founders of the Conservatoire Royal. Taken up by the critic Jules Janin at the beginning of her career, she went from strength to strength, reviving the classics, playing Hugo and Dumas, and putting the Théâtre Français on its feet again. Spiteful revelations of her private life marked the beginning of her decline. (*Dictionnaire de biographie française*)

CHAPTER 18

[1] Dr A. C. Brownless practised at 18 Lonsdale Street East and the surgeon Richard T. Tracy at 139 Brunswick Street, Collingwood.

[2] Édouard Adet was a partner in the firm of Curcier, Adet & Co., merchants and importers, listed in Melbourne business directories 1857–66. He served several times as vice-consul for France, most notably after Lionel's death until the arrival of the next appointee. He not only witnessed Lionel's will, but was executor for probate. The *Argus* of 30 November 1903 announced his death in Bordeaux and commented on his commercial activities and vice-consular service in Melbourne.

[3] See Appendix V for a translation of Lionel's will, witnessed by his secretary Phillips and Fauchery. It begins with a touching reference to Céleste: 'My only regret in leaving this life is dying far from my wife and not leaving her in the situation that I would have wished her to have.' He asks Edouard Adet to send her his personal effects and sell the rest, acknowledging only four debts totalling £336, among them £80 for jewellery. When Adet had sold everything and paid all outstanding debts, the balance in hand was £394/17/9 and probate was duly granted.

[4] In fact, Lionel was in his *forty-first* year.

[5] A full but less fulsome account of Lionel's funeral appeared in the *Age* and the *Argus* on 1 January 1859. (See Appendices IVA and IVB.)

[6] After Lionel's death, Fauchery left Australia for Manila, having found that 'the people of Melbourne did not understand all that was legitimate in [his] desire to photograph them' (quoted in the *ADB*, vol. 4, p. 158).

[7] Lionel's brother, the marquis Marie-Olivier-Théodore de Chabrillan, was head of the family and a member of the Council of State.

[8] Édouard de Naurois tried to dissuade Lionel from marrying Céleste, but offered his help at any time. He did not recognize the woman weeping in the park as Céleste, but met her again many years later when he was an old man. One of the properties owned by this very wealthy aristocrat was the Théâtre des Nouveautés where, in April 1870, he noticed good reviews of *L'Américaine* starring the author Madam Lionel de Chabrillan. A strong friendship developed between them based partly on their mutual love of Lionel and partly on the stimulus she gave him. Céleste persuaded him to take an interest in improving his properties, whereupon the Count made her manageress of the theatre. When the Franco–Prussian war was declared, he gave her a present of 1500 francs before she went to Le Vésinet and he to England. (Haldane, *Daughter* . . . .)

[9] There is no trace of the urns and funerary ornaments Céleste claims to have sent to Australia. Lionel's grave had fallen into complete disrepair until the Institute for French–Australian Relations restored it with the aid of a grant from the French Government and the assistance of the Alliance Française. A ceremony was held in November 1992, in the presence of the French Consul, to celebrate the restoration of the grave and the service of Lionel de Chabrillan as first French consul in Melbourne.

[10] Similar in style and format to the *Illustrated London News*, *L'Illustration, Journal Universel* was a paper generously illustrated with etchings, specializing in current events of interest, reviews and stories from around the world. The tribute to Lionel did not gloss over all his misadventures, but interpreted them in the best light possible. It appeared on 30 April 1859 with a reproduction of Fauchery's handsome photographic portrait of Lionel in consular dress.

[11] The novel *Est-il fou?* was published by A. Bourdilliat in 1860.

EPILOGUE

[1] See Clancy & Thornton-Smith, *Analytical Checklist* . . . .

[2] C. de Chabrillan, *En Australie*, p. 15.

[3] *The New Grove Dictionary of Music and Musicians*, vol. 2, p. 755.

[4] She also continued to write her memoirs, ostensibly with the intention of publication. According to her biographer Françoise Moser, there were fifteen notebooks of almost illegible writing covering the years from 1859 until Céleste's death. These journals are now untraceable.

[5] Haldane, *Daughter* . . . , p. 245.

[6] *En Australie*, p. 8.

[7] C. de Chabrillan, . . . *Soeurs* . . ., p. 280.

Appendices

APPENDIX I:

A Newspaper Account of a Dinner to Celebrate the French Emperor's Name Day

The *Argus*, 16 August 1855, page 5:

BIRTHDAY OF THE EMPEROR OF THE FRENCH

The anniversary of the nativity of his Majesty, the Emperor of the French, was celebrated yesterday evening by a grand entertainment given by M. Le [*sic*] comte de Chabrillan, Consul of France, to his Excellency Sir Charles Hotham, and the consuls representing the various European nations in this colony.

The Criterion Hotel was chosen as the scene of the festivities, and the hall was decorated with a degree of taste worthy of the occasion. Around the room were disposed vases of artificial flowers, so arranged as to produce a very pleasing but simple effect. The arms of England figured at the lower end of the room, executed on rather a large scale, whilst the initial letter N was executed in gold along the sides. The decorations were entrusted to M. Varannes [*sic*]. An efficient band was in attendance in the orchestra. At half past six o'clock his Excellency and suite arrived and were received by a company of the 40th regiment, drawn up at the door of the hotel. His Excellency was also escorted to the spot by a small guard of troopers. He was received at the door by M. Le comte de Chabrillan.

At seven o'clock precisely, the company assembled in the hall. There were about fifty guests present. Amongst the gentlemen present on the occasion we observed:—The Hon. the Collector of Customs; the Hon. Colonial Treasurer; the Roman Catholic Bishop; the Hon. the Colonial Secretary; the Secretary to the Gold Commission; Consul of the United States; Major Hodgson, V.V.R.R.; his Reverence the Vicar–General; Consul de Belgique; Consul de Hollande; Consul de Portugal; Dr. Collins of the 40th Regiment; Lieutenant Richard of the 40th Regiment; Lieut.-Colonel Anderson, V.V.R.R.; his Honor Justice Williams; his Right Worshipful the Mayor; Colonel Macarthur; his Honor Justice Barry; Captain of H.M.S. Electra; Captain McMahon; Captain Hotham; Captain Vereker, of the 12th regiment; Captain Kay; Lieut. Leeson, of the 12th Regiment, E. Montefiore, Esq., W. Badcock, Esq., W. Beyfus, Esq., N. Costello, Esq., Ant. Read, Esq., E. Cotton, Esq., G. Evans, Esq., R. Down, Esq., G. Henelle, Esq., E. Dubois, Esq., A. Greeves, Esq., M.L.C., W. Sturt, Esq., W. Westgarth, Esq., E. Chaine, Esq., E. Cargill, Esq., W. Hammill, Esq.

Grace was said by his Reverence the Vicar–General.

The dinner served was very creditable to the resources of the establishment. Not only was the table tastefully decorated, but the viands were well selected and served.

The cloth having been drawn,—

M. Le comte de Chabrillan proposed—'The Health of her Majesty Queen Victoria.'

The toast was enthusiastically responded to.

'The National Anthem.'

Sir Charles Hotham proposed—'The Emperor of the French,' and three times three.

Air—'*Partant pour la Syrie.*'

The toast having been duly honored, Sir C. Hotham proposed—'The Health of the Empress of the French,' which was warmly received.

M. Le comte de Chabrillan proposed—'The healths of Prince Albert and the rest of the Royal Family.'

This toast was also drunk and duly honored.

M. de Chabrillan proposed—'The Navies and the armies of the Allies.'

The toast was drunk with great applause.

Airs—'*Marseillaise*' and '*Rule Britannia.*'

Colonel Macarthur, in returning thanks, trusted that the English and French might long drink each other's health; and he was glad that he had an opportunity of expressing that sentiment on such an occasion.

The Commander of the Electra returned thanks in behalf of the navy, and expressed his strong admiration and respect for the gallantry and ability of our allied in naval warfare. He had served against them when young, and was now proud to serve with them now.

M. De [*sic*] Chabrillan proposed—'The Health of Sir C. Hotham,' which was drunk with all the honors.

Air,—'For he's a Jolly Good Fellow.'

Sir C. Hotham, in returning thanks, said that he believed he was the officer present who had served the most with the French, and he had invariably found them the most forward in the path of honor and duty. He hoped they might often have occasion to interchange the friendly sentiments of that evening. He need not say more, for they met for a particular purpose for which no long speeches were needful.

M. De Chabrillan proposed—'The Prosperity of the Colony of Victoria.'

Air,—'*Cheer, Boys, Cheer.*'

His Honor Judge Barry, in returning thanks, said that the intimate alliance which existed between this colony and England, rendered her deeply interested in the allies of the English, and no expression of good will towards the colony by the representative of the French nation would be lost on them.

Sir C. Hotham proposed—'The Health of M. Le Compte [*sic*] De Chabrillan.'

The toast was duly honored, Sir Charles himself leading the cheers.

M. De Chabrillan said he did not accept the toast as an individual, but as the representative of France in Victoria, and as an expression of their sympathy with that nation. (Cheers.) He thanked them for the honour conferred on him, and on the nation he represented. (Cheers.)

M. De Chabrillan proposed—'The Members of the Committee of the Patriotic Fund and the Members of the Committee of the Ball.'

Mr. Westgarth returned thanks for the honor done to the members of the committee, and hoped that the body to which he belonged would not be found wanting. He had reason to believe that the ball would come off with great eclat [*sic*], and the committee were very well satisfied with the preparations. The success of the arrangements, he believed, were chiefly due to M. Le Compte de Chabrillan himself. (Hear, hear.)

M. De Chabrillan proposed—'The Health of Lady Hotham and the Ladies.' The toast was received in the way in which toasts usually are.

Sir C. Hotham returned thanks in behalf of Lady Hotham and the ladies. He had no doubt they would all show their sympathy in the undertaking in which they were then engaged, by taking their places on the following evening at the Exhibition Ball.

Air, '*Here's a Health to all good Lasses.*'

His Honor Mr. Justice Williams proposed—'The Health of Madame de Chabrillan.'

The toast was loudly cheered.

M. de Chabrillan responded for Madame de Chabrillan, and expressed his feeling that she was most anxious for the success of the patriotic ball.

This concluded the list of the toasts, and his Excellency Sir C. Hotham soon afterwards withdrew. His example was imitated very soon after by the gentlemen present, who separated after a very pleasant evening.

APPENDIX II:

Newspaper Reports on the French Ball in Melbourne, 17 August 1855

A: The *Argus* of 18 August 1855, page 5:

THE FRENCH BALL

The tone of the pulse at the wrist indicates to physicians the condition of the body, and in like manner the expression of public opinion, at the extremities of a State denotes the true position of a nation in respect to the popular sympathy or dislike. The decisive effect of a Parisian revolution upon the whole of France is less extraordinary than it would be, were it not a fact that its inauguration invariably occurs exterior of the capital; so that, in truth, the opinion of the provincial population, with regard to a contemplated movement, is ascertained prior to its consummation, and may be relied upon to support it. The same principle will equally apply to English politics, although, doubtless, they have a less central determination than those of their French allies, and a memorable and familiar instance may be adduced in illustration of the origin and progress of the Anti-corn Law League, which at once showed the vigor and general importance of a provincial movement.

The above remarks are suggested by the character of the public sympathy in this colony in favor of the extraordinary, but to all appearances, fast alliance, which at present exists between the greatest nations of Europe,—historically and by tradition foes. The copartnership of Great Britain and France in those tremendous efforts in behalf of political justice which are now agitating the whole world, is so significant of its originality and evidently genuine character, that the future historian will have to rely for his deductions entirely upon the evidence furnished by the period itself, there being nothing in the historical antecedents of either nation to justify the conclusion which we now witness. The understanding which now exists between the two nations is not of that after dinner character which Phillip de Comines, in his quaint and gossiping way, denounces as spurious and to be suspected. Being totally irrespective of dynastic influences, it is consequently the more to be counted upon for permanency. It has been cemented by the liberal outpouring of the best blood of both empires in front of the mightiest fortress in the world, and it is supported by the wishes and sympathies of the people of both. May it endure to lead the van of civilisation, and to furnish matter and example to the other nations of the earth to adopt and follow!

That the new relationship established by the mother country towards France is applauded in this outwork of the British Empire, the thoroughly successful issue to which the ball in aid of the wounded and invalid French soldiers of the army of the Crimea has been brought, will substantially prove. Upwards of a thousand pounds sterling, it is said, will be remitted by M. le Comte de Chabrillan to the French Minister of War, in aid of the fund now being collected by that functionary for the purpose referred to. This sum includes an amount of 230 pounds, which had been previously received by the French Consul in the shape of private donations; and in mentioning this, we are particularly gratified to remark the handsome manner in which the officers of the Melbourne garrison have evinced their liberality and cordial cooperation on behalf of the worthy object of this movement. In order to do full justice to every one, we publish the following list of subscriptions, as furnished to us by M. le Comte de Chabrillan:—Germain Nicholson, Esq., 50 pounds; an Englishman, 2 pounds; Lieutenant-Colonel Valiant and the officers of the 40th Regiment, 88 pounds; the Abbe [*sic*] Bourgeois, 5 pounds; Kay and Butchart, 21 pounds; the officers of the 12th Regiment, 57 pounds; a British general officer, 40 pounds; the Belgian Consul, 2 pounds 18 shillings; a clerk in Messrs. Montefiore and Co.'s office, 1 pound; and Mr. Griffiths, 5 pounds. There are additional donations, of which we are unable, in consequence of the accounts not being at present made up, to give particulars.

The ball of Thursday evening was, without exception, the most brilliant that has taken place in this city. The attendance numbered fully 1500, and included the Governor and Lady Hotham, the judges and the 'elite [*sic*]' of Melbourne society. We have already described in this journal the decorations, which were even improved by the effect of the illumination. The programme gave a list of twenty-four dances, and was scrupulously adhered to. So great was the satisfaction of the company, that towards the close of the entertainment the provision in this respect was even deemed to be hardly sufficient, the demand for a supplementary supply being very general. This was partially met by the co-operation of the band of the Volunteer Rifle Corps, who were in attendance, in addition to the musical staff of the 12th and 40th regiments, and which, in the handsomest manner, complied with the loudly expressed demands of the company, by playing one or two additional pieces of dance music. The mysteries of the Tombola, a new feature introduced by the Comte de Chabrillan, were unravelled about the 'witching hour' of midnight, and the hundred successful competitors were invested with the prizes amid the general applause of the company. The lots were drawn by Signor Carandini, 'maitre [*sic*] de ballet' of the Theatre Royal, and who also acted in the responsible capacity of Master of the Ceremonies. The first dance was announced about ten o'clock, and the programme was concluded at four o'clock by the performance of the British and

French National Anthems, which were received by the Company in the most enthusiastic manner. There was a great improvement upon the Rifle Ball arrangement in respect to the custody of cloaks, hats, &c., there being a well-organised staff of attendants, under the orders of Mr. Pain, and anything like a rush being provided against by the depositary being partitioned off in a substantial manner. The refreshments, were supplied by Mr. Purssell, of Collins-street, were 'recherche [*sic*]' and ample; and in reference to this portion of the arrangements we must express our approval of the plan, which we sincerely trust will become the rule on similar occasions, of the exclusion of spirits. It prevented the occurrence of scenes which should never take place anywhere, or under any circumstances; but which at a ball should be specially provided against. The utmost order prevailed throughout, and the thorough enjoyment of the company was manifested by the spirited manner in which the calls of the M.C. were responded to.

The enthusiastic manner in which the people of Melbourne have met the appeal of the French Consul will have its due effect upon the cordial understanding which exists between the allied nations. It is the 'petits soins' of our friends which exhibit their friendship, and so with nations. A minute part of the British people separated from the mother country, and occasionally supposed to have different interests from those of their native land, have shown in an unmistakeable manner their adhesion to the policy of its rulers. The alliance of England and France is no longer a question of names: it is the earnest effusion of the popular sympathies of both countries, and with the assistance of the Most High is evidently destined to advance His name, and the civilisation of the human race.

B: *The Melbourne Punch*, January–July edition 1855, page 25:*

THE FRENCH BALL

We have the pleasure in responding to a request made by the editors of our contemporaries, Judge Barry, and several other well disposed persons of neglected education, to offer a few hints for the guidance of parties attending this Evening's festive and patriotic entertainment; but, who are unfortunately unacquainted with the conversational elegancies and graceful idioms of the French tongue. We need scarcely observe, that as the dancing only commences towards evening, and the company may be assumed to be fashionable; every lady and gentleman must commence with the ordinary salutation pronounced—'bung swaw'.

Those who may have the honour to be introduced to the Consul should of course make some complimentary allusions to the success attending the ball which he has inaugurated.

'Ma parole, c'est la fromage, entierement, ma tulipe!' Would probably be the remark of one of the French noblesse under such circumstances.

To express a modest assent, the Count will probably reply,——'Je vous believa, mon garcon,' and he will then ask in French, what you will take to drink? There are various expressions which convey this meaning, and we therefore give none of them. Your answer, if intended to be a courteous refusal, should be 'Fermez en haut.'

'Comment faites vous faire mon coeury' is all that ladies need absolutely say to their partners; should the room feel hot, perhaps 'Il est sanguinairement chaud' may be added.

In case of misunderstanding arising between any gents, at this entertainment, it will be the pleasing duty of their partners to appease their wrath. 'Prenez le froidement,' is perhaps, under the circumstances, the most affecting appeal that can be made to the combatants.

'Crochez le' is an elegant rendering of the English vulgarism 'hook-it'. There will be no impropriety in the use of this expression, on the part of a lady refusing a partner.

Sir Charles Hotham will not be present, there will therefore be nothing approaching to sarcasm in the statement of a weakness for beer; and to ask for it, will flatter a French prejudice. 'Ne volez pas un pauvre homme de sa biere,' is the burthen of a social, national melody, ranking in the devotion of the people, with the more political '*Marseillaise*'—all parties would be propitiated by a demand for 'La biere Murphien.'

If, after supper, any difficulty should arise between gentlemen, as to their claim to partners, a gentlemanly warning will be conveyed to an antagonist, in the words 'Esprit Votre oeil.' 'Vous sois Souffle' will be the appropriate reply.

Should you be introduced to Judge Barry, you must avoid the use of monosyllables. As we have not a dictionary by us, and our polyglot editor is unwell, we cannot be perfectly certain that we accuratively [*sic*] render the language in this case,—but his honor will be so pleased with the subject as to lose sight of the idioms. Tell him that you are deeply interested in 'les Sousteltes accumenatedes d'Empiricisme Alchemiquale,' and he will probably continue to talk to you for some hours; but never mind, if it is after supper, you need only listen while he is talking French, and he will soon lapse into Celtic. His honor would be complimented, but that it is a monosyllable, by your telling him as you part, that he is a 'Rhum vieux bec.' He is not vain, but all of us are open to flattery.

'Bon achete, ancien bouffer' will be your farewell to the Comte. 'Vous etes un autre' your defiance to the cloak room man who asks for sixpence.

---

*Authors' note: We acknowledge the errors in French grammar and spelling, but the heavy-handed, deliberate 'franglais' used in the article does not warrant individual correction or comment.

APPENDIX III:

Criticism of the Count de Chabrillan in his Role as French Consul

The *Argus*, 15 March 1856, page 4:

CONSULAR DIGNITY

Some time ago a novel was published in England entitled '*The Warlike Adventures of a Peaceable Man.*' A work might here be written under the title of '*The Warlike Adventures of a Functionary of Peace,*' describing the proceedings of the Comte de Chabrillon [*sic*], the French Consul. That it is his province, as the representative of our great ally, to set an example of deference to the law,—still more so to abstain from becoming a law-breaker, or abettor in the breaking of the law himself,—seems to find no formal demonstration. That within the last few days he has sinned against this rule has become a matter of public notoriety, and is recorded among the archives of that not very exalted tribunal, the Police Court.

It seems that two gentlemen, named Chaine and Piocotti, countrymen of the French Consul, had a quarrel, which they proposed to settle according to the ancient custom, 'more honored in the breach than the observance,' of trial by combat. This romantic mode of adjustment was, however, unfortunately, spoiled by the interference of a prosaic policeman, who arrested M. Chaine, and brought him before the Police Court on Wednesday. But M. Piocotti was not at the same time forthcoming, as the French Consul had withstood the arrest, and taken the belligerent gentleman under his protection, scaring the unfortunate constable from his quarry by a profuse waving of the tricolor. The Court, very properly and naturally, laughed at this proceeding, and told the policeman to take M. Piocotti into custody. If M. de Chabrillon liked to drag the French flag into Police Court rows, the responsibility rested with him. If he so little understood the nature of his position and privileges as to think he had a right to afford an Alsatia to common offenders against the law, the Court could not help the injury that might accrue to his feelings in affording him a better knowledge of his duties. The Consul, however, just managed to 'save his distance' in the race of dignity, by himself bringing up M. Piocotti before the Court, and that gentleman and M. Chaine entered into bonds to keep the peace towards one another. And so we may presume that for the present the pistols have been replaced in their cases, and the coffee countermanded.

The perfect respect and regard which we and almost all our countrymen are known to feel for the French nation, and the French flag enable us to speak more freely on the present matter, and with less fear of being misunderstood, than would otherwise have been the case. We regret to see the representative of a great nation—a man who, in that capacity, has been treated here with a distinction to which the small consular dignity would of itself never have entitled him, forcing us by his conduct to dissociate our ideas of himself and the French people, and forbidding us to develop farther any possible vanity in the individual by lavishing upon him as the symbol of France the expressions of our cordial respect for that great country. We regret that the accredited representative of that nation here should have condescended to wave back a policeman from 'the execution of his duty' in the Alma road with the same flag which was borne beside our own to victory on the heights over the Alma River.

This is not the only occasion on which M. de Chabrillon has displayed a somewhat morbid idiosyncrasy, and has misinterpreted the respect of the colony for the French people which has manifested itself in complimentary observances towards himself. Some time ago the officers of the garrison, it will be remembered, got up some theatrical entertainments for the benefit of the Patriotic Fund. M. de Chabrillon was invited, and the committee of management set apart for him a box similarly placed to that ordinarily occupied by her Majesty in her state visits to English theatres. One would have thought that there was nothing in this arrangement to have offended the 'amour propre' of even a consular Comte; but he thought otherwise, explaining in an indignant letter to a contemporary, that he (the Comte) did not attend the performance because a suitable place was not accorded to him. Not long afterwards, disgusted with his appearance in the portrait gallery of an illustrated Melbourne periodical—somewhat given, it must be owned, to slight exaggerations in depicting public men—the Comte, we are credibly informed, was proceeding to hostilities of a similar kind to those in which Messieurs Chaine and Piocotti were interrupted, one of these identical heroes appearing as friend when the representative of France proposed to act as principal. Other transactions have also reached our ears, rendering it apparent that M. de Chabrillon is not a person with strength of mind to bear the 'eclat' [*sic*] with which he has here been surrounded.

We regret to have to observe that the misunderstanding of his true position as a consul which has been so marked in M. de Chabrillon's case has not been confined to him

(. . .)

If the two consuls to whom we have referred will take the trouble to study any competent authority on consular duties and privileges, they will find that one of them has grossly and illegally exceeded the former in attempting to resist the ordinary course of the laws of the country in which he resides; and that both, out of respect for the nations they respectively represent, have been treated with distinction far beyond any to which their mere consular office entitles them. We would, in conclusion, in the most friendly spirit, point out that they will best uphold the true dignity of the countries which they serve if they more fully appreciate the kind and cordial feelings of the colonists, and content themselves with reciprocating the amenities which distinguish the intercourse of private gentlemen.

APPENDIX IV:

Newspaper Reports of the Count de Chabrillan's Funeral

A: The *Age*, 1 January 1859, page 5:

FUNERAL OF THE LATE FRENCH CONSUL

The funeral of the late Comte Lionel de Morton [*sic*] de Chabrillon [*sic*], Consul of France for this colony, took place yesterday afternoon.

The procession left the residence of the deceased gentleman at half past two o'clock, in the following order:—

First came two private carriages, containing Dr. Brownless, Dr. Tracy, Dr. Macadam, and Dr. Mackenzie. Next in order came the Rev. Dr. Geoghegan, the Roman Catholic Vicar-General, the Rev. Dr. Barry, the Rev. Fathers McEvoy, Sheil, Power, Stack, Lane, and Hayden. After this came the hearse, drawn by four horses, and attended by D. Phillips, Esq., secretary to the late Consul; M. Adet, Acting French Consul, M. Fauchery; and followed by fifty French gentlemen on foot. In the carriages which came next in order we noticed Judge Barry, –Beckx, Esq., Belgian Consul; –Passmore, Esq., Sardinian Consul; –Hentech, Esq., Swiss Vice-Consul. His Excellency the Governor–General's carriage followed. Next came General Macarthur, commander of the forces, Col. Leslie and officers of the 40th Regiment. Col. Neil's carriage followed, with several other private carriages. In this order the funeral cortege proceeded to St. Francis' cathedral, where a solemn requiem mass was performed over the body by the Rev. Dr. Geoghegan, and the other clergy in attendance. The coffin, covered with the French flag, upon which was placed the cocked hat and sword of the deceased, was then replaced in the hearse, and the procession moved on towards the Melbourne cemetery, which was reached shortly after four o'clock. The following gentlemen officiated as pall-bearers: General Macarthur, Commander-in-chief; –Cooper, Esq., Portuguese Consul; J. Tarleton, Esq., American Consul; J. B. Were, Esq., Danish Consul; Capt. White, Aide de Camp to Gen. Macarthur; –Damypen, Esq., Russian Consul. The usual religious rites were then performed, and the coffin was lowered into the grave prepared for it in the Roman Catholic burying ground.

The arrangements were conducted by Messrs. Bramston and Marshall, of Collins Street east, who provided the whole of the funeral equipments. The cortege presented a most imposing appearance, the hearse in itself being probably unsurpassed by any in the colonies.

B: The *Argus*, I January 1859, page 5:

FUNERAL OF THE FRENCH CONSUL

The funeral of Monsieur le Comte Lionel de Moreton de Chabrillan, Consul of France, took place yesterday afternoon.

The cortege, which included a large number of carriages, as well as gentlemen on foot and horseback, moved from the Consul's late residence in Spring-street, at about a quarter past two o'clock, and arrived at St Francis's Cathedral shortly before three. At the entrance porch of the cathedral, it was received by the Rev. Dr. Barry bearing the cross, the Rev. Dr. Shiel, and other persons connected with the church. The procession proceeded, chanting, up the body of the church to a space that had been prepared for the coffin, immediately in front of the sanctuary. Around the coffin were placed a number of lighted candles, and upon it were laid the uniform, coat, hat, and sword of the deceased, together with the French tricolor. The church was completely thronged by the personal friends of the late Count, as well as by those who, without being personally known to him, wished to testify their respect for the manner in which the Count had ever conducted himself as a public man. There were a number of others also who had been drawn to the church from curiosity, and a desire to see the funeral service of the Roman Catholic Church performed, as was naturally to be expected, with unusual grandeur. It had been surmised, from the announcement in yesterday's paper, that the body would be conveyed to St. Francis's Church at 9.30 a.m., that a solemn 'requiem' would be sung for the departed, together with the whole of the office of the dead; but only that portion of the latter which is more generally used was sung. The officiating priest, in the absence of the Right Reverend Dr. Goold, now in Europe, was the Very Reverend the Vicar-General, Dr. Geoghegan, assisted by Drs. Shiel and Barry, as deacon and sub-deacon; the Very Reverend Dean McEvoy was director of the ceremonies, the Revs. M. Stack, M. Downing, W. Lane, and J. Hayden assisting. There were present in the church as mourners, Major-General Macarthur, Lieutenant-Colonel Leslie, commanding the 40th regiment; Brigade-Major Hare, Captain White, Captain Hall, Quartermaster Varrance, together with other staff and regimental officers; Captain Lascazas; the American Consul, J. W. Tarleton, Esq.; the Consul General of Austria [*sic*], J. B. Were, Esq.; the Consul General of Portugal, J. Cooper, Esq.; the Consul General of Russia, W. Damyon, Esq.; the Consul General of the Argentine Republic, J. W. Mackenna, Esq,; the Hanoverian Consul, J. Kaufman, Esq.; Drs. Tracy, Brownless, and Macadam; Messrs. Hutt, Pinnock, and Cotton; and many others of our trading merchants and other citizens, together with a large number of the countrymen of the Count.

The performance of the funeral service lasted nearly three-quarters of an hour, and at the conclusion the coffin, with the mementos laid upon it, was carried back to the hearse, which was covered with plumes and drawn by four horses, and the cortege then moved slowly up Elizabeth-street and along Sydney-road, until it reached the New Cemetery, a little after 4 p.m. The coffin was then lifted from the vehicle, and carried from the gates to its final resting place, attended by the large body of mourners who had followed it from town, and having for pall-bearers Major-General Macarthur and the Russian and Austrian Consul-Generals on the one side, and on the other Captain White, the Consul-General of Portugal and the American Consul. The remaining portion of the funeral services was here read over the body by the Very Rev. Dr. Geoghegan, V. G., assisted by the other clergymen who had been present in the Cathedral, and the coffin was then finally committed to the earth.

APPENDIX V:

Translation of Count Lionel de Chabrillan's Last Will and Testament

Consular Agency of France   27th December 1858

    My only regret in leaving this life is dying far from my wife and not leaving her in the situation that I would have wished her to have.

    I empower my friend and interim successor <u>Edouard Adet</u>, a French merchant in Melbourne, to liquidate any possessions I may leave in Melbourne. I request him to send my wife my personal effects as well as the Indian curios, such as the ebony wood chairs, boxes, parasols etc. etc. brought back by me from my last voyage.

    Monsieur Adet will kindly dispose of the furniture, silverware and merchandise in my house to my best advantage. The sum of this liquidation should be sent to my wife.

    Similarly, I empower Mr Adet to dispose of any goods which should or could be sent to me from Europe. Finally, I authorize Mr Ed. Adet to settle my account with the Oriental Bank.

    I recognize the following creditors only:

Mr Walsh, Jeweller	£80 Sterling
Money deposited by Coulon	£50 Sterling
Bill due 13th January next to Monsieur de Lascazas	£140 Sterling
Mr Joseph Wilkie	£66 Sterling

Balance of purchase price of a piano

Witnesses:

Antoine Fauchery   Comte de Moreton

F. H. L. Phillips   This is the proper writing referred to   Order no. 681
Secretary   in the annexed affidavit of Edouard   Tariff no. 18
   Adet sworn before me this 3rd day of   Solvit 18f.
   February AD 1859. Robt. Caddy
   A Comm[sr]

Bibliography

Works by Céleste de Chabrillan

Memoirs

Adieux au monde, mémoires de Céleste Mogador. 5 vols, Locard-Davi et de Vresse, Paris, 1854.

Mémoires de Céleste Mogador. 2nd edn, 4 vols, Librairie Nouvelle, Paris, 1858.

Mémoires de Céleste Mogador. 3rd edn, 2 vols, Librairie Nouvelle, Paris, 1876.

Un Deuil au bout du monde, suite des mémoires de Céleste Mogador. Librairie Nouvelle, Paris, 1877.

Novels

Les Voleurs d'or. Michel Lévy, Paris, 1857. Trans. Lucy and Caroline Moorehead, *The Gold Robbers.* Sun Books, Melbourne, 1970.

La Sapho. Michel Lévy, Paris, 1858.

Miss Pewel. A. Bourdilliat, Paris, 1859.

Est-il fou? A. Bourdilliat, Paris, 1860.

Un miracle à Vichy. Bougarel fils, Vichy, 1861.

Mémoires d'une honnête fille. A. Faure, Paris, 1865.

Les Deux soeurs émigrantes et déportées. C. Lévy, Paris, 1876.

Une méchante femme. C. Lévy, Paris, 1877.

La Duchesse des mers. C. Lévy, Paris. 1881.

Les Forçats de l'amour. C. Lévy, Paris, 1881.

Marie Baude. C. Lévy, Paris, 1883.

Un Drame sur le Tage. C. Lévy, Paris, 1885.

Plays

(Titles without bibliographical details cannot be verified, but have been listed in secondary sources, notably Moser.)

En Australie. 1 act vaudeville. Th. des Champs-Elysées, 19 July 1862. Cosson, Paris, 1862.

Les Voleurs d'or. 1 act. Th. de Belleville, 28 May 1864. Michel Lévy frères, Paris, 1864.

Chambre à louer. 1 act. Th. des Folies-Marigny, 20 Oct. 1865.

Les Crimes de la mer. 5 acts. Th. de Belleville, 8 May 1869. Morris père et fils, Paris, 1869.

L'Ambition fatale. 5 acts. Th. Beaumarchais, 15 April 1875.

Pierre Pascal. 5 acts. Music by M. Senée. Ambigu-Comique, 4 Aug. 1885. Chaix, Paris, 1885.

Le Drame de Louvier. 5 acts.

Forgeron d'Ardentes. I act.
Les Petits de Beaufort. 4 acts.

Comedies

Bonjour au vaincu. I act. Th. des Champs-Elysées, 19 April 1862. Cosson, Paris, 1862.
Querelle d'Allemand. I act. Th. des Champs-Elysées, 28 Oct. 1863. Librairie des Deux-Mondes, Paris, 1864.
L'Amour de l'art. I act. Th. des Folies-Marigny, 4 June 1865. Alcan-Lévy, Paris, 1865.
Un homme compromis. I act. Th. des Folies-Marigny, 4 Sept. 1865. Alcan-Lévy, Paris, 1868.
Les Revers de l'amour. 5 acts. Th. des Nouveautés, 28 Jan. 1870. The author, Paris, 1870.
L'Américaine. 5 acts. Th. des Nouveautés, 3 April 1870. Estienne, Paris, 1870.
La Plaideuse. I act. Ambigu-Comique, 20 Dec. 1874.
Le Bonnet d'âne. I act. 1876.
Entre deux balcons. Fantaisies-Parisiennes, 7 March 1880.
Ma'am Nicole. 3 acts. Folies-Dramatiques, 4 July 1880. Barbré, Paris, 1880.
L'Amour et la rose. 3 acts. Th. des Arts, 10 July 1880.
Cordon, s.v.p. Revue. Th. Pépinière, 26 Dec. 1886.
Bastienne.
Le Dernier rendez-vous. 3 acts.
Marie Margotte. I act. Th. des Nouveautés.
Regain d'amour.
Le 31 de victoire. I act.

Operettas

Nédel. I act. Music by Marius Boullard. Th. des Champs-Elysées, 23 May 1863.
Militairement. I act. Music by Marius Boullard. Th. des Champs-Elysées, 28 Oct. 1863. Librairie des Deux-Mondes, Paris, 1864.
En garde. I act. Th. des Champs-Elysées, 14 Jan. 1864. Librairie des Deux-Mondes, Paris, 1864.
Les Pierrots en cage. I act. Music by Kriezel. Th. des Folies-Marigny, 9 Sept. 1865.
A la bretonne. I act. Th. des Folies-Marigny, 10 Sept. 1868. Morris père et fils, Paris, 1868.
La Tirelire d'Yvonne. I act. Music by Georges Rose.

Poems

Un chien trouvé
Échange d'âmes
Les Églises
La Légende du Soldat Pierre
Le Marseillais
La Mère du Mobile
Mes Soeurs de France
Mon Petit-fils le Potache
Les Orphelins de la guerre
Paris captif

L'Union
Les Volontaires de 1870

Songs
L'absolution (Music by E. Gambillard)
Adieu romance (Music by Avray)
L'amour, c'est des bêtises (Music by G. Rose)
Attends un peu (Music by E. Gambillard)
Battez tambours (Music by Avray)
Le chapeau rond (Music by G. Rose)
Le dimanche (Music by Comte Lionel de Chabrillan)
Encore moi (Music by G. Rose)
La fête de Jean-Pierre (Music by G. Rose)
La Gauloise (Music by G. Rose)
Le grand cousin (Music by G. Rose)
L'heure (Music by G. Rose)
J'ai battu mon homme (Music by G. Rose)
Je l'ai lâché (Music by E. Gambillard)
Laissez-moi pleurer (Music by G. Rose)
Ne boudez pas (Music by G. Rose)
T'as du chagrin (Music by G. Rose)

ARCHIVAL MATERIALS AND MANUSCRIPTS

Archival material from the Public Record Office of Victoria is listed numerically by series (VPRS) number.

Biddle, Thomas Edgar. 'Transactions of British Ships between Ports in the United Kingdom and the Port of Melbourne, 1840–1859', 1962, La Trobe Library, Victoria.

Index to the *Argus* 1855–April 1859, microform.

Panton, Joseph Anderson. 'Autobiography 1840s–1860s'. Typescript, La Trobe Library, Victoria, MS 652.

PROV, VA 628 Criminal Law Branch, Law Department VPRS 30 Criminal Trial Briefs—Supreme Court, 1855–1961.

——VA 914 Law Department, VPRS 76 Court of Insolvency Correspondence Files, 1842–76.

——VA 433 Prothonotary of the Supreme Court, VPRS 264 Capital Case Files, 1852–1925.

——VA 864 Crown Law Department, VPRS 266 Inward Registered Correspondence 1852–1938.

——VA 466 Governor's Office, VPRS 1092 Governor's Letters Books, 1853–1908.

——VA 466 Governor's Office VPRS 1096 Inward Correspondence, 1857–1910.

——VA 860 Chief Secretary's Office, VPRS 1189 Inward Correspondence Registers 1856–63.

——VA 606 Department of Trade and Customs, VPRS 3501 Passenger Lists of Immigrants (unassisted) from United Kingdom, microfilm copy, 1852–1923.

——VA 433 Prothonotary of the Supreme Court and VA 683 Public Record Office, VPRS 5136 Criminal Record Books, microfilm copy, 1841–1940.

——VA 862 Registrar General's Office and Office of Titles and VA 983 Office of the Government Statist and Actuary; Registry of Births, Deaths and Marriages, VPRS 7291 Index of Deaths, microfiche copy, 1853–95.

——VA 862 Registrar General's Office and Office of Titles, VPRS 7292 Index of Early Church Records, microfiche copy, 1837–54.

Sexton's Books, Melbourne General Cemetery.

Newspapers and Periodicals

The *Age*

The *Argus*

The *Ballarat Times*

The *Daily Mirror*

The *Express*

Le Figaro

L'Illustration, Journal Universel

The *Melbourne Punch*

La Presse

The *Sydney Morning Herald*

The *Victorian Review*

Reference Works and Published Documents

Australian Dictionary of Biography (ADB). vols 1–6. Melbourne University Press, Melbourne, 1967–76.

Australians: A Historical Dictionary. G. Aplin, S. G. Foster and M. McKernan (eds). Fairfax, Syme & Weldon, Broadway NSW, 1987.

Catalogue général des livres imprimés de la Bibliothèque Nationale. 231 vols. Imprimerie Nationale, Paris, 1897–1981.

Chisholm, A.R. 'Céleste de Chabrillan and the gold rush'. *Meanjin Quarterly*. June 1969, pp. 197–207.

Clancy, P. A. & C. B. Thornton-Smith. *Analytical Checklist of French Fiction and Pseudo-Memoirs Set in Colonial Australia*. ISFAR & The Australian Centre (University of Melbourne), Melbourne, 1991.

The Cyclopedia of Victoria. James Smith (ed.). 3 vols. The Cyclopedia Company, Melbourne, 1903–05.

Dictionnaire de biographie française. Librairie Letouzey et Ané, Paris, 1933– .

Encyclopedia Britannica. 15th edn. 30 vols. Encyclopedia Britannica, Chicago, 1974.

Featherstone, Guy Fontaine. *Victorian History 1835–1900. A Bibliography of Bibliographies and Works of Reference*. Red Rooster Press, Melbourne, 1979.

The French Presence in Victoria, 1800–1901. Catalogue of an exhibition by the Alliance Française of Victoria and the French Consul General to mark Victoria's 150th anniversary. Victorian Artists' Society, Melbourne, 1984.

La Grande Encyclopédie, inventaire raisonné des sciences, des lettres et des arts. 31 vols. Société anonyme de la Grande Encyclopédie. Paris, 1882–1902.

Melbourne Commercial and Squatters' Directory for 1854. James J. Blundell, Melbourne, 1854.

Melbourne Commercial, Professional and Legal Directory for 1855. James J. Blundell, Melbourne, 1855.

Melbourne Commercial, Professional and Legal Directory for 1856. James J. Blundell, Melbourne, 1856.

New Grove Dictionary of Music and Musicians. Stanley Sadie (ed.). 20 vols. Macmillan Publishers Ltd., London, 1994.

Nouveau Larousse illustré. Dictionnaire universel encyclopédique. 2 vols. P. Augé (ed.). Librairie Larousse, Paris, 1897–1904.

Nouveau Larousse universel. Dictionnaire encyclopédique en deux volumes. Paul Augé (ed.). Librairie Larousse, Paris, 1949.

Nouvelle biographie générale depuis les temps les plus reculés jusqu'à nos jours. 46 vols. Firmin Didot frères, Paris, 1855–66.

Petit Larousse. 24th edn. Librairie Larousse, Paris, 1966.

Phaidon Book of the Opera: A survey of 780 operas from 1597. Phaidon, Oxford, 1979.

Sands & Kenny's Commercial and General Melbourne Directory. Sands & Kenny, Melbourne, 1857–61.

Syme, Marten Adlington. *Shipping Arrivals and Departures, Victorian Ports.* 2 vols. Roebuck, Melbourne, 1987.

Thornton-Smith, C. B. *Analytical Checklist of First-Hand Accounts in French of Colonial Australia.* Revised & enlarged edn. English Department, Monash University, Melbourne, 1986.

Victoria Government Gazette. Government Printer, Melbourne, 1854–59.

Contemporary accounts of Australia
in the 1850s

Beauvoir, Count Ludovic de. *Voyage autour du monde: Australie.* Henri Plon, Paris, 1869.

Cannon, Michael (ed.). *The Victorian Gold fields 1852–53: an original album by S. T. Gill.* Currey O'Neill for the Library Council of Victoria, Melbourne, 1982.

Carrières, A. C. de la. *Voyage aux pays aurifères, Afrique, Mexique, Californie, Pérou, Chili, Nouvelle-Calédonie, Australie, Russie.* A. Courcier, Paris, 1855.

Castella, Hubert de. *Les Squatters australiens.* Hachette, Paris, 1861. Trans. C. B. Thornton-Smith, *Australian Squatters.* Melbourne University Press, Melbourne, 1987.

——*Notes d'un vigneron australien.* George Robertson, Melbourne, 1882. Trans. C. B. Thornton-Smith, *Notes of an Australian Vine Grower.* Mast Gully Press, Melbourne, 1979.

——*John Bull's Vineyard. Australian Sketches.* Sands & McDougall Ltd, Melbourne, 1886.

Chavannes, Herminie. *Un jeune Suisse en Australie.* Émile Bérous, Genève, J. Grusard, Marc Ducloux, Paris, 1852.

Clacy, Mrs Charles. *A Lady's Visit to the Gold Diggings of Australia 1852–53.* [1853] 2nd edn. P. Thompson (ed.), Angus & Robertson, London, 1963.

Dumas, Alexandre. *Journal de Madame Giovanni.* A. Cadot, Paris, 1856. Trans. M. Wilbur, *The Journal of Madame Giovanni.* Hammond, London, 1944.

Duyker, Edward (ed.). *A Woman on the Goldfields. Recollections of Emily Skinner 1854–1878.* Melbourne University Press, Melbourne, 1995.

Fauchery Antoine. *Lettres d'un mineur en Australie.* Poulet-Malassis et de Broise, 1857. Trans. A. R. Chisholm, *Letters from a Miner in Australia.* Georgian House, Melbourne, 1965.

——*Sun Pictures of Victoria.* D. Reilly and J. Carew (eds). Library Council of Victoria, Melbourne, 1983.

[Fenton, Elizabeth]. *Mrs. Fenton's Tasmanian Journal 1829–1830.* Sullivan's Cove, Adelaide, 1986.

Finn, Edmund. *The Chronicles of Early Melbourne, 1835 to 1852: historical, anecdotal and personal by 'Garryowen'.* 3 vols. Fergusson & Mitchell, Melbourne, 1888.

Hargraves, Edward Hammond. *Australia and its Gold fields.* H. Ingram, London, 1855.

Howitt, William. *Land, Labour and Gold or Two Years in Victoria: with visits to Sydney and Van Diemen's Land.* 2 vols. Longman, Brown, Green & Longmans, London, 1855.

Huber, Thérèse. *Adventures on a Journey to New Holland.* Trans. R. Livingstone, L. Bodi (ed.). Lansdowne Press, Melbourne, 1966.

Journet, Ferdinand. *L'Australie: description du pays, colons et natifs, gouvernement, institutions, productions, travaux publics, mines.* J. Rothschild, Paris, 1885.

Kelly, William. *Life in Victoria or Victoria in 1853* and *Victoria in 1858.* [1859] 2 vols. Lowden Publishing, Kilmore, Vic., 1977.

Lang, John Dunmore. *The Australian Emigrant's Manual or A Guide to the Gold Colonies of New South Wales and Port Phillip.* Partridge & Oakey, London, 1852.

McCombie, Thomas. *The History of the colony of Victoria from its settlement to the death of Sir Charles Hotham.* Sands & Kenny, Melbourne, 1858.

——*Australian Sketches.* Sampson Low, London, 1861.

McCrae, Georgiana. *Georgiana's Journal [1841–65].* Hugh McCrae (ed.). Angus & Robertson, Sydney, 1934.

Maynard, Félix. *Les Baleiniers, voyage aux terres antipodiques.* Pub. Alexandre Dumas. A. Cadot, Paris, 1859. Trans. F. W. Reed. *The Whalers.* Hutchinson, London, 1937.

O'Rell, Max (pseud. of Blouet, Léon Paul). *La Maison John Bull & Cie: les grandes succursales, le Canada, l'Australie, la Nouvelle-Zélande, l'Afrique du Sud.* C. Lévy, Paris, 1894.

Salisbury, Robert marquis of. *Lord Robert Cecil's Gold Fields Diary,* with introduction and notes by Ernest Scott. Melbourne University Press, Melbourne 1935.

Sherer, John. (ed.) *The Gold Finder of Australia: how he went, how he fared and how he made his fortune.* Clarke, Beeton & Co., London, 1853. Trans. R. Bourdier, *Les Chercheurs d'or.* Gustave Barba, Paris, n.d. [1856?].

Smith, James, 'Melbourne in the Fifties', *Centennial Magazine,* vol. II, no. 5, December 1889, pp. 344–9.

——'Recollections of an Octogenarian', no. 5, 'Bygone Celebrities', *Leader,* 27 July 1907, p. 43.

Sutherland, Alexander. *Victoria and its Metropolis: past and present.* 2 vols. McCarron, Bird, Melbourne, 1888.

Westgarth, William. *Victoria and the Australian Gold Mines in 1857.* Smith, Elder & Co., London, 1857.

——*Personal Recollections of Early Melbourne & Victoria.* George Robertson & Co., Melbourne, 1888.

Withers, William Bramwell. *The History of Ballarat, from the first pastoral settlement to the present time.* Ballarat Star, Ballarat, 1870.

SECONDARY SOURCES

Adcock, W.E. *The Gold Rushes of the Fifties.* E. W. Cole, Melbourne, 1912.

Anquetil, Louis Pierre. *Histoire de France jusqu'à la révolution de 1789.* 4 vols. Garnier frères, Paris, 1853.

Bagot, Alec. *Coppin the Great, Father of the Australian Theatre.* Melbourne University Press, Melbourne, 1965.

Bate, Weston. *Lucky City: the first generation at Ballarat, 1851–1901.* Melbourne University Press, Melbourne, 1978.

Brisbane, K. (ed.). *Entertaining Australia.* Currency Press, Sydney, 1991.

Cannon, Michael. *Old Melbourne Town Before the Gold Rush.* Loch Haven Books, Victoria, 1991.

Charlwood, Donald E. *The Long Farewell.* Allen Lane, Melbourne, 1981.

Chisholm, A. R. 'Céleste de Chabrillan and the gold rush', *Meanjin Quarterly*, June 1969, pp. 197–207.

Clark, Charles Manning Hope. *A History of Australia.* Vol. 4, 1851–1888. Melbourne University Press, Melbourne, 1978.

Cooper, John Butler. *The History of St Kilda from its First Settlement to a City and after, 1840 to 1930.* 2 vols. Printers Pty Ltd, Melbourne, 1931.

Crowley, Frank. *A Documentary History of Australia.* 5 vols. Thomas Nelson, Melbourne, 1980.

D'Auvergne, Edmund B. *Lola Montez, An Adventuress of the Forties.* London, T. Werner Laurie, n.d. [1909?].

Denholm, David. *The Colonial Australians.* Allen Lane, Melbourne, 1979.

Dunstan, David. *Better than Pommard! A History of Wine in Victoria.* Australian Scholarly Publishing, Melbourne, 1994.

Fredman, L. E. 'Melbourne Bohemia in the nineteenth century', *Southerly*, no. 2, 1957, pp. 83–91.

Frost, Lucy. *A Face in the Glass: the journal and life of Annie Baxter Dawbin.* William Heinemann Australia, Melbourne, 1992.

Haldane, Charlotte. *Daughter of Paris.* Hutchinson, London, 1961.

Holdredge, Helen. *Lola Montez.* Alvin Redman, London, 1957.

Lapierre, Alexandre. *La Lionne du boulevard.* Robert Laffont, Paris, 1984.

Leclercq, Pierre-Robert. *Céleste Mogador, Une reine de Paris. Biographie.* La Table Ronde, Paris, 1996.

McLean, Jeanne. 'Céleste de Chabrillan', *Margin*, no. 26, 1991, pp. 1–9.

——La Véracité des *Voleurs d'or* (1857) et d'*Un Deuil au bout du monde* (1877) de Céleste de Chabrillan comme témoignages sur l'expérience vécue dans le Victoria des années 1850. M.A. thesis, University of Melbourne, 1990.

McWilliam, G. *Hawthorn Peppercorns.* Brian Atkins, Hawthorn, 1978.

Montez, Lola. *Lectures of Lola Montez, including her autobiography.* Written by C. C. Burr. Woodfall & Kinder, London, 1858.

Moser, Françoise. *Vie et aventures de Céleste Mogador, fille publique, femme de lettres et comtesse (1824–1909).* Albin Michel, Paris, 1935.

Murger, Henri. *Histoire de Mürger.* Hetzel, Paris, 1862.

——*Scènes de la vie de bohème.* Michel Lévy frères, Paris, 1851.

Musset, Alfred de (attrib.). *Gamiani, ou Deux Nuits d'Excès, par A.D.M. avec un épisode de la vie de l auteur, extrait des mémoires de la Comtesse de C********.* 2nd edn. Lesbos Institution Méry—Pavillon Baudelaire, Paris, n.d.

Niall, Brenda. *Georgiana. A Biography of Georgiana McCrae, Painter, Diarist, Pioneer.* Melbourne University Press, Melbourne, 1994.

Penauille, E. *Mme Lionel.* (Coll. Biographies contemporaines.) Chez tous les libraires, Paris, 1869.

Quérard, Joseph Marie. *Les Supercheries littéraires dévoilées.* [1847] 2nd edn. 3 vols. G. P. Maisonneuve & Larose, Paris, 1964.

Bibliography

Reilly, Dianne. The Life and Times of Antoine Fauchery. M.A. thesis, Monash University, 1984.

Richardson, Joanna. *The Courtesans: the demi-monde in nineteenth-century France.* Weidenfeld & Nicholson, London, 1967.

Serle, Geoffrey. *The Golden Age: A History of the Colony of Victoria 1851–1861.* Melbourne University Press, Melbourne, 1963.

Seymour, Bruce. *Lola Montez: A Life.* Yale U.P., New Haven & London, 1996.

Stuart, Lurline. *James Smith, the Making of a Colonial Culture.* Allen & Unwin, Sydney, 1989.

Stuer, Anny P. L. *The French in Australia.* Department of Demography, Institute of Advanced Studies, A.N.U., Immigration Monographs Series 2, Canberra.

Thornton-Smith, C. B., 'A true account in which only the facts are wrong—Hubert de Castella's *Les Squatters australiens* (1861)', *Explorations*, Monash University, no. I, May 1985, pp. 3–5.

——'French perceptions of the Colony of Victoria—facts, fictions and euphoria', *Explorations*, Monash University, no. 2, December 1985, pp. 114–25.

Turnbull, Clive. *The Melbourne Book.* Ure Smith, Sydney, n.d. [1948?].

Uhl, Jean. *A Woman of Importance: Emily Childers in Melbourne 1850–1856.* Jean Uhl, Melbourne, 1992.

Viel-Castel, Horace de. *Mémoires sur le règne de Napoléon III, 1851–1864.* G. Le Prat, Paris, 1942.

Index